Green tracers were coming from both sides of the canyon, and they were all coming up at me. Both of my door guns were firing as fast as they could, trying to suppress some of the enemy fire. Just before I reached the sandbar I heard one of the F-4s on the VHF radio: "Lead's in."

As I pulled the aircraft into a hard flare and let it settle onto the sandbar, I heard a sudden roar. The F-4 passed over me, followed by a loud swishing sound. Looking up, I saw two silver cylinders passing above my rotor blades. The cylinders slammed into the wall of the canyon and burst into a raging fireball that climbed up the canyon's sheer cliff. It seemed to suck the air right out of my lungs. Immediately, the green tracers stopped coming from the south wall and seemed to slacken from the other side of the river. I knew that would not last, but it gave me a breather. As soon as the shock wore off and Charlie got his shit together again, the enemy fire would pick up once more. . . .

LEST WE FORGET

The Kingsmen, 101st Aviation Battalion, 1968

William C. Meacham

IVY BOOKS • NEW YORK

An Ivy Book
Published by The Ballantine Publishing Group
Copyright © 1999 by William C. Meacham
Introduction copyright © 1999 by W. T. Grant

www.randomhouse.com/BB/

Library of Congress Catalog Card Number: 99-90740

ISBN 0-8041-1917-1

Manufactured in the United States of America

First Edition: December 1999

10 9 8 7 6 5 4 3 2 1

To My Wife, Carole

Carole came to my rescue in 1961, and we were married in February 1962. She supported me throughout my military career. Carole assisted me in almost all of my actions during the aftermath and recovery from the Vietnam experience while I was trying to put the violent years behind me. Without her encouragement, support, gentle pushes, harder shoves, and many hours of editing, this document would still be an unfulfilled dream.

Introduction

by
W. T. Grant

Lest We Forget . . . The title sums up the purpose not only of this book but of many like it as well. It is important to document the sacrifices of men and women called to the service of their country, the many who have gone forward in answer to that call with fear and reluctance, particularly in the case of the Vietnam War. A war derided by so many that, in our history, it can be equaled only by the Civil War. Owen Lock and Ivy Books deserve a great deal of credit for ensuring that the story of the soldiers who answered the call is recorded for future generations. I have always favored accounts of history written by those who made it. Such writings allow an insight that cannot be emulated by historians removed from the events. Viewing the war in Vietnam from the perspective of its participants is extremely important because the war's character not only varied by location but with the passage of even small amounts of time.

William Tecumseh Sherman reminded those under his command that "war is hell," and the truth of his words is undeniable to anyone who has suffered through one. The perception of glory attached to it emerges only after time, from the courageous deeds of those who fight to survive the agonies of war. Many go off to war waving the flag and full of patriotic notions only to discover, after being immersed in the reality, that the "glory" of war is frequently little more than a struggle to survive until the next day while helping those around you to survive that same challenge. For some, personal survival is eventually surrendered to God or to fate. Those soldiers then fight for the protection of their comrades with a tenacity that is almost always poorly documented by award commendations. It is in the soil of shared and desperate determination that the seeds of brotherhood among warriors germinate, then grow into trees of such strength that those who have not experienced it find hard to comprehend. The brotherhood of Vietnam veterans has even deeper roots because of the ungrateful reception and hardship with which they were greeted on their return. That reception has created some of the more tragic casualties of the war. Some Vietnam veterans feel that it is *us* against the world. Some take the entire burden upon themselves, denying access even to their brothers in combat. I hope that books like this one can burrow into that shell and show those veterans that they are not alone, that there are many who appreciate the sacrifices they made, the difficulties they endured.

When I was growing up, there were many times that I would have benefited from having a big brother. It was not until I was twenty years old and in Vietnam that I found one. He came in the form of a captain named William C. Meacham, "Wild Bill." Wild Bill took me under his wing; he trained, chided, scolded, encouraged, and sometimes ridiculed me. As a matter of fact, Wild Bill taught me everything I know. I'm sure of that because he often reminds me. On occasion, I remind him that what he taught me was everything *he* knows and it only took two minutes. As is evident, Bill Meacham is still my big brother. The years that have passed since we met in dusty, dirty, damp, smelly Camp Eagle have not changed that, nor will the passage of many more.

Wild Bill has always been a grand storyteller, and now through the efforts of many, including his lovely wife, Carole, he has been motivated to write and share his adventures with you. I am sure that the reader will be enthralled as he relates stories of men of great courage who were just doing their jobs. The reader will discover that Wild Bill is a skilled aviator, a leader who leads from the front, or alongside, but never from the rear. Meacham's style of leadership never allows him to look over his shoulder; he assumes that those who are supposed to follow will be there, as he is for them. I don't recall ever hearing Wild Bill say, "I love my country." But his patriotism shines like the brass on a soldier's uniform on parade day—bright, without the tarnish of adversity or disappointment. If the demons of Beelzebub were to threaten America, Bill Meacham would stand facing the gates, waiting for the hounds of hell, telling those with him, "This Army is all right!"

Lest We Forget. Over the years I have heard those words many times from the lips of William C. Meacham in a toast to those who fell and those who survived the horrors of war. Now share in the experience and always remember the legacy that those patriotic Americans have left you.

W. T. Grant
Kingsman One-eight, *out!*

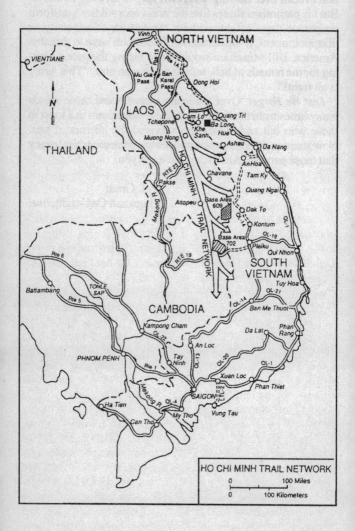

HO CHI MINH TRAIL NETWORK

Prologue

It was the strangest feeling. The aircraft was descending out of five thousand feet on a heading of 042 degrees for Runway 03L. Everything was so quiet. As I looked out the window at the city lights below, there were no tracers, no flares, and no explosions. You couldn't see Puff working out somewhere on the horizon. Then I realized that the aircraft was not the UH-1 helicopter I'd been flying for the past year, but a Braniff 707. And the city I was flying over was not Hue/Phu Bai, but Fairfield, California, on final approach to Travis Air Force Base.

Just forty-eight hours before, I had been flying in Vietnam on a night combat assault involving the 101st Aviation Battalion. The battalion consisted of three lift companies of twenty UH-1 helicopters each, a gun company of three light fire teams (each fire team consisting of two UH-1C gunships), and a Chinook (CH-47) company. The year I'd been there was one of the biggest clusterfucks I was ever involved in. I had finally realized it was time to go home.

My final operation was supposed to have been simple: three lift companies—Alpha, Bravo, and Charlie—going into three separate LZs; Alpha into LZ 1, Bravo into LZ 2, and Charlie into LZ 3. The gun company was to break up into three sections to support each lift company, while the Chinooks were scheduled to come in after the slicks. My role in the mission was to insert three Pathfinder teams, each composed of three men. We'd picked up nine people and made the insertions with no problem. Then the fun began. Alpha Company ended up on LZ 3, Bravo Company on LZ 1, Charlie

1

Company dropped its passengers in LZ 2, and nobody knew what the hell was going on.

Unfortunately—or fortunately, depending on your point of view—soldiers rotated home after one year in country and took their experience with them. Luckily, on that mission the LZs proved to be cold—meaning the "bad guys" were not on the ground waiting for us. At least, they weren't inclined to make contact.

After we inserted the Pathfinders, I returned to my unit, which was Bravo Company (unit call sign the "Kingsmen"). There I joined as Chalk 5 with the second platoon to put in the ground troops. After the troops were dropped off and secured the LZs, all other aircraft were released back to their parent units. However, I stayed behind to pick up the Pathfinders and return them to their compound.

Because I was not sure where the Pathfinder headquarters was located, I contacted Hue/Phu Bai tower and requested guidance as to where those people were to be set down.

There was a CH-46 in the traffic pattern whose call sign was "Scarface." He came up on the net and advised me that the Pathfinder compound was about four miles down Highway 1 on the right-hand side. I started talking to Scarface a little, and he wanted to know what we were into and what was going on. I told him, then advised him it was to be my last trip; I was going home the next day. His answer was that he couldn't believe anyone would be stupid enough to be flying a night combat assault with less than forty-eight hours left in country. By God, when I stopped and thought about it, it really wasn't too bright.

My copilot on that mission, Warrant Officer (WO) Jim Weaver, was also a short-timer. He'd been in country almost as long as I had and was also due to rotate home in less than a week. When the Operations officer, at the last minute, asked if we would fly the mission, nothing said we had to, especially since we'd already turned in our gear. But a maximum effort was needed for the operation, and I guess we were just too dumb or too loyal to say no.

It was over. A year had passed, and we were coming back

home on a 707. We stopped in Honolulu and were briefly allowed off the plane, but instructed not to leave the passenger area. We were on a military charter, not a civilian flight, so we wouldn't have to clear customs in Honolulu, but at our arrival at Travis Air Force Base in California.

When we deplaned in Honolulu, people looked at us as if we'd just arrived from some alien planet. Maybe it was something they saw in our eyes, or maybe it was our mannerisms. Whatever, we were somehow different than before we'd gone to Vietnam.

None of us had known one another. We were two hundred total strangers crammed into a "people mover" with nothing in common but our service in Vietnam. When we'd left for Southeast Asia a year before, there was a lot of nervous joking. We'd been excited and scared—and worried—all at the same time. There had been a lot of chatter on the aircraft.

Coming back, we were still a group of strangers, but all of us shared a bond. We were each imbued with the knowledge that we'd survived a year of terror and were now going home—home to a life of "normalcy." The stewardesses on the plane seemed nice, but they were a little standoffish, as if getting too close to us might cause them some kind of physical pain. Maybe it was fear—or respect—for what we'd been through. There was no horseplay, no joking around, and no talking; no noise at all. Everyone seemed lost in his own thoughts.

On the final leg of the trip, from Honolulu into Travis, I arranged with four of my fellow passengers that the first person to clear customs would grab a cab for the five of us. Then we'd split the fare to Oakland Airport, where we would grab flights to our final destinations. The last part of my trip would be relatively short, from Oakland to Los Angeles, no more than an hour's flight away.

We landed at Travis at nine P.M. on December 24, 1968. Clearing customs proved to be merely a formality. The inspectors seemed anxious to get home for Christmas Eve, so they ran us through, spot-checked our luggage, and sent us on our way.

Our group of five piled into a cab and headed for Oakland. We told the cabdriver, "Get us to the airport as fast as possible, and if you get a ticket, we'll pay for it." He didn't get a ticket, but he did get one hell of a tip.

Except for the ticket agents, the Oakland terminal was almost deserted. It was almost ten P.M. I yelled, "Who has a plane going to L.A.?" Continental Airlines at the far end said they had one ready to depart right away. As I hurriedly paid for my ticket, I asked if I had time to make a quick phone call. The ticket agent said I didn't but told me to ask again at the departure gate and they would let me know if there was time for the call then.

When I got to the departure lounge, nobody was there except for the boarding attendant. I asked him if there was time for a call, and he too said no. However, he did offer to place the call for me if I would give him a name and phone number. I quickly gave him the information and boarded the plane.

At 11:15 P.M. my flight landed at Los Angeles International Airport. I called my wife at home in Santa Ana, about an hour's drive from the airport, but there was no answer. I hoped the Continental agent had been able to reach her by phone.

I grabbed my parachute kit bag, which had just a very few things in it—it was amazing just how little you brought home after a year overseas—and walked outside. I stood there in my khaki uniform in the cold December night and casually observed the few people moving about the airport.

There was one particular individual whom you might call a "flower child." If the sun had been shining, and it had been warm, there probably would have been flies buzzing around him. Anyway, he was one pathetic-looking human being. But that was okay by me. I was perfectly willing to allow each to his own.

While I was standing there, a security guard came up to speak to me, an elderly (at least to my twenty-eight-year-old eyes) gentleman in his sixties. He took one look at the flower child, then looked at me and asked, "Captain, is that what you were fighting for?"

I had to stop and think for a minute before replying, "No, it wasn't. Now let me ask you a question. Do you have any children?" When he said he did, I continued, "Do you have any grandchildren?"

"Yes, I do," he replied.

Nodding toward the hippie, I said, "Are they *that* type of person?"

"Hell, no!" came his immediate response.

"Well, your children and grandchildren are what I was fighting for."

With tears in his eyes, the old security guard said, "Thank you!" then turned and slowly walked away.

As I stood waiting for my wife, the thought crossed my mind: Do I really want to remember any of this, or do I want to forget what transpired over the last year? The more I thought about it, the more I realized that I would never forget. I didn't want to forget. I could never forget.

Chapter One

For as long as I could remember, I'd wanted to be a soldier. I'd been brought up on John Wayne movies, the kind where the good guys always won. My family was not traditionally a military family. However, they had always answered the call to arms.

My great-grandfather, George Furman Parrott, Captain, South Carolina State Militia, Confederate States of America, was the first member of my family that I was aware of who served under arms in a cause he felt was right.

My father had served in the Merchant Marine during World War II, and had seen action in both the Atlantic and the Pacific. His five brothers had also served during that war, and one had even gone on to retire from the Navy as a full commander.

Of my mother's two brothers, one was a naval aviator serving in the Pacific, the other, Fred Ross Jackson, had joined the Army and gone into the paratroopers. He'd been assigned to the 504th Parachute Infantry Regiment, "The Devils in Baggy Pants," a unit I would later serve in.

When I entered high school, I enrolled in the California Cadet Corps at Anaheim Union High School. That was my first experience in a military uniform. Little did I realize at the time that I would be spending the next thirty-five years in uniform.

I made my first parachute jump when I was fifteen years old at Lake Elsinore, California. That was before the Parachute Club of America came into existence and established age limits and safety regulations. The basic block of instruc-

6

tion for my first jump consisted of: "That thing on your back is a parachute, and that thing out there is an airplane. The airplane will take you up, and the parachute will bring you down." Brief but effective!

When I was sixteen, I enlisted in the California Air National Guard in Santa Ana. In July 1957, I departed for Lackland Air Force Base in San Antonio, Texas, for basic training. I remained with my unit—the 222d Radio Relay Squadron—for four years, but it was not really what I was looking for.

In February 1962, I enlisted in the United States Army at Fort Jackson, South Carolina, for "Airborne Unassigned." In basic training I met Sergeant First Class Hawkins, my platoon sergeant and the first of many individuals who would influence my military career. Since I'd already been to Air Force Basic Training, I was immediately made platoon guide.

About one week after the beginning of training, we were standing Reveille formation at 0500 hours. It was a very cold February morning. SFC Hawkins asked me a question, and I gave him some wise-ass answer. Without batting an eye he instructed me to send the troops to chow, then said he would like to talk to me.

SFC Hawkins walked around the corner of the barracks, and I, like a damn fool, followed him. As I turned the corner, out of sight of everyone, the lights suddenly went out. SFC Hawkins had hit me as hard as I'd ever been hit. As my eyes returned to focus, I saw him silhouetted against the gray light of the false dawn. He stood with his hands on his hips, his Smokey the Bear hat pulled down over his eyes. He looked down at me and said, "Son, you can do this one of two ways—your way or mine. Do it your way and you will lose. Do it my way and you will make it through without too much trouble. How do you want it to be?"

I decided to do it his way. That was my introduction to the Army that I would grow to love and respect.

A week later SFC Hawkins called me into his office and told me that I was to go to the Post Education Center to take a battery of tests for my high school diploma. (I'd quit high school in my senior year.) With that "gentle" push in the right direction, I managed to acquire my high school diploma and continued my education. By the end of my military career I would earn a Bachelor of Science degree.

Upon completion of Basic Training and AIT, I was assigned to Fort Benning, Georgia, where I went through jump school. Although I'd been jumping out of airplanes for about six years in civilian life, I was in for one hell of a shock when I began airborne training.

The Airborne School at Fort Benning is the best in the world. It is where they literally separate the men from the boys. Fort Benning in July is hotter than the hubs of Hell, and the training is hard and intense. We began training before the sun was up, running everywhere we went, and were dropped for push-ups for every infraction, imagined or real. By the end of the second week the cadre in the jump committee had worn us down to the worst physical condition any of us had ever been in. Then they began to build us back up again.

Although the physical training was important, the airborne instruction was even more so. I think the most important lesson I learned there was to react on command. That ability was to save my life later. I would see others, who had not received the benefit of such preparation, die needlessly.

The training tested us on many different types of equipment. The one I disliked the most was the suspended harness, more commonly called the "Nutcracker." That device was used to teach us how to control the direction of the parachute while descending. A similar device allowed us to practice PLFs, parachute landing falls. Then there was the mock door, used to demonstrate the correct manner of exiting an aircraft.

The one that was the most fun for me was the thirty-four-foot tower. The tower had cables attached to it that ran down to a point on an earthen berm about three hundred feet away. The parachute risers coming off our harnesses were hooked to the cable. Then we stood in the door of the tower and jumped. When we exited, we fell ten feet before the slack in the risers drew taut and stopped the fall.

The last piece of equipment we trained on before the actual

parachute jump was the 250-foot tower. There, we were attached to a parachute that was already deployed and hooked to a metal frame. Then we were lifted 250 feet off the ground. When the parachute was released, we were required to guide it as necessary and perform a PLF on making contact with the ground. That was one way of determining if we'd paid attention in the other classes.

Then it was time for our first actual parachute jump from a military aircraft. We were sitting in the "Sweat Shed"—a tin-roofed, open-air structure mounted on wooden poles. As we waited for the planes, the guy sitting next to me, who was as nervous as I was, said to one of the instructors, "Look, Sarge, I know that we've had the best training in the world, because you told me so. And I know that we have the best equipment in the world, because you told me so. But goddamn it, I have to know what happens if this son of a bitch doesn't work!"

The instructor smiled and answered, "Well, son, I'll tell you. You are going to unass that aircraft at 1,250 feet above the earth. You will exit with a good body position, get a three thousand count, and check your parachute. If you have a problem, then you will deploy your reserve parachute. If that doesn't work, you will be exactly three feet off the ground. Now, any damn fool can jump three feet!"

Over the next four days my class completed five successful parachute jumps and graduated as United States Army Paratroopers. Along with the silver wings they pinned on my chest, I immediately received my orders for Germany.

Standing in the quadrangle at Robert E. Lee Barracks in Mainz, Germany, home of the 1st of the 504th Airborne Battle Group, I knew I was finally where I belonged. I was no longer a student or a trainee, but a fully qualified Airborne Infantryman in the United States Army. I had the world by the tail, or so I thought, until I was assigned to Charlie Company, 1st of the 504th, and met First Sergeant Pulliam.

First Sergeant Thomas W. Pulliam was to be the second person to make a lasting effect on me during my career in the Army. He had survived both World War II and Korea, and it seemed he was constantly blaming that on me. God, how I hated that man. For about eighteen months I would have gladly killed him. Then one day it dawned on me that he was only teaching me what being a good soldier was all about, and that by being that kind of a soldier, I would have a much better chance of staying alive.

Most of the training was at platoon (forty-four men) and squad (eleven men) level. These were small units that worked independently. They had the capability of determining their own course of action and acting accordingly. At any time during our training exercises, the platoon leader, or whoever was in charge, could be, and most likely would be, "killed," and someone else had to be designated to take command.

After about two years of this I felt for the first time that I was "ready." During this time I first became aware of what I considered a lack of leadership in the officer and noncommissioned officer ranks. And like a lot of people in my platoon, I bitched and complained, only to discover there was nothing I could do about it.

Like any good first sergeant, Pulliam knew the mood and temperament of his company. He was well aware of the strong leaders and the weak leaders within the command structure, and Pulliam was the first to tell someone that if he thought he could do better, he should stop complaining and do something about it.

In June of 1965, I was promoted to sergeant, and in August of that year I rotated from Germany to Fort Campbell, Kentucky. When I arrived at Fort Campbell, I went to the post locator on the off chance that I might find a friendly face I'd served with in Germany.

The first person I came across was the Supply sergeant, Paul Clark. So I went over to Paul's unit to see him. We were sitting there bullshitting and drinking coffee when the door opened and there stood the devil himself, Thomas Pulliam. He took one look at me and said, "What the hell do you want?"

Without thinking, I replied, "Well, damn it, Top. I'm looking for a job." With that, he walked over to the telephone and placed a call to the post sergeant major.

"Sergeant Major, First Sergeant Pulliam here," he said. "There's a buck sergeant here by the name of Meacham. I want him." And that was how I was assigned to Bravo Company, 2d Battalion 502d Airborne Infantry, 101st Airborne Division.

After about four months with 2/502, I was called to the Orderly Room one morning by the first sergeant. When I reported to him, he pointed to a stack of papers on his desk and instructed me to sign them. When I asked what I was signing, he merely replied, "Goddamn it, Sergeant, just sign the damn things."

After I'd completed signing the forms (shit, there were a lot of them) I asked the first sergeant what the hell I'd just signed. Pulliam looked at me for what seemed like ten minutes, then said, "Sergeant, I told you some time ago that if you thought you could do a better job, don't talk about it, do something about it. Well, I think you can do a better job than some of the officers I know. You've expressed a desire to go to OCS"— Officer Candidate School—"well, now you're going."

January 1966, Fort Gordon, Georgia—Signal Corps, Officer Candidate School

OCS was not an easy school. It wasn't as intense as jump school, but it lasted a lot longer. Jump school had been only three weeks long, while Officer Candidate School took a minimum of six months to complete. At one time OCS was a three-month course, but not long before my class began, it had been combined with the Officer Basic Course, which also lasted three months.

My first impression was, "What in the hell have I gotten myself into?" The OCS cadre did their very best to make you quit. We were put under so much pressure right from the start that it was almost unbearable.

My class began with sixty-four students. We would later pick up twenty-seven others who were sent back from classes ahead of us. Out of these ninety-one students, we graduated thirty-two in June 1966. I graduated in the lower one-third of the class. Oh, well, what the hell. They didn't engrave your class standing on the back of your second lieutenant's bars! I guess for a high school dropout, it wasn't too bad.

My next stop was Fort Hood, Texas. With fifteen days time-in-grade as a second lieutenant, I reported to the 57th Signal Battalion, at Fort Hood, and was assigned as the company commander of Headquarters and Headquarters Company. This was where I first met M.Sgt. Andy Camp, an old soldier who had fought in World War II and was captured by the Germans. Later he fought in Korea and was captured again, that time by the Chinese. In 1966 he was my first sergeant.

When I first met Andy Camp, he looked at me and said, "Lieutenant, I don't know anything about being a first sergeant."

I replied, "That's good, because I don't know anything about being a company commander. So let's get on with it."

Boy, what a learning experience it turned out to be! With the help of some good senior NCOs, it didn't take me very long to get things going in the right direction.

Probably the thing that concerned me most was knowing that sooner or later we would be going to Vietnam. Although second lieutenants are supposed to make mistakes, I didn't want anyone to get wounded or killed because of my inexperience. I felt comfortable being an officer, but not a Signal Corps officer. I guess I still wanted to be with the same type of unit I'd been with prior to attending OCS.

I had already requested a transfer back to an airborne unit, but it came back disapproved. My next alternative was flight school, so I applied with the knowledge that upon completion of the course I would be sent directly to Vietnam. In February 1967 my application for flight school was approved.

Chapter
Two

U.S. Army Primary Helicopter School, Fort Wolters, Texas

Holy shit, I was in hog heaven! Up to that time, all the military schools I attended—Basic Training, Advanced Infantry Training, Leadership School, jump school, and Officer Candidate School—had been designed to eliminate the student through physical and academic pressure. It was thought that if a person could not perform under heavy pressure in a training environment—where the threat to his life was usually small—he would not be able to perform well under combat conditions.

At Fort Wolters, I found myself in a "Gentlemen's Course." As commissioned officers, we had already been through the physical harassment and the other assorted bullshit. At Helicopter School we were allowed to live off post and work a five-day week with no additional duties. And money! My God, I never had so much money in my life. I was drawing base pay, quarters allowance, flight pay, and per diem (a special allowance paid to those on temporary assignment away from their home base). Hell, the per diem pay was more than all my other pay combined! I didn't know what to do with it all, but my wife, Carole, took care of the finances and ensured that I didn't buy everything in sight.

Although we were in the Gentlemen's Course, it was no free ride. Out of about one hundred commissioned student pilots, we lost close to one-third of our class. Some failed academically, some could not master the aircraft controls, and others discovered they were afraid of flying.

The elimination rate for the warrant officer candidates (WOCs) was even higher. They had the same academic and flying schedule we had, but after they left the flight line and the classroom area, they received the kind of treatment I'd gotten going through OCS. I had the highest respect for anyone who had the ability to learn how to fly while undergoing that type of harassment.

I did get one free ride in flight school—the orientation ride. It would be my first, and only, nongraded flight in a helicopter for nine months.

The first, and probably most important, lesson I learned was that a goddamn helicopter had absolutely no respect for rank. That Hiller OH-23 showed me right up front who was boss, and it sure as hell wasn't me.

There were both civilian and military pilots who served as instructor pilots (IPs). They must have all had secret death wishes, for teaching nonaviators how to fly a helicopter was indeed a dangerous profession. For the civilians, I guess the pay was sufficient incentive, because the pay was good. But for the military, it was just an assignment—the luck of the draw.

The military IPs were officers and warrant officers who had returned from Vietnam and were using the experience they acquired there to teach us the art of helicopter warfare. Although we did not realize it at the time, some of those men were already burned out. Some would yell and scream at us, and cuss us out over the intercom. Others would just sit, shake their heads, and look at us as if to say, "Why are you trying to kill me?" They would then take the controls and show us where we'd just made what they believed was a premeditated attempt on their lives.

The average time to solo (fly without an instructor on board) was fifteen hours. I soloed in fifteen and a half hours. On my first flight as a solo student, my IP told me to go to a certain training area and practice a given maneuver. "Yes, sir! Yes, sir! Three bags full!" And off I went.

As soon as I was out of sight, I put the aircraft into a climb and asked myself, How high will this son of a bitch go? Well, hell, I had an hour and a half of fuel, so I'd find out. When that poor little helicopter finally reached ten thousand feet, it was enough for me. I had never been that high before in anything by myself. All I wanted then was to get back down to where I belonged.

After we soloed, we started flying more often. Each day I would fly one hour with my IP and then one and a half hours solo to work on any errors the IP had pointed out during the first hour. When we next flew dual, the IP would expect me to demonstrate correctly the maneuvers where errors had been made earlier, and he expected marked improvement.

Learning to fly was a lot of fun. Learning to hover was a real bitch. Hovering the aircraft was defined as the ability to hold it in a stationary position above a designated spot on the ground at a height of three feet. With a helicopter, you usually try to keep the nose pointed into the wind when hovering. Well, without belaboring the point, they gave me the whole state of Texas in which to learn how to hover, and I ended up in Oklahoma!

I didn't think I would ever be able to make that damn aircraft stay over one spot. My IP kept telling me not to worry about it. The plan was, one day I would pick the aircraft up and, lo and behold, it would be at a three-foot hover. He said that from that point forward, I would not have a problem with that maneuver again. How right he was! It must have been magic.

The flying portion of the course consumed only half of each day. The other half was the hardest part for me: academics. In the academic phase, we received instruction in aerodynamics (what makes it fly), weather, cross-country navigation, maintenance, and a multitude of other subjects. Maintenance was my worst subject.

One day the course of instruction was on the internal working of the combustion engine. I was sitting in the back of the classroom, and not paying any attention whatsoever.

The instructor asked, "Lieutenant, aren't you interested in the internal working of the combustion engine?"

I said, "No, sir. If I wanted to be a mechanic, I would have gone to mechanic's school. If I wanted to be a crew chief, I would have gone to crew chief's school. If the son of a bitch breaks, and the crew chief can't fix it, then we'll call someone who can." I didn't make any points with the instructor that day.

Our time at Fort Wolters was almost over. Four and a half months of defying the laws of gravity, cheating death every day, and sitting in hot, stuffy classrooms wishing we were on the flight line, were coming to an end. My academic grades weren't great, but they were sufficient.

The last obstacle to graduation was a one-hour check ride with a "standardization pilot." The stan-pilot's job was to evaluate our flying ability to determine if we had progressed far enough to move on to the advanced phase of flight school.

The afternoon before my check ride, my IP said he wanted me to leave all my books and study material in my locker, go home, get a bottle of good booze, and get loaded. That was not a difficult order to follow.

At 0900 hours the next morning, the check ride began. A hot, sweaty hour later, although I didn't see any flying colors, I'd passed my final check ride in the primary phase of flight school. My next stop would be Fort Rucker, Alabama, for the second phase.

Fort Rucker was deep in the heart of Dixie. It was there that all fledgling helicopter pilots came. We were under the impression that since we'd completed the primary phase of flight school, the second phase would be easier. However, we soon discovered that though we'd soloed in the primary phase and felt we were already the cream of the crop, we hadn't even come close to paying the price of admission into the world of Army Aviation. At Fort Rucker we thought we would learn the tricks of the trade, at least as far as combat flying was concerned.

Fort Rucker was the advanced phase of our training. Unless you were going to transition into another type of aircraft such as the CH-47, or to gunnery school, you could plan on going directly to Vietnam upon graduation. The instructor pilots, most of whom had already served at least one tour overseas, were dedicated and professional aviators. They were concerned not only with the flying ability of the commissioned-officer student pilots, but also their attitude.

However, it was (and remains) very unfortunate that some officers, with little or no experience of their own, still consider themselves more knowledgeable than someone of a lesser rank and far greater experience. When a commissioned officer, such as a second lieutenant, was assigned to an aviation unit, he was normally assigned as a section leader. It was safe to say that there were usually many more highly qualified pilots in that section, and many—if not most—would be warrant officers, by definition lower ranking than *any* commissioned officer. If the lieutenant did not have the common sense to listen and learn from the people who had that knowledge and experience, whatever their rank, there was a high probability he would soon be instrumental in causing death or injury either by accident or by enemy fire. I had seen that as an enlisted man, and the IPs had seen it in Vietnam. Attitude was an extremely important factor in leadership and survival.

The OH-13 helicopter was used as an instrument trainer. Helicopters are normally flown in what is known as visual flight rule (VFR) conditions. This means that the pilot maintains eye contact with the ground at all times. If the weather begins to deteriorate, then the pilot flies lower to maintain ground reference. In the States, when the weather becomes too bad to fly VFR, it's necessary to land somewhere—even in an open field—and wait until the weather improves. However, our helicopters were going to war, and in that environment, landing in a field was not conducive to health and longevity.

Learning to fly by instruments was foreign to all of us. It had been proven in tests that even the most experienced pilot, when put in a situation where there were no instruments nor any ground reference, would lose control of his aircraft within three minutes. The condition when flying without ground reference was known as instrument flight rule (IFR). This was often referred to as: "I follow roads, rivers, and railroad tracks."

Instrument training was very hard for me, and I really had to work at it to pass that part of the course. I had to get into the aircraft with my instructor, put on the hood—a device that restricted my vision to the inside of the cockpit—fly all over Alabama, make practice approaches to airports I never saw, and return two hours later having never once seen the ground or sky. The only clues I had that I was actually flying were the moving needles and gauges in the instrument panel, and the radio conversations with various control towers and approach-control centers.

Upon completion of my instrument training, I was still not a fully rated instrument pilot, but was issued what was known as a Tac Ticket (tactical instrument rating). I guess this was designed to give me enough confidence so that if I was unfortunate enough, or dumb enough, to get myself into an inadvertent IFR situation, I would be able to do a 180-degree turn and get the hell out of there. For many pilots, including myself, that training would later prove to be a lifesaver.

In August 1967, I was introduced to my second true love. I had been seeing her from a distance for a long time, and the time had come for us to finally meet. She was so beautiful, so sleek and trim, and she was going to be mine. I knew that once I had put my hands on her, the affair would begin, and there was nothing, absolutely nothing, I or anyone else could do about it. I also knew that the affair was something I could not, would not, ever be able to let go; it was destined to last a lifetime.

Now I had what most people only dreamed of. I had a mistress, and my wife approved of her. My mistress was a Bell UH-1 helicopter, the Huey, the Army's latest utility helicopter. It was capable of carrying eleven troops on a standard day, plus performing many other missions. The basic weight was 4,900 pounds, and it could carry a payload of 3,116 pounds. The overall length was fifty-seven feet and one inch, with a rotor diameter of forty-eight feet.

We were in the last phase of our training. There were so

many subjects to cover that they all seemed to run together: route reconnaissance, low-level navigation, formation flying, instrument flying, confined-area operations, forced landing; the list went on and on. The syllabus was set up to teach us the "school solution," but if you were lucky, your instructor would deviate from the written lesson plan and show you some of the maneuvers that were never mentioned in a study guide. In combat, there was no such thing as a "school solution."

The last week at Fort Rucker was spent at Tac X (tactical field training site), where we lived and flew under simulated combat conditions. There we utilized all of the training we'd received in the past nine months in order to give us a little insight into the world we were about to enter. We were given missions such as reconnaissance, resupply, formation combat assaults, night formation flying, perimeter defense, and E&E (escape and evasion). That was a very busy week, but it was also very rewarding.

On November 17, 1967, my twenty-seventh birthday, we had a formation fly-by of fifty aircraft over the main post of Fort Rucker. This was to signify that another class of rotary-wing aviators was about to graduate. What a beautiful sight it was!

The twenty-first of November that year was a most memorable day for me. I received my silver wings as an Army Aviator, and my orders. I was to report to Travis Air Force Base, California, for transport to the Republic of South Vietnam. Why was I not surprised!

You know, it was funny. Yesterday I couldn't even spell Aviator, and today I are one.

Chapter
Three

The passenger terminal building at Travis Air Force Base was an absolute zoo. There must have been over a thousand people milling around. Some were trying to get manifested on their scheduled flights or check their baggage. Others were just trying to find a place in which to wait. They all looked the same: khaki uniforms, identical short haircuts, bewildered expressions. I wondered if I had that same look. And young! Christ on a crutch, they were so very young. Most of them looked to be no more than eighteen or nineteen years old. I felt like an old man.

By the time I completed the check-in process, it was already 1000 hours. My flight would not depart until 1600 hours. I had to be back at the terminal two hours before departure, so I still had four hours to kill. I had to decide what to do with it. I decided, All right, let's put all my training to some good use.

Small-unit operations? There was nothing smaller than a one-man operation.

Evaluate the situation? The place was a madhouse.

Solution? Get the hell out of there.

Objective? Find the nearest Officers' Club. Have a few drinks, a good meal, and then some more drinks.

Course of action? Evade and escape.

Options? I could walk! Too far. Take a cab! That cost money. I could walk out to the parking lot where Carole was waiting and drive! I selected the third option.

Execution? I returned to the parking lot and completed a map recon. (We had picked up a map of the base when we came through the main gate.) We then located the Officers' Club, and proceeded on our route of march. Mission complete. Brilliant! Absolutely, by God, brilliant!

My delusions of grandeur were dispelled as soon as we walked into the O-Club. The place was packed. Most of the officers there were infantry officers. However, after further observation, I determined there were some "friendlies" in the area.

In the far left rear corner were ten to fifteen helicopter pilots with whom I'd gone to flight school. It had been only thirty days since we had graduated, but damn, it was good to see them again.

There were family, friends, wives, and girlfriends there to see their young warriors off to some faraway land. It was so sad to see the false front they all put on, Carole included. They seemed to be so happy and carefree, yet when you looked into their eyes, you could see the worry and heartache they really felt. All of them seemed to be wondering if it would be the last time they'd ever see their loved ones alive. It had to have taken more courage than I would ever have just to sit there and not show the fear they really felt.

After much hand-shaking, backslapping, and introducing, we got around to comparing notes as to who was on which flight. It did not surprise me at all to find out that no one there was on my flight. The Army had a program known as the Buddy System, where you could enlist with someone you knew and go through your training together. I had enlisted "Airborne Unassigned" and gone to jump school. Since I hadn't been able to find anyone dumb enough to jump out of a perfectly good aircraft who wanted to enlist with me, I ended up going to jump school by myself. My assignment to Germany was the same, as were the reassignments to Fort Campbell, OCS, and flight school. I had attended all of those schools alone. And I was going to war the same way.

The memories of those last six hours quickly faded as the airplane climbed to a cruising altitude of 37,000 feet. We left the coast of California behind, and if all went as planned, we would reach our final destination, Bien Hoa Airfield in Vietnam, in about sixteen hours. There would be one refueling stop at Kadena Air Force Base on Okinawa. It was going to be one hell of a long trip.

With nothing better to do, I began observing the other people on board the aircraft. As I said before, most of them were young, and like me, this was their first trip to Vietnam. I wondered how many would be returning on that type of plane in 365 days. How many would come home wounded? How many would return in body bags? How many would not come home at all? And the ones who did make it back, what would their minds be like? Could they overcome what they had seen and lived through? What of me? Would I be coming home in one piece, and would I be sane after those 365 days? Damn, what morbid thoughts! I had to knock that shit off.

All right, I told myself. Let's just kick back, relax, and enjoy the flight. After about an hour, I felt myself falling asleep as the airplane chased the sun descending in the west. We never did catch it.

We landed at Bien Hoa Airfield in the Republic of South Vietnam on January 2. After sitting so long in an air-conditioned jetliner, I found the heat and the humidity almost unbearable. By the time I reached the bottom of the boarding ramp, my shirt was soaked with sweat. I was born and raised in South Carolina, and thought I knew about humidity. But damn!

There was a terminal building on the field, but it was not for our use. We were directed to an area about three hundred yards to the north that reminded me of the Sweat Shed we'd used in jump school. The main difference was that the roof and walls, which were only four feet high, were made of sandbags.

We moved into the shade of the open-air building for two different reasons. First, we were following the instructions of the NCOs who had met us at the plane. Second, we wanted to get out of the sun and find a cool place to wait. We were all wondering what we were waiting for.

It took a little over an hour and a half to get us sorted out, but that gave us a chance to recover our baggage. By the time the process was complete, the buses had arrived and we were loaded on for transportation to the 90th Replacement Battalion (90th Repo Depot). Eight or nine standard Army buses were standing by, just regular school buses that had been painted OD green. They had wire mesh over the windows to prevent the Viet Cong from throwing hand grenades into the buses. That had a sobering effect on us.

The trip from the airfield to the Repo Depot was about fifteen miles. It proved interesting but totally uneventful. The road itself was lined with hootches constructed out of tarpaper, cardboard, plywood, flattened beer cans, and anything else that could be begged, borrowed, or stolen. Where there were no hootches, the road was bordered by short, stubby palm trees known as nipa palms. Their large, broad leaves hung down to the ground, and would have given excellent cover to anyone waiting in ambush. Evidently, the road was considered secure, for no one, including the driver, had a weapon of any sort. That bothered me.

The compound at the 90th Replacement Battalion reminded me of something out of *Hogan's Heroes*. I couldn't figure out if it was meant to keep the bad guys out or keep us in. There was a sandbagged bunker on each side of the front gate. An eight-foot fence topped with concertina wire ran the length of the perimeter. Four-man bunkers were spaced every thirty to forty yards around the perimeter and set up for interlocking fire. The only problem with the setup was that less than a quarter of a mile away was another compound organized the same way. It didn't take a military genius to see that if the bad guys positioned themselves between the two compounds and started shooting in both directions, it wouldn't take long before the two compounds would be shooting at each other. And, of course, that's exactly what happened shortly after my arrival.

At the 90th Repo Depot, the in-processing began. Although it was still daylight when we arrived, it proved to be a very long and tiring night. I finally got to bed around three o'clock in the morning. Then, three hours later, I was wide-awake. For some reason, I just could not sleep. I didn't know if it was excitement or anxiety that kept me awake, but whatever it was, I was not alone. It seemed that most of the people I'd arrived with were also up and moving around.

We had to stay close to the barracks area because we had no idea when we would be shipped out to our units of assignment. There really wasn't much to see or do in the compound. There was a PX, but it was so crowded that I couldn't get into it. The situation was the same at the mess hall. I could stand by the fence and watch the Vietnamese watching me, or I could sit on my bunk in the hootch and stare at the wall. Luckily, the Officers' Club was what I considered close at hand. So guess where I spent most of my time? The O-Club was air-conditioned, had young Vietnamese waitresses, a good selection of food, and plenty of booze. How could I go wrong?

But after two days of waiting, even the club got boring. I couldn't understand what was causing the holdup. Finally, in the early evening hours of the third day at the 90th Replacement Battalion, I was summoned to the Orderly Room. My original orders had me assigned to the 4th Aviation Battalion, 4th Infantry Division, at a place called Pleiku, somewhere up in III Corps. The Army, in its infinite wisdom, had decided that I no longer needed to go where I'd been ordered to go.

The captain who had called me in began by telling me what a great deal I was getting. I had been in the Army long enough to know that when you start getting *that* line of shit, you had better start looking over your shoulder. He told me I didn't really want to go to III Corps and fly in the mountains and how dangerous it was. The captain was not an aviator, and I knew he would not know the first thing about flying in the mountains or anywhere else. But he was, as I would find out later, what was generally known as a REMF—a rear echelon motherfucker.

He said they were sending me to a unit just six miles up the road, and what a great unit it was. Again I wondered how in the hell he would know that. He said that my transportation would pick me up at 0700 hours the next day. He also asked if I had any objection to the assignment. As I had no choice whatsoever in the matter, I said, "No, sir," thanked him, and left the Orderly Room.

The 17th Assault Helicopter Company, 214th Combat Aviation Battalion, 1st Aviation Brigade, was to be my new unit. With nothing left to do (my bags had never been unpacked), it was back to the club until it closed, and then try to get a few hours sleep. But I knew that sleep would not come.

Chapter Four

Just like the man said, at exactly 0700 hours, on January 6, 1968, the company commander's driver pulled into the parking lot at the 90th Repo Depot to take me to the 17th Assault Helicopter Company. The ride in the open-air jeep proved to be a lot more interesting than the ride in a crowded bus. Due to the large amount of traffic, mostly military vehicles, we had to travel at a relatively slow pace, but that gave me a good opportunity to look around.

The area didn't seem too bad. There were a great many buildings on the east side of the road, all behind the same type of eight-foot fence that surrounded the 90th Replacement Battalion. Evenly spaced along the fence were the usual four-man bunkers. However, on the west side there was nothing but open fields running back about five hundred yards from the road. No trees, no buildings, no brush. I mean nothing! Great fields of fire.

After traveling north about two miles, we passed II Field Force Headquarters. Damn, what a complex that was. From the road I could see the headquarters building and its helipad, large enough to hold six helicopters. There were two-story wooden barracks for the enlisted troops. The officers were housed in single-story, six-room buildings, with one officer per room. The PX really surprised me. It was as big as any PX I'd seen in the States or in Germany. I didn't know what time it opened, but at 0800 there must have been three hundred people already waiting in line just to get in.

As we continued north I couldn't help but wonder about the place. There were more and more buildings. There were motor pools, storage yards, supply buildings, and even a library. If it was as luxurious as what I was seeing, maybe that captain back at 90th Repo Depot hadn't been so dumb after all.

After we traveled another two or three miles, the large complex ended, but the fence line and the bunkers continued. Much of the area was under construction. My curiosity led me to ask the driver what was being built there. His response was that, when complete, it would be Plantation Army Airfield. However, it was obviously a long way from being completed.

By then we were in the town of Long Binh. It was easy to see where the airfield construction project ended and where a tent city began. Tents! I wondered who the poor bastards were who had to live in them. I was still wondering about it when the jeep made a right turn onto a dirt road that went right between two large groups of these tents. You've got to be shitting me! I thought. With all of those nice wooden buildings just down the road, they surely were not going to have an aviation company living in such an encampment! It didn't take me long to find out just how wrong I was.

The Orderly Room was located in a GP-medium tent. The offices of the company commander and the executive officer were in the rear. I gathered my gear and reported to the company commander, Major O'Connor. He welcomed me aboard and quickly told me that I would be assigned to the second platoon. After we talked for a few minutes about my military background and what my duties would be, he gave me a brief history on the 17th AHC.

The advance party had arrived at Bien Hoa, RVN, on September 25, 1967. They immediately began to establish the company's permanent quarters at Long Binh. The main body arrived during the first week of October.

The 17th AHC was assigned to the 12th Aviation Group. The call sign of the two lift platoons was the Kingsmen. Their gun platoon was known as the Lancers.

While the tent quarters were being built, the unit began a period of intensive in-country training. Members were sent to the 118th AHC, the 240th AHC, the 191st AHC, and the 334th Assault Helicopter Company, where they received area orientation and proficiency check rides with combat-experienced pilots. After that brief but rigorous period, the battalion commander pronounced them ready for combat and assigned them their first missions.

During the last days of November a select group of pilots and crews was assigned to special duty, working with Special Forces long-range patrols. They studied and practiced insertion techniques for placing small patrol teams on the ground undetected. Some of the methods used were rappelling (from helicopters), rope ladders (ditto), low-level approaches into confined areas, and the McGuire rig.

These techniques were soon put into use when the company was assigned to support Operation Rapid Fire III near the Cambodian border, not far from the city of Tay Ninh. During that operation, the company also worked with Free Cambodian units, which were aggressive, quick to learn, and eager to fight.

After returning from Tay Ninh, the company was ordered to deploy to Bao Loc to support the 101st Airborne in Operation Klamath Falls. This operation marked the 17th AHC's first experience in mountainous terrain. Headquarters and support detachments were maintained at Long Binh, and a full complement of ten slicks and five gunships were committed. That was where most of the unit was deployed.

Up to my arrival, the company had supported units from the 101st Airborne Division, 9th Infantry Division, 1st Infantry Division, 199th Light Infantry Brigade, 58th Infantry (Long Range Recon Patrol), 18th ARVN, 25th ARVN, the U.S. Navy SEALs, U.S. Army Special Forces, and Australian units. They had flown close to twenty thousand sorties, carried 33,000 passengers and 450 tons of cargo in 7,500 hours of flying.

The 17th AHC had been in Vietnam for four months, but had already established a fine reputation as a fighting unit. Damn, I was impressed!

After leaving the CO's office, I began the company in-processing. The first sergeant took care of most of the details. He had the normally boring, days'-long routine down to a science, and it took less than an hour.

I was shown to my quarters, which consisted of a canvas cot, a metal wall locker, and a wooden footlocker in a GP-medium tent. After dropping off my bag, I went down to the supply tent to draw my initial issue. It took two trips from the supply tent to my hootch to transfer all the equipment I was issued. I was glad I hadn't brought much in the way of clothing with me because I sure as hell wouldn't have had any place to put it.

Most of the issue was standard military equipment. However, there were some items I hadn't seen before. For instance, there was the ballistic helmet, which weighed close to four pounds and was designed to deflect a 7.62mm round (the caliber of a Soviet AK-47 bullet). It was heavy, but if it worked as advertised, it would be well worth it.

Next was the body armor. This was nothing more than a chest protector, more commonly called a "chicken plate." This equipment was also quite heavy, weighing approximately eight pounds. It was designed to stop the same type of round at point-blank range. I wondered if they were trying to tell me something.

The next item of issue that concerned me was a Smith & Wesson .38 caliber pistol. The .38 fired a relatively small projectile. If I had to shoot somebody with the damn thing, I didn't want to make the son of a bitch mad; I wanted to kill him. I asked if I could get a .45 caliber automatic but was told that there were none available. However, there were always "other" ways of getting nonissue weapons, and I knew that to find out how to do so, I simply needed to talk to the veteran pilots.

That afternoon I was sitting on my bunk wondering what to do with all of the crap I had been issued when a young warrant officer walked in carrying his helmet and chicken plate. He dropped them on his bunk, walked over to the small refrigerator in the center of the tent, took out two beers, and walked over to where I sat. He looked at me for a few seconds before he sat down.

When he finally spoke, he was no longer looking at me. "Well, Lieutenant, I guess you're the FNG I've heard about." Without waiting for an answer, he handed me a beer and said, "Looks like you could use one of these."

I had just met WO1 John Dean, one of the second platoon's aircraft commanders. I had a million questions, but this guy looked like his butt was dragging. He had just brought his aircraft back from Bao Loc for maintenance after flying missions all day. Dean was one of the pilots who had come over with the company. As we sat drinking our beer, I let him talk about whatever he wanted to while I kept my mouth shut and listened. John didn't waste any time letting me know how the system worked and what was expected of me. As we talked it became apparent that John was referring to the aircraft commander's (AC's) policy, rather than the company policy.

It had been determined that a pilot would gain the experience needed to become an aircraft commander within three months, or three hundred hours of flight time as a copilot. During that time, the copilot would fly with different ACs on a rotating basis. That would allow him to be evaluated by each aircraft commander. More important, the copilot would have the opportunity to see the strong points, as well as the weak ones, of each of the ACs. Needless to say, some pilots were stronger in their flying ability, and used sounder judgment than others.

As the afternoon wore on, a few other pilots returned from their daily missions. Richard "Dick" Washburn, William "Bill" Turner, and Jerry Seevers. These men were all WO1s,* and all were aircraft commanders. Each one of them greeted me in the same way: "Hey, look what we got, an FNG." Much

---

* In the Vietnam era, there were four grades of warrant officer, pay grades WO1 through WO4. "Warrant" officers found themselves in the area between enlisted men and "commissioned" officers and, formally, even the most senior warrant officer was outranked by the most junior commissioned officer.

of what they had to say just reconfirmed what Dean had already said.

I remembered what my IP had told me in the advanced part of flight school about learning from the mistakes of others. I was doing just that! Sure, those guys had learned the hard way. Although I had been with the unit less than twenty-four hours, I made one of the most important decisions I would ever make. My resolve was to keep my mouth shut, my eyes open, and listen to what I was told.

The light had faded as we talked. I was amazed at how much information I'd gained in such a short period of time. Nobody seemed to be bragging; they were just discussing the missions they'd flown in the past few days. For the most part, after the introductions, they paid little or no attention to me. It was as though I were not even in the tent. They talked of units they had supported, LZs they'd taken fire in, who had taken hits, and the amount of hours they had flown. The only thing no one seemed concerned with was tomorrow. It seemed as if they took only one day at a time. They continued talking long after I had gone to sleep.

I could hear the sound of helicopter rotor blades making their distinctive "popping" sound somewhere in the back of my mind. Why in the hell was I hearing helicopters? I opened my eyes and tried to figure out where I was. Then it came back to me. I was in a tent with a dirt floor, lying on a canvas cot on top of a sleeping bag.

The only other person in the tent was a Vietnamese girl, about nineteen or so, sweeping the dirt floor with a brush broom. The girl was what the guys in the unit called a "hootch-maid." They were paid to do our laundry, shine our boots, and take care of our tent, for about six dollars a month.

I looked at my watch and saw it was 0645. I couldn't believe it! I had finally gotten a good night's sleep. It was the first one since I'd arrived in country five days earlier, and I was damned if I hadn't slept like a baby.

While trying to tie my boots and wondering what to do with my day—most of the platoon, including the platoon leader, was still at Bao Loc—I got the feeling someone was watching me. Looking up, I realized there really was a God. There stood WO1 Dick Washburn with a cup of coffee in each hand. With a silly grin on his face, he said, "Hi, Lieutenant. You looked a little strung out last night. I thought you might be able to use this." How right he was!

Dick was a little older than the other pilots I'd met. He didn't have much to say about what he'd done. He just sat and listened. Lord only knows why! But at that time I really needed someone with whom I could talk. The main question I had was, "Okay, coach. What do I do now?"

Dick sat back and grinned. "All right, sir. First things first. Let's go see if there is anything left to eat at the mess hall. Then we'll stop by the Orderly Room to see if the Old Man has anything for you to do."

The only thing left at the mess hall was some cold toast and lots of coffee. The mess sergeant told me, "Lieutenant, you want hot chow, you get up and eat with the rest of the troops." Lesson learned.

Sitting there drinking our coffee, Dick and I were trying to get to know each other. I got the feeling that I wasn't learning a whole hell of a lot about Mr. Washburn, but he was getting a pretty good picture of me. I didn't know whether I liked this or not. I was telling my whole life story to a guy I'd just met and whom I outranked. What in the hell had gotten into me? Shit! I didn't know, but it seemed perfectly natural.

After about an hour, the mess sergeant finally got the message across to us: "Would you please get the hell out of my mess hall?" Believe me, it was, without a doubt, his mess hall.

We walked into the Orderly Room a few minutes after 0800 hours. The company commander was already in his office and saw us enter. The CO called to Washburn, "Dick, are you scheduled to fly today?"

When Dick replied, "No, sir," the major asked him if he had time to help me get squared away. Dick's response was, "Sir, the lieutenant looked kind of lost and I was the only one around, so I kind of figured it was left up to me." As we were leaving, the CO instructed me to report back to the Orderly Room at 1300 hours.

We went back to the tent, where I picked up the four sets of jungle fatigues I'd been issued and took them to a small shop set up just inside the wire. I had nine items to be sewn on each of the four uniforms. The Vietnamese tailor told me they would be ready in an hour. The cost would be under seven dollars. Unreal! I guess inflation hadn't yet caught up with us on that side of the world.

Dick gave me the Cook's tour. There were two dirt roads, one on each side of our company area. The one to the south separated us from our sister company, the 195th Assault Helicopter Company. The lift platoon's call sign was "Sky Chief," and the gun platoon's was "Thunder Chicken." The unit to the north, the 199th Light Infantry Brigade, was much larger. It consisted of four infantry battalions plus support units. Located adjacent to us was the brigade headquarters, one infantry battalion, plus some of their support units. This should have made me feel very secure. However, when looking at their perimeter defense setup, I could see they had a bunker line facing our bunkers across the road, with a separation of about five hundred feet. Shit, I hoped they didn't get mad at us.

When I reported to the Orderly Room at 1300 hours, the CO called me into his office and told me that an Aircraft Accident Investigation Board was being formed. I was to be the investigating officer. He told me he was sorry to do that to me before I had a chance to get my feet on the ground, but with the unit supporting the missions at Bao Loc, I was the only commissioned officer available. I would have ten days to complete my portion of the investigation.

The unit that had lost the aircraft was the 240th Assault Helicopter Company out of Bear Cat. The aircraft was a Charlie-model gunship that had been working as part of a heavy-fire team.

After picking up the stack of DA (Department of the Army) forms required for the investigation—Jesus, the goddamn

Army would fall apart without paperwork—and the appropriate regulations, I went back to my hootch and spent the rest of the afternoon deciding what needed to be done first.

I decided I had to go to Bear Cat, about twenty air miles to the southeast of us, interview the crews of the other two aircraft, and take their written statements. I talked to the Operations officer. He arranged for me to be dropped off at Bear Cat in the morning and picked up late in the afternoon. I then called the 240th to find out if the air crews would be made available. I was assured they would be there. With that taken care of, I was free for the rest of the afternoon. It was Miller time!

The next morning we departed Long Binh at 0700 hours. The view from the air was spectacular. The road was already crowded. Approximately two hundred meters on each side had been cleared away before the jungle began. Just looking at it made me wonder how many "bad guys" were sitting below the green canopy. The jungle seemed to go on forever.

After I reported to the 240th Orderly Room, the company runner escorted me to the gun platoon's quarters. Boy, those guys lived well! No tents for them. They had the same type of wooden barracks I'd seen on the trip to my company. Well, the battalion headquarters was located there, so I guessed the closer you were to the flagpole, the better you lived.

The 240th company commander had already had each of the eight crew members write out their individual eyewitness statements. First, I had to interview each witness separately. Later on, I interviewed them again, as a group.

All of the crew members told the same story. The "heavy" (three gunships) fire team had been in contact with an enemy force of unknown size for about fifteen minutes. The area they were working had been single- and double-canopy jungle, with only a few small clearings where you could land a helicopter.

The aircraft that had gone down, Mad Dog Three-three, had just completed a rocket run. He was in a right-hand turn, climbing to one thousand feet to be in position to cover Mad

Dog Three-six when the latter commenced his gun run. The third aircraft in the heavy fire team was Mad Dog Three-four.

The platoon leader, Mad Dog Three-six, had just started his gun run when the radio came alive with a call from Mad Dog Three-three.

"Oh, shit! Three-six, Three-three, I got a problem. I'm going down."

"Three-three, this is Three-six. What is your problem?" No answer. "Three-three, Three-six. What is wrong?" Still no answer.

"Three-four, this is Three-six. Do you have Three-three in sight?"

Mad Dog Three-four had just completed his gun run and was in a climbing right-hand turn. "Roger that, Three-six. Three-three is going down to the east of the target area. Looks like he's trying to make the clearing at about a quarter mile."

"Okay, Three-four. I've got him in sight. Break. Three-three, this is Three-six. Can you make the clearing?" Mad Dog Three-three did not respond.

The UH-1C helicopter, flown by two warrant officers, with a crew chief and door gunner on board, entered the 100- to 150-foot trees fifty meters short of the clearing. All eight crew members of the other two aircraft agreed that when Three-three went into the trees, his main rotor blade was turning so slowly they could count the revolutions.

As the helicopter settled into the trees, the main rotors broke off at the mast. The aircraft started to spin, causing the tail rotor and part of the tail boom to break off. The helicopter then rolled over on its back and fell inverted to the jungle floor eighty feet below.

A ready reaction force was inserted to secure the wreckage and to search for survivors. There were none. After the bodies were recovered and flown back to Bear Cat, the weapons systems, radios, and ammunition were removed from the crash site. The wreckage of the aircraft was determined to be non-repairable and it was left in place.

One of the main concerns on my mind was the slow-turning main rotor blade. If that was in fact true, it indicated a transmission problem. What would have caused it? Was it a material failure, faulty maintenance, battle damage, or did the pilot fail to execute a proper autorotation? I requested and received the aircraft maintenance records for the previous sixty days. There was no history of transmission problems, and all the scheduled maintenance had been performed as required.

At the Flight Operations office I checked the flight time for the pilots. They had both flown less than one hundred hours in the past thirty days, well within the guidelines for proper crew rest; 140 hours within a thirty-day period was the maximum allowed. I was to find out later that most of the flight-total boards were pure bullshit.

Next, I talked to the battalion flight surgeon. I asked to review the medical records of the four men who had died. There was no evidence of drug or alcohol abuse, and it had been determined that they had not died of bullet wounds. Death had occurred from injuries sustained when the helicopter impacted with the ground.

Over the next four days, I spent most of my time in my hootch trying to decipher all of the information I'd gathered. This was not easy; it was the first time I had been involved in that type of investigation. Of course, there was a DA form that was used as a checklist. As each requirement was completed, I had to initial the block at the end of that requirement. I was to initial all of the blocks, with the exception of one. After all the other forms had been completed, including those with my findings, I took the report to the Orderly Room to be typed. The next afternoon I picked up the completed report and made arrangements to go to Bear Cat the following day.

At 0900 hours the following morning I handed the Aircraft Accident Report to Major Jessup, the president of the board. After he reviewed it, he told me there was one block on the checklist that had not been initialed, and therefore the report was incomplete. I could see right from the start that it was not going to be a good day. The one requirement I'd failed to comply with was to visit the crash site.

Major Jessup was insistent that I go out to the site where

the aircraft wreckage was located. I made my reasons for not going very clear: (1) The aircraft had been shot down. (2) The people who shot it down could very easily still be in the area. (3) There was a good chance the wreckage would be booby-trapped. (4) I didn't think I would be able to find a pilot dumb enough to go out in a single ship to put me in a clearing that would more than likely be booby-trapped. And (5) I sure as hell wasn't dumb enough to go out there by myself. For some reason, I got the feeling that the major did not like me.

In the space on the report marked "Findings and Recommendations," I had used just the "Findings" portion. I found that, based on all the evidence, records, and interviews, the aircraft had been shot down while engaged with a hostile enemy force. I had not filled in the "Recommendations" block. Once again the major was having none of that. At his insistence, I took the report and wrote in the "Recommendations" block in large bold letters: STOP THE FUCKING WAR. . . .

Chapter
Five

I believe that, from the beginning of time, every young man who is about to go into an armed conflict has the same feelings. Whether the conflict is a feud between two men or a world war, it always breaks down to the case of young men trying to kill other young men. So the emotions are always the same: self-doubt (Can I do what is required of me when it's time to face danger?) and fear (Will I be dreadfully injured or die?).

The aircraft accident investigation had intensified my worries. I had just gotten a firsthand look at what could, and very possibly might, happen to me. As far as my fear of death, there was none. If death comes, there is nothing you can do about it. You simply die. However, being wounded, possibly crippled for life, did bother me. I couldn't bear the thought of having to depend on someone else to take care of me for the rest of my life.

But the most terrifying of all was the fear of the unknown. Would I be able to take another human life? Would I be able to be a soldier? Would I be the man I thought I was? And when would those doubts and fears go away so I could be at peace with myself?

Fifty-three days after I had last been in the front seat of a helicopter, I finally got word that I would get to fly the next day. Lieutenant Dave Greenlee, one of the section leaders of my platoon, came in from Bao Loc in the afternoon, and I was told I would be going back with him the following morning. As far as I was concerned, the next morning couldn't come soon enough. Our flight was also going to serve as my orientation ride.

We had to be at Bao Loc at first light, so we were in the air at 0530 hours for a ninety-minute flight. Dave told me to get used to the early morning get-ups; most of the units we supported wanted us on station at first light. The location of the units and the flight time to get there would dictate our get-up time. Shit! I never had been a morning person.

Early the next morning on the flight line, Dave gave me a map and told me to give him a heading that would take us to Swan Lock. After about fifteen minutes of him flying and me looking at that damn map—he was flying on a heading of 355 degrees, so I knew what part of the map to look at—I told him, "Dave, there ain't no such place."

He just shook his head and said, "Sure there is," while pointing to a place on the map. And there it was: Xuan Loc. Another lesson learned. Most of the names of places in Vietnam didn't sound at all the way they were spelled.

We landed at Bao Loc at 0700 hours, just in time for breakfast. All of the other aircraft were preflighted and ready to go. We refueled our aircraft, then joined the rest of the company.

I was in hog heaven. I was with a combat unit in a real war. They didn't call it a war at the time, but people involved were killing each other. The only thing that could have made it better was if I'd been assigned to the 101st Airborne Division. Although we were supporting them, that was not the same thing. Once Airborne, always Airborne.

After finishing breakfast, I was sitting on the ground smoking a cigarette and drinking a cup of coffee when up walked Jack Schlater, Captain, United States Army, my new platoon leader. "Shaky Jake" (not used in the derogatory sense whatsoever) looked just like the Texan he was. He was about six-foot-one and weighed somewhere around 165 pounds. His face looked weather-beaten and hard, but his eyes always seemed to be laughing.

Jack introduced himself and sat down to talk with me. He started asking questions about my military background and what my thoughts were on the Vietnam conflict. When he found out that I'd been on active duty for six years, he seemed relieved. Jack told me that Lieutenant Greenlee had one section of the platoon's aircraft, and I would have the other. Each section had five helicopters and ten pilots; that is, a pilot and copilot for each.

As I'd already been informed, I would fly in rotation with each of the platoon's aircraft commanders. When they thought I was ready, I would be put up for an aircraft commander's check ride. There would still be an initial in-country check ride, which would qualify me to fly as copilot. I was surprised to learn that the check ride would take place that very day in conjunction with the mission.

Normally, when a pilot passed his aircraft commander's check ride, he was given a call sign and assigned an aircraft and a crew for which he would be responsible. However, since I was a section leader, I would be given my call sign immediately: Kingsman Two-five.

The use of company call signs was designed for simplicity and ease of control. In a training environment, such as flight school, we would use the last three numbers of our aircraft tail number. If my aircraft tail number was 66-12345, then the aircraft call sign would be Army 345. As you can imagine, when working with ten or fifteen helicopters at one time, it would be almost impossible to keep track of who was in which aircraft by tail number.

The unit call sign was used for quick identification. An example would be the call sign "Kingsman Two-six": "Kingsman" identified the 17th AHC, "Two" identified the second platoon, and "six" identified the platoon leader. So when I heard someone call Kingsman Two-six on the radio, I knew they were calling the platoon leader, Captain Jack Schlater.

The support mission for the 101st was winding down, and the day was to be spent extracting the infantry companies from the jungle areas they had been working and returning them to Bao Loc. The unit we would be working with was only about twenty minutes' flight time away. We were to extract 140 men, using ten helicopters with an ACL (aircraft load) of seven men per aircraft. We would be flying two formations of five aircraft each. If all went according to plan, it would take two trips to get them all out.

I was flying with Lieutenant Greenlee, and we were the lead aircraft in the second flight. There was a three-minute separation between flights. This allowed enough time for the first flight to load and depart just as we were ready to touch down. We would also have a pair of gunships covering the extraction.

This was my first flight into a combat area. I was so damn excited that I could hardly sit still. Hot damn! I was going out to do battle with the bad guys and win the war.

The first flight of five took off and headed west into the mountains. We followed three minutes later. After we had lifted off and turned to the west, I could just make out the five distant specks that were the aircraft of the first flight. Ten minutes later we heard the first flight call the ground unit and report that they were three minutes out. The ground unit reported that the LZ was cold. The first flight called "one minute out." We could see them on short final in a trail formation.

The LZ was a large clearing in the jungle that ran east to west. There was a group of four men in the center of the LZ, and five groups of seven spaced out along the long axis of the LZ. I could see five more groups just coming out of the jungle.

As the aircraft of the first flight touched down, the five groups on the LZ moved to the aircraft and boarded. The second group, coming out of the jungle, took their place on the LZ. The first flight had just departed as we touched down. The troops were on board and we were off the ground in less than a minute. These guys seemed to know what they were doing.

We returned to Bao Loc, dropped off our troops, and started back for our second lift. It looked as though it would be the same type of run as the last one, so I started to relax a little bit. That was when Dave told me there was a good possibility that we would take some fire on this lift. The VC (Viet Cong) liked to wait until the last aircraft was coming out of the LZ before opening fire. Maybe it wasn't the time to relax, after all.

Once again I could see the first flight on short final, and see the five groups of men waiting to board the helicopters when they landed. But something was missing. Where the hell were the rest of the troops? The only other people in the LZ were the four-man command group. Even I knew that you didn't need five helicopters to extract four people.

The first flight picked up their load and departed just as we landed. I looked around and could still see only the four people in the middle of the LZ, and they were not moving. What the hell was going on? Where was everybo— *Son of a bitch!* What in the hell was happening? There were explosions all around the LZ. Then I saw people running out of the jungle, heading toward the aircraft.

The radio started to blare in my ears, "Kingsman Two-seven, this is Lancer Three-three. I will be making my gun run from east to west. Will be hitting both sides of the LZ. Call when ready to lift off."

"Three-three, Two-seven. Roger."

I looked out the right window and saw one of the gunships firing rockets into the jungle about fifty meters back from the edge of the LZ. The ground troops were on board, and the door gunners were firing into the tree line.

Dave called, "Lancer Three-three, Kingsman Two-seven. Coming out with a flight of five to the west."

"Two-seven, Three-three. Roger that. Lancer's going high and dry."

As we cleared the trees and were heading back to Bao Loc, I was still trying to figure out just what had happened. I looked in the back of the aircraft and saw that we had seven people on board, including the four-man command group. I couldn't understand what had taken place. I hadn't heard anyone call that they were receiving fire, and I hadn't seen any muzzle flashes.

After about ten minutes I finally looked at Dave and asked, "Dave, I don't want to sound too much like a fool, but would you mind telling me what that was all about?"

He looked at me and laughed. "Okay. The grunts had set up a defensive perimeter around the LZ. As we landed, the company commander, who was with the command group, told them to blow their claymores and make for the aircraft. Those were the explosions you saw around the LZ. The gunships and the door guns were putting down suppressive fire just in case the VC decided to come in close when we were on our way out."

"Why in the hell didn't you tell me what was going to happen before we landed?"

Dave stopped laughing. "I wanted to see your reaction. You didn't panic. Hell, you didn't even get excited. That's what I wanted to see."

So now I had made my first extraction with people shooting. Of course, it was only the good guys shooting, but at the time I didn't know that. Dave said I'd done a good job and hadn't gotten excited. Shit, if he only knew! It was a good thing I had my seat belt and shoulder harness fastened when those claymores went off or I would have gone right through the goddamn overhead.

I couldn't think of any reason to let him know what my inner reactions really were, so I just sat there with my mouth shut, an unusual occurrence for me. Other than having the shit scared out of me, the mission was a piece of cake.

We spent the night at Bao Loc and returned to Long Binh early the next morning. Three new warrant officers—Jim Weaver, Mike Ware, and Robert L. Smith—had arrived in the short time I'd been gone. Weaver and Ware were assigned to the second platoon; Smith had been assigned to the gun platoon. I had been with the unit for only a week, but it felt good not to be the newest guy in town.

R. L. Smith, the last to be assigned, was given the additional duty of seeing that the Vietnamese women that took care of our quarters were brought onto the compound in the morning and escorted off in the afternoon. He would be given a "Lancer" call sign, but for those of us who flew with Smith for the next year, the only call sign we would use was "Hootchmaid."

For the short time I was with this unit, everything had been very properly military. The warrant officers, surprisingly, extended every military courtesy to us officers. It was, "Yes, sir." "No, sir." "Would the lieutenant like this?" "Would the lieutenant like that?" It was so much by the book that it started to scare me. That was another one of those times when you know you should keep your back up against the wall.

Captain Jack called me into his tent and offered me a drink. Washburn was already sitting there with a drink in his hand. Jack informed me that Dick was to be my primary aircraft commander and would be responsible for my in-country training. With that bit of information, and the look on Dick's face, I could easily understand why he needed a drink. Well, back to the drawing board. When was I ever going to get out of the training stage?

Every day it was: At 0400, get up; at 0500, departure; at 0600, on station, supporting units of the 9th Infantry Division south of Saigon. That was what the mission sheet read. So at 0400 hours it was rise and shine. (I was still not a morning person.) First stop was the mess hall to grab a quick cup of coffee. Then we went to the flight line to preflight the aircraft. It was still, "Yes, sir. No, sir. Three bags full." I didn't know what to think.

One morning at 0445 we started the aircraft, did the engine run-up, and got a commo check with Operations. Ready to go, we were sitting in the revetment with the engine at flight idle. Dick Washburn, WO1, aircraft commander, with four months in country, looked at me with the most serious look I'd ever seen. Then he stated in a very quiet voice, "Now, you dumb son of a bitch, I want you to sit there with your mouth shut, your feet on the floor, and your hands in your lap. I don't want you to say anything, do anything, or even move unless I tell you to. I am going to try to teach you how to stay alive." Well, so much for military courtesy. I could see that it was going to be a very long day.

And a long day it was, but a very beneficial one. We were supporting one of the infantry battalions of the 9th Division working southwest of Saigon. We arrived on the scene at

0550 and they put us right to work. It was a single-ship "ash-and-trash" mission. Ash and trash could be anything from carrying empty plastic water bottles to acting as a medevac aircraft for wounded soldiers.

First off, we had to pick up and deliver hot breakfast, in metal food containers called mermite cans, to their night defensive positions (NDPs). There were three line companies with three platoons each in the field. Each of these units had to be fed. Later, we would go back, pick up the empty mermite cans from each unit, and return them to the battalion headquarters area. Lots of takeoffs and landings.

Dick was not an instructor. He was a teacher, and a damn good one. All the while he was flying, he explained what he was doing and why he was doing it. He showed me how to approach a position that was surrounded with tree lines. On any approach, there was the possibility of a VC popping out of his spider hole, firing off a thirty-round magazine of 7.62mm ammunition, and then dropping back into his hole. He would be back in his hootch, eating his goddamn fish heads and rice, before the noise died down. The VC were ingenious little bastards. Dick kept telling me, "Don't underestimate 'em. It will get you killed."

The rest of the day was more of the same. Take this to that unit; take these people to another unit; back-haul equipment and people to the battalion staging area.

There was also a lot of shutting down and standing by between missions. Dick used standby time to explain what we were doing and why. There was so much to learn, but Dick made it look and sound so simple.

After we had shut down and eaten lunch, we were sitting by the aircraft waiting for another mission when a funeral procession moved into a graveyard located just down the road from the battalion staging area. Dick asked me if I saw anything that looked out of place. All I could see was a long line of Vietnamese civilians with a coffin being carried at the front of the procession. It looked normal to me.

Dick then told me, "Look at how the people are walking." Most of them were kind of shuffling along, taking small steps. "Now look at those two guys, the one near the front and the other in the rear of the procession. Notice how they're taking full, steady steps. They're pacing off the distance. This place will get mortared tonight." It was.

What a hell of a way to fight a war. You knew what they were doing, but there was nothing you could do about it. Dick told me, "If you think this is bad, just wait. You ain't seen nothin' yet!"

Later that afternoon, I found out what the real cost of this small part of the war really was. We were resupplying one of the infantry companies with water and C rations when we got a call that one of their patrols had run into a sniper. They had one U.S. KIA (Killed in Action) that they needed to have picked up. Needless to say, they couldn't leave him out there, and they couldn't move until he was gone.

A hundred thoughts ran through my mind. I had tried to prepare myself mentally for that moment from the time I first joined the Army. How would I react? Did they get the sniper? Was there more than one sniper? Oh well, all of these questions would be answered in their own good time.

We were less than five minutes from the patrol's location. As we started our approach we could see red smoke, indicating the area was still considered hot—the bad guy was still there. We landed about twenty meters from the nearest tree line. God, what an awful feeling! I could feel the rifle being aimed directly at my head. I just sat there waiting for it to fire. I didn't like that shit one bit.

I don't know what I expected, but I sure as hell wasn't prepared for what actually happened. I guess I thought they would have the body in a body bag or something, and all I would see would be a black rubber bag. As we landed, four men came running out of the tree line toward the aircraft carrying the dead soldier between them. They loaded him on board, turned, and without a backward glance, returned to the tree line.

Dick was on the controls of the aircraft, and departed as soon as the body was aboard. At that point I made one of the biggest mistakes of my life; I turned around in my seat and looked at the dead soldier. It was a kid, only eighteen or nineteen years old. Hell, he didn't look old enough to shave. His hair was blond, and he had the whitest teeth I'd ever seen. He had a single bullet wound in the center of his chest. Surprisingly, there was very little blood.

But what bothered me the most were his eyes. When he was loaded on the helicopter, his head rolled to an angle, and now it seemed he was looking directly at me. His eyes were open, and he was staring right into my eyes. I will never forget those blue eyes. He looked so peaceful. If his eyes had been closed, he could have been in a very deep, restful sleep.

I'd never seen the kid before. I would never know his name. But I knew I would never forget him. On that day, the war became very personal for me. Now it was my goddamn war.

Dick must have seen the look on my face because he said, "Don't worry, Bill. You'll get used to it." Christ, how can a person ever get used to something like that? But he was right. I did get used to it.

We were released at 1800 hours. It took us an hour to fly back to Long Binh, and after getting the helicopter post-flighted and put to bed, I finally got back to my hootch fifteen hours after getting up. That was something we definitely had not heard about in flight school.

We had logged seven hours of flight time and made close to forty takeoffs and landings. The mental strain of the missions was staggering. Man, my ass was dragging. I was so tired that I didn't even stop at the mess hall for chow, but instead went straight to my hootch. Now I knew what Dean must have felt like the first time I'd seen him.

As I walked in and dropped my gear on my bunk, Jim Weaver looked at me and said, "Jesus Christ, Lieutenant, you look like shit." With that, he opened his footlocker and brought out a quart bottle of Bacardi rum. He looked at me, took the cap off, threw it away, and said, "Let's have a drink."

Well, hell, it had been a long, hard day! I couldn't think of anything better to do, so I joined him. This started a tradition with Jim and me. It got to a point where every night we would open a bottle of rum, and when the bottle was empty we would call it a night and go to bed. That went on for nine months.

We continued to work with the same units for the next four days. I was getting familiar with the area, and Dick was letting me do more of the flying. It sure felt good to be in control of the aircraft. It seemed that all the "tricks of the trade" Dick had been teaching me were as much common sense as anything else.

On any of the approaches we made to the units in the field, we could expect to take fire. In the area we were working, the terrain consisted of flat rice paddies with bordering tree lines. We knew that most of the VC in the area were just local farmers who could blend into the countryside whenever it suited them.

In flight school, we were taught that all approaches were made at eighty knots forward airspeed and five-hundred-feet-a-minute descent. If you tried to do that in II Corps, you would most likely get your ass blown out of the air. Most of our approaches were either low-level or high overhead.

I was still concerned about having only a .38 caliber pistol as my individual weapon. Most of the pilots who had been in country for any length of time had acquired a nonissue weapon. There were many different makes and models. AK-47s, .30 caliber M-1 carbines, and the 9mm Swedish-K submachine gun were a few of the more popular.

I asked Dick where all these weapons came from. He told me that most of the AK-47s and the carbines could be picked up from the infantry units we were supporting. However, if I wanted something other than those firearms, it would be necessary to go to the Army Special Forces camp at Ho Ngoc Tao, located between Long Binh and Saigon.

The .30 caliber carbine did not have enough killing power for my taste. Although the AK-47 was a very good weapon, it had a very distinctive sound. I did not think it would be a very smart move to have that type of firearm in a firefight at night. The AK-47 was the main weapon used by the enemy. If somebody heard the gun being discharged, they would most likely shoot at the sound without knowing who was firing the weapon.

The following day was a no-fly day for Dick and me, so we took advantage of the time off to get away from the company area. We borrowed the XO's jeep and headed south toward Saigon. It was the first time I'd been out of the company area other than in an aircraft. We went past the 90th Repo Depot, where I'd processed in after arriving in country. Although it had only been three weeks, I felt that I had been there forever.

The Special Forces compound was located on the west side of the highway next to a river, the name of which I don't recall. As we turned into the compound it looked no different from any of the other gates we'd seen on our fifteen-mile trip. But once we were inside, it was clear the place was a goddamn fortress. The guards at the gate were not Vietnamese, but Cambodian mercenaries. Dick told me that the Cambodes and the Vietnamese hated each other passionately, which was why the Special Forces used the mercenaries.

After checking in at the Orderly Room to let them know we were in the area, we went to the Team Room, an area set up for relaxation and entertainment. The walls were decorated with VC and NVA flags, as well as almost every kind of weapon you could imagine. There were weapons from the USA, USSR, China, Germany, France, England, and many other countries.

It was mind-boggling to think that a lot of the weapons on display were war trophies. There was also enemy equipment, uniforms, letters, and diaries. They even had an NVA skull wearing a pith helmet. The skull had a cigarette stuck between its teeth.

The refrigerator—a large civilian-style reefer—was full of whiskey, beer, soft drinks, and almost anything a hungry airborne soldier could possibly want to eat. And it was all free! Since we had the day off, I couldn't think of any reason not to have a drink. A very tall rum and Coke seemed to be in order.

Dick seemed to know most of the people there. Needless to say, I didn't know anyone, so I felt a little out of place. Then, much to my surprise, bigger than shit and twice as ugly, in walked S.Sgt. E-6 Jerry "J.J." Johnson.

J.J. and I had served together as E-5s in Germany. In fact, he was the one who'd taken Carole and me to the Frankfurt airport the day we rotated back to the States. Damn, it was good to see him; I didn't feel so out of place. It didn't take us long to catch up on what had happened in our lives over the last three years. Jerry requested Special Forces training while still in Germany, and was assigned to Fort Bragg, North Carolina, when he rotated back to the States.

We both still liked to drink, so we just picked up where we'd left off in Germany. The only thing wrong was that we didn't have any of the good German beer we'd grown to enjoy so much. Oh, well, we just learned to make do with what we had!

Jerry had been in country for about six months, and he told me he couldn't have had a better assignment. He planned to extend for at least another six months when his year was up. He really loved that shit.

A couple of hours and many drinks later, I finally got around to telling him the purpose of my visit to the unit. Since Jerry and I had served for two and a half years in the same airborne unit, he knew I was a soldier first and a pilot second. When I told him what I needed, he burst out laughing. It just so happened that he was a light weapons specialist, and so had access to damn near every type of weapon there was in Vietnam.

Jerry took me to the arms room, where I looked over the assortment of weapons he had under his control, and my mind went into overdrive. If I'd been able, I would have taken one of each. Jerry just sat back and grinned.

We went over the pros and cons of all the weapons I thought I wanted. One of the most prized "souvenirs," other than a Chicom pistol, was the Swedish-K submachine gun. It was lightweight, fast-firing, and very accurate. The only bad thing about it was that it fired 9mm ammunition. Unless you were working for an SF unit such as his, ammunition was in very short supply.

After we'd gone over eight or ten different weapons, it finally dawned on me that J.J. was letting me ramble on because it amused the hell out of him to see me so undecided. And, boy, was I ever undecided! Either Jerry grew tired of me making a fool of myself, or he needed another drink, or possibly both, because he finally said, "I've got just what you need."

With that, he walked over to a locker that hadn't been opened before and took out two weapons. The first was a Thompson submachine gun with the stock removed. I had fired that type of weapon before and knew that the recoil would make the weapon climb up and to the left. If you fired it out of the window of a helicopter, and let it climb, there would be a good chance of shooting off part of your main rotor blade—not a real good idea. You normally don't do it more than once. But, J.J. explained, if you laid the weapon on its side, instead of climbing it would pull itself forward. This was what I'd been looking for all the time, but hadn't realized it.

The next weapon he brought out was really a hog leg! It was a British-made Webley .38 caliber revolver that had been chambered for U.S. .45 caliber ammunition. God in heaven! I knew that if I hit somebody with either one of those weapons, there was no way in hell they would not go down.

Now I was happy. My U.S. Army–issue Smith & Wesson .38 caliber revolver would find a nice home in the bottom of my footlocker for the remainder of my tour. The new guns gave me more confidence than I'd ever dreamed of having. Along with the two weapons, J.J. gave me ten twenty-round Thompson magazines in a claymore bag, two magazines turned and taped together in the submachine gun, plus one thousand rounds of .45 caliber ammunition for the pistol. What more could a person ask for?

It was getting late and we still had to drive back to our company area. Although the road was considered safe during the day, it was not a good idea to travel on it by yourself after dark. As we prepared to leave, J.J. told me not to let anyone know where my two unauthorized weapons came from. The only people they would help with that kind of support were the air crews who flew for them. But I knew that he'd helped me because we'd known each other for such a long time. I couldn't help saying, just to mess with his mind, "Well, hell, Jerry, I don't fly for you."

He looked at me and said, "Bill, I know you. You'll fly for us. This is your kind of work. There is no way you'll be able to stay away."

Dick was very quiet for the first half of the trip back to the company area. Then out of the blue he told me, "Bill, you've been flying with me for the last week, and you've done real good. Now I'm going to put you up with some of the other ACs. If you do as well with them, I'll recommend that you start flying some of the FOB [Forward Observation Base] missions. We don't normally let the new pilots work these missions this soon, but after the way you handled yourself with Lieutenant Greenlee, and working with me the way you have, I think you might be ready. I've already talked about this with Staff Sergeant Johnson."

I didn't know what to say. Nobody had told me exactly what those missions were, but I had a pretty good idea. I did know they were strictly voluntary. Christ on a crutch, what a compliment.

The rest of the trip was made in silence. By the time we arrived, I knew J.J. had been right. There was no way in hell I could stay away.

The next day, I flew with John Dean, supporting the 199th Light Infantry Brigade. The area we were working was to the northwest of Long Binh. The terrain was rolling hills with scattered trees that grew to a height of about twenty feet. There were a lot of open areas to use as LZs. It was an excellent area to be flying because with so many open areas, the VC couldn't watch or booby-trap them all.

John flew all of the approaches for the first hour. He explained how and why he made each approach the way he did. This was a much different type of terrain than I'd worked with Dick Washburn, so a different technique was used. After the first hour John said, "You have the controls. Let's see if you can earn your flight pay." Once again there was none of the typical flight school bullshit.

Although John stayed close to the controls, as he had me do when he was flying, he let me do all of the approaches. If he saw me getting myself into a situation that could prove dangerous, he recommended an alternate approach. For example, when I'd been into an LZ twice and was on my third approach, I was set up to use the same flight path, altitude, and airspeed. Not a good idea! As John pointed out, if you set a pattern and kept using it, Chuck would eat your lunch for you. You tried never to give the bad guy a chance to figure out what you were going to do.

The next day with John was very busy. We didn't even notice how fast the time passed. It was one approach after another, and I don't think we ever got above one hundred feet altitude. We were continually on the go, moving people and material from one place to another. As far as I knew, we never got shot at. I commented about this to John. He looked at me, shook his head, and said, "Don't get in too big of a hurry. Before this is over, you'll get shot at more than you can imagine—if you live that long." The man sure had a way with words.

Chapter
Six

The following day was spent in support of the 9th Infantry Division. I was flying copilot with Captain Schlater. It was a ten-ship mission, five out of the first platoon and five out of the second. We also had four gunships from our gun platoon, plus the company commander in the command and control (C&C) ship.

We departed Long Binh at 0445 for the ninety-minute flight to Dong Tam. This gave us time to reach our destination, refuel, and be mission-ready by 0730 hours. It was my first real night formation flight since flight school.

Damn, it was dark. There was neither moon nor stars visible in the sky. I was sure glad we were following the first platoon. They were about a half mile ahead of us, and all I could see were their navigation lights. Captain Jack had briefed me the night before that I would be doing the navigating and taking care of the radios for most of the time during the flight. If we had been in the lead, and I'd been navigating, God only knows where we would have ended up. I had no way in hell of knowing where we were. I couldn't see the ground, and there were no navigational aids or roads to follow. How in the holy hell did anybody know where they were or where they were going?

As we continued to fly, the night sky started to get lighter as the sun came closer to the eastern horizon. I had the map in my hands. I knew where we were going, and I knew where we'd departed from. I also knew what heading we were flying, and for how long, and at what airspeed. It seemed reasonable that with all that information I should be able to at least come close to locating myself in the air relative to my position over the ground. As I took all of these things into account and applied all my training, I came to the only conclusion possible. Shit, I was still lost! The guy I felt sorry for was the copilot in the lead aircraft, especially if he was an FNG like me.

As the sky became still lighter, I began to make out some of the terrain features. It was just as mind-boggling as if it had still been dark. As far as I could see there was nothing but flooded rice paddies whose coloring varied from light blue to dark emerald green. And each seemed to have a small piece of man-made high ground with a grave on it.

The paddies were separated from each other by low built-up earthen berms, known as "dikes," that ran the length of the paddy. These rice paddy dikes were two to three feet wide. A lot had trees or nipa palms planted along them. The vegetation was so thick that it couldn't be walked through. From our altitude of two thousand feet, there must have been over a thousand square miles of rice paddy dikes in sight. It seemed as if they went on forever in all directions.

I still didn't know where we were. Then Jack pointed out a small brown area off the nose of the aircraft about ten miles ahead of us: Dong Tam, home of the 9th Infantry Division. We landed at its refueling point, hot refueled (with the turbine whining), then relocated to an open area, where we shut the aircraft down.

Needless to say, this was an entirely different environment from what I was used to. I had never seen anything like it in my entire life. Everything was so flat, and it all looked the same.

The CO came over to brief us on how the operation would be conducted. It was going to be like a big chess game. We would be inserting platoon-size units into an area. They would sweep the tree line or the small villages, then we would pick them up and reinsert them into another area, to do the same thing all over again. The first platoon would be working separately from the second platoon. We would each have a light fire team (two UH-1Cs) flying cover for us. Our CO would be flying C&C for both platoons. I could see that this might turn into a really bad situation rather quickly.

At 0830 the C&C ship took off with the company commander and his counterpart from the unit we were supporting. They were to identify the LZ for the gunships to prep. Then the CO would vector the lift ships, a flight of five, which would be coming low-level into the AO. The C&C would then make a pass over the LZ and drop a smoke grenade to mark the spot where the lead aircraft was to land. After the first lift had made its insertion, the C&C would then move to the second LZ and repeat the process.

Five minutes after the CO departed, the first platoon's five aircraft, carrying eight troops each, departed Dong Tam for the LZ. Everything went as planned and the insertion was completed without a hitch. The C&C then headed for the next LZ.

The second flight of five, my platoon, was still at Dong Tam, loaded and ready to go. The guns departed, and we were on our way two minutes later. We took off on a heading of 060 degrees and remained under fifty feet en route to the LZ. It was only a fifteen-minute flight, and by staying low we kept our exposure time to a minimum.

We also tried to avoid overflying as many of the tree lines as possible, as the bad guys owned the tree lines. This was all really exciting for me. It was my first real live combat assault (CA), and I was in the lead aircraft.

This insertion also went as planned. While we were putting in our troops, the first platoon had returned to Dong Tam for another load and to wait for the C&C to call them off. As soon as we completed our insertion, we headed back to pick up another load of troops. We were about five minutes out from Dong Tam when I heard the C&C instruct the first platoon to head for its next LZ.

That was the way things would continue until each platoon had made six insertions. Then we would go back and pick up the first group we'd put in and reinsert it into another location. Except for occasional sniper fire, the LZs were quiet. The VC didn't seem to want to come out and play.

Major O'Connor was flying the C&C ship with WO1 Mario "Butch" Meola as copilot. At about 1300 hours they

were vectoring my flight into an LZ. We were in a trail formation, ninety knots forward airspeed and about fifty feet altitude. As Jack had me working the radios, I was using my call
sign, and did that ever make me feel good. I could see the
C&C aircraft at about fifteen hundred feet off my nose, and
made radio contact.

"Kingsman Six, this is Kingsman Two-five."

"Two-five, this is Six. Go ahead."

"Six, Two-five. We are two minutes out. Have you in sight
at my twelve o'clock high."

"Roger, Two-five. I have your flight in sight. We are going
down to mark the LZ. Your guns are on station at your eleven
o'clock."

"Roger, Six. Two-five has the guns in sight. Break. Lancer
Three-four, Kingsman Two-five is inbound with a flight of
five."

"Roger, Two-five. We've got you covered."

I could see the C&C ship descending and watched as the
smoke grenade fell into the rice paddy. The procedure was to
identify the color of the smoke, then the C&C would confirm
the color. I could see the smoke starting to rise and called,
"Kingsman Six, this is Kingsman Two-five. I identify goofy
grape [purple]."

"Roger, Two-five. Confirm purple."

Jack was flying and I had a chance to watch the C&C ship
as it completed its run across the LZ. There was a tree line at
the far end of the LZ, and the C&C seemed to start a climbing
left-hand turn right before the trees. The aircraft had climbed
to about seventy-five feet when I saw a line of green tracers—
the NVA/VC used green tracers and the U.S. used red—come
out of the tree line reaching up toward the C&C ship. I
couldn't see how in the hell they could miss. They didn't.
Then I could hear Kingsman Six calling that they were receiving fire and had taken some hits. At that point the world
went to hell in a handbasket for the rest of the day.

Kingsman Six had taken a tracer round that entered the
bottom of the left door, traveled upward, and lodged in the
upper part of the door frame. As Kingsman Six broke away

from the tree line, the gunships rolled in and shot the shit out of the area where the VC fire had come from. There was no more fire to be seen coming out of that area, but we still avoided the tree line.

By the time we reached Dong Tam to refuel, Major O'Connor had already shut down and was checking his aircraft. He had taken only one hit. Fortunately, the aircraft was still flyable.

After refueling, we headed back to the AO to move one of the platoons to a different location. We picked them up and headed for the next LZ. Once again I could see the C&C ship, but he looked to be a little higher, maybe two thousand feet. I called Kingsman Six and let him know we were about a mile out.

Major O'Connor replied, "Roger, Two-five. The LZ is the green rice paddy at your twelve o'clock and one mile."

What in the hell is this shit? I wondered. The C&C was still at two thousand feet and all the rice paddies were green. So where in the hell was I supposed to land?

"Kingsman Six, this is Two-five. Which one of the paddies do you want me to put the troops into?"

"Two-five, this is Six. I want you to land in the green paddy with the grave in it."

Well, I'd be a son of a bitch. All the rice paddies had graves in them. "Okay, Six, we are on short final. Is this where you want them?"

"Negative, negative, Two-five. That's the wrong place."

"Roger, Six. We're making a go-round. Break. Kingsman flight, this is Two-five. We are going around with a right break."

So off we went. A flight of five with forty troops on board, and absolutely no goddamn idea where in the hell we were going.

"Kingsman Six, this is Two-five. Are you going to mark the LZ for us?"

"Two-five, Six. Negative on marking the LZ. I'll vector you into the landing zone."

"Six, Two-five. Roger that. We'll be coming around for another approach."

And that's the way it went for the rest of the day. The only time the C&C got below two thousand feet was when he was landing at Dong Tam to refuel. Jack hadn't said anything throughout this whole fiasco. He just sat there and let me muddle through as best I could.

Around 1700 hours the 9th Division released us, so we would still have some daylight left after our ninety-minute flight back to Long Binh. On our return trip my flight was in the lead. Jack allowed me to fly the first forty-five minutes, then told me to sit back and relax. I didn't argue with that at all. Damn! It had been a long day, and I'd been given one hell of a workout.

The farther we flew to the north, the more familiar the terrain became. I could see Saigon in the distance. Due to the amount of jet traffic coming out of Tan Son Nhut Airport, we had to descend to five hundred feet or below to stay out of the way of the Air Force fighter-bombers taking off and landing there. The company was strung out for over a mile. My platoon was in the lead, then came the first platoon, followed by the four gunships. The command and control ship brought up the rear.

We were about five miles south of Saigon at four hundred feet, and I was doing what I'd been told by the other ACs: sitting there with my hands in my lap, my feet on the floor, and my mouth shut. Looking down through the chin bubble, I could see a small figure standing in the middle of a dry rice paddy. The closer we got to the paddy, the larger the man became. I could make out something in his hands. Then I couldn't believe what I was seeing. That silly son of a bitch was standing there, right out in the middle of the rice paddy, shooting at us.

From where Jack was sitting on the left-hand side of the aircraft, he couldn't see the man. I told him what I was watching, and he told me to notify the C&C.

"Kingsman Six, this is Kingsman Two-five. We are receiving fire. I have the target in sight."

The response I got sure as hell wasn't what I expected. "For God sakes, don't shoot. You might hurt somebody."

I was so dumbfounded that I couldn't even respond. I just looked silently at Jack. I assumed that my mouth was hanging open. Jack just shook his head, keyed the radio, and said, "Kingsman Six, this is Kingsman Two-six. I understand do not return fire."

"Two-six, this is Six. That's affirmative. Do not fire."

Wasn't this a bitch? Fifteen helicopters, sixty men, and they wouldn't let us kill this little bastard who was shooting at us! It made me wonder what his rules of engagement were.

We'd been told that afternoon that Major O'Connor was being transferred to Group Headquarters at Bear Cat. Maybe that's why he got a little "cautious" on the mission. But even if that had been the reason, it sure didn't make it any easier on us. Maybe it was just as well he was being transferred, as there were some pretty hard feelings when we landed.

Our new commanding officer was Major Donald G. Andrews. He had been born and raised in Miami, Florida. He majored in psychology at the University of Florida and, upon graduation in 1954, was commissioned a second lieutenant of Artillery through the ROTC program. He attended Artillery Officers' Basic at Fort Sill, Oklahoma, then proceeded to flight school, graduating in 1956. After serving as an Army aviator with various units in both Europe and the United States, he was assigned to Vietnam in 1963 as a staff officer, Joint Staff J-3, MACV. Upon completion of his first combat tour, he was reassigned to Fort Bragg, North Carolina. In 1967 he returned to Vietnam as the XO of the 116th AHC at Cu Chi. On January 20, 1968, he became commanding officer of the 17th AHC.

You could tell right from the beginning that this guy was no joke. He was a professional. He wasted no time letting us know what he expected of us. That did not seem to present a problem, as far as the aviation part of the operation went.

If there was to be a problem, it would occur during the off-duty time. I had discovered that after a hard day at the office, these guys liked to kick back, relax, drink, play cards, and just raise a little hell in general. After flying with them for a couple of weeks, I couldn't agree with them more.

Even with the new CO, the missions went on as before. It seemed that the amount of contact with the VC was dropping off slightly in all areas we worked. That had us wondering a little. Everybody was talking about the Vietnamese Lunar New Year, which the Vietnamese called Tet. In the past, everyone had simply called a truce. The VC and the ARVN soldiers just quit fighting and went home for the holidays. Tet was only a few days off, and if things went as they had in the past, it would be nice to have a couple of days of light flying.

I continued flying with different aircraft commanders, supporting mostly the 9th Division out of Dong Tam. But the area seemed really quiet and no one could understand why. Normally, the VC would be active enough to keep us wary; lately there'd been nothing. With so little activity, we were released early enough to return to our home station well before dark.

The thirty-first of January was a light day of flying, only four and a half hours. We returned to Long Binh early, at 1600 hours, and Operations released us from duty for the day. Not being used to having this much time off on a day we were supposed to be flying until dark, we just stood around looking at each other. Then someone, I think it was Dick Washburn, came up with a brilliant idea. The way he put it was, "The dinks are going to celebrate the Lunar New Year, so let's get a head start on them."

The party was on.

Chapter
Seven

The partying went on until approximately 2200 hours, when most of the pilots decided to call it a night. A poker game had started in my tent with six of us playing. The stakes were nickel, dime, and quarter. There was nothing to get excited about. You could play all night and win or lose only twenty dollars. It was a very relaxing evening.

The poker game gave everyone a chance to forget what they'd been going through the last couple of months. It also gave me an opportunity to see what those people were thinking.

It was interesting to hear them talk. Those kids were just that—kids. They talked about their girlfriends, their cars, whose car could outrun whose, and what they thought they'd do when they got home. Most of them didn't know the first thing about playing poker. I saw from the beginning that if I really wanted to, I could make a lot of money just by letting them think they knew what they were doing.

The game started breaking up a little after midnight. Off in the distance we could hear the *crump* of mortar rounds impacting. There were just a few at first, then more and more. I'd heard incoming rounds before, but there had only been three or four. This was much more intense.

Then we heard the sound of incoming rockets. The 122mm rockets made a hell of a lot more noise when they exploded than the mortar rounds. There were a lot of explosions and they seemed to be getting closer. All of that took place within a two-minute period. It sounded like one hell of a fight was taking place only a short distance away.

Then we heard the crackle of small-arms fire erupting just down the road. The card game broke up and everyone immediately headed for their hootches. All of the lights had gone out in the company area. I went outside and saw the tracers going out into the darkness. Gunships were making gun runs. I could see the flashes of exploding mortars and rockets as they impacted within the perimeter. It looked a lot like the fireworks display at Disneyland.

Captain Schlater walked over from the direction of Operations. He didn't know what was going on except that there was fighting all over the place. He stayed for a few minutes before heading back to Operations. He hadn't yet given any instructions. So with nobody to tell me what I was supposed to do, and no one else in sight—I guess they'd all headed for the bunker—I simply sat down on the sandbag blast wall that went around my hootch and watched the war go by.

Soon, the sound of small-arms fire seemed to get closer and more intense. After sitting there for a short time, I went inside and put on my flak jacket and steel pot, picked up my weapons and ammunition, and returned to my ringside seat. I figured that sooner or later Captain Jack would be back to let me know what was happening.

When I first processed into the company, I was taken on a tour of the perimeter. They'd shown me the area we were supposed to defend in case of a ground attack. I'd been led to believe that a ground attack was so unlikely that none of the pilots took the perimeter defense seriously. Now I was beginning to wonder if I should stay where I was or go where they'd shown me. Or should I go to the flight line in case we had to get the aircraft off the ground? I hadn't seen any of the other pilots heading that way. The flight gear was still in the hootch. Shit, I had no idea what to do.

So I just did what any good soldier would do. I waited. The only helicopters taking off and landing at our airfield were the flare ship and the gunships. The gunships were the Lancers from my company and the Thunder Chickens from our sister company. A steady stream of them appeared to be leaving the area; they weren't going very far. They would take off, turn to fly along the perimeter, expend their rockets and minigun ammunition, then land to rearm. It was quite an impressive display of firepower.

It must have been around 0100 hours when a brilliant white flash came from the southeast. It was brightest thing I'd ever seen. After the initial flash, it was still bright. Then I could see the shock waves coming toward me. It looked like the newsreels at the movies of the atomic bomb test at the Bikini Atoll in the early fifties. It scared the living hell out of me. I knew that I was going to die. Thirty days in country, and I was going to die. Now wasn't that a bitch! But I didn't die. As the shock waves reached me, I simply fell backward off the sandbag wall. After I hit the ground, the tents around me appeared to try to take flight. I was afraid the wall would fall over on top of me. Then it was over. The tents were still standing, the wall hadn't fallen on top of me, and I was still alive. Maybe there was a God, after all. I don't remember praying, but I'm sure I did. I think it was then that I confirmed the popular saying that there were no atheists in a foxhole.

I found out later that the explosion and shock wave had been caused by the Long Binh ammo dump blowing up. Although the entire complex hadn't gone up at one time, a good portion of it had. Most of the remaining ammo-storage bunkers exploded later that morning.

I moved out from behind the sandbag wall into what I guess would be called the company street, the thirty-foot space between the two rows of tents. I'd taken only two or three steps when a string of red tracers came right down the middle of the damn street. I dove back behind the sandbags. Two things got my attention right off the bat: first, the tracers were red; and second, they came from the area across the road that belonged to the 199th Light Infantry Brigade.

After crawling out from behind the sandbag wall, I took a few minutes to try to figure out just what the hell had happened. That was not why I'd attended flight school; if I wanted to get shot at on the ground, I would have gone back to the infantry.

I knew I couldn't stay where I was, but I didn't know what

else to do. Somewhere, I'd read words that I believe were attributed to General Custer: "Always ride toward the sound of the battle." It sounded like one hell of a battle was going on along parts of the perimeter. So that's where I headed.

I took my time moving away from the tents. It was the first ground attack in the area, and a lot of very nervous people were out there. I sure as hell didn't want to get shot by my own folk.

I reached the bunker line in about twenty minutes. A few other people were moving in that direction. They were going into the bunkers. I stopped at the nearest one to let them know I was going to move about midway between where they were and the bunker to their left.

I moved into the position I'd picked out for myself, a place that looked like it might be in a blind spot, where a person could position himself and not be seen from either bunker. I couldn't see anyone else on the line. It was kind of lonely out there by myself, but I didn't like the idea of being inside one of the bunkers. They made too good a target; one B-40 rocket would take out the whole structure, and the people inside as well.

The gunships were still making their runs, working out about two hundred meters from the berm. The flares were now being dropped on the other side of the compound, so there was a small amount of light to my front, but not very much.

I kept looking over the berm, but it was still too dark to see anything. I couldn't stand up without exposing myself, so I leaned against the berm and raised my head just far enough so my eyes could see over the top. After I'd been staring out into the darkness for about fifteen minutes, my eyes began playing tricks on me. I would think I saw something move, and when I looked again, nothing would be there.

I turned around and looked back toward the billeting area just as a flare went off. That shot the hell out of my night vision, and it would take another ten minutes or so of looking into the darkness to regain it. In the meantime I would have to make sure I didn't look at the flares being dropped behind me.

It seemed to take forever for the flare ship to work its way back to our side of the perimeter, but eventually I saw it coming our way. When the first flare went off, I spotted something moving in the wire approximately thirty meters to my right. There was a group of people there, eight or ten VC, about ten meters from the berm, out in the wire. Evidently, they had found a blind spot and already moved through it, to within fifty meters of the barbed wire, and were about to get inside our perimeter. How in the hell could they have gotten that far without being seen by someone?

Now what was I going to do? I was out there by myself with no way of getting any help, and scared out of my everloving mind. All I had with me were the weapons I'd gotten from J.J.—the pistol and the Thompson submachine gun. The one thing I needed, and didn't have, were hand grenades. With a couple of those, I could have done some real damage.

As it was, I would have to move; if they got over the berm, I would be in real trouble. While moving, I would have to stay down behind the berm, where the VC would be out of my sight. Well, so be it! I checked the submachine gun, made sure the safety was off, and, staying below the top of the berm, started running.

I didn't have to move far, but it seemed to take forever. I tried to judge where to stop and yet still be as close as possible to where the VC were, since I hadn't decided what I was going to do when I got there. I did know that the effective range of the Thompson submachine gun wasn't very far, and with the stock removed it was even less. If I was going to use the damn thing, I would have to be close.

Lying there, I took a deep breath, wondering if it would be my last, and looked over the top of the berm. The VC were huddled together about twenty feet away. They looked as if they were getting ready to make their final rush to break inside the wire.

I brought my submachine gun up, pointed it to the lower right-hand side of the group, and fired. I had loaded four tracers, the first two rounds and the last two rounds, into the thirty-round magazine. The first two would allow me to see if

I was shooting where I wanted to, and the last two would let me know when the magazine was going dry.

The first rounds hit right where I wanted them. As the weapon started to climb, I could see the bodies begin to jerk, twist, and tumble as the .45 caliber rounds tore into them. I released the pressure on the trigger and the weapon stopped firing. I brought it back to bear, then fired again. I continued firing into the pile of bodies until the thirty-round magazine was empty. Dropping down behind the berm, I ejected the empty magazine and inserted a fresh one.

I moved a short distance to my left, then came up firing into the pile of bodies again. After using half my ammunition, I stopped. There was no movement. Instead of looking like people, it was like looking at a pile of bloody rags. The dead VC were lying in the weirdest positions. I don't think they ever knew what hit them. They never fired a round at me. At least, I didn't think they did.

At the time, I didn't even know how many people I'd just killed, and I guess it didn't matter. But I'd just answered one of the questions that had been bothering me: Could I take a human life? I knew I wouldn't have to worry about that one anymore.

The flares were still burning as I sat down behind the berm. I was surprised to find that I could see my hands shaking. I tried to light a cigarette and couldn't. I hadn't noticed the people who had come out of the bunker until one of them handed me a lighted cigarette. I guess they had heard the sound of the gunfire and came out to see what was happening. The one thing that I did know was that I sure was damn glad to see them.

I just sat there. I couldn't help thinking it was almost like in the movies. However, there were some big differences. In the movies, everyone would get up and go home after the end of the show. And here you had the smells. I could still smell the burned gunpowder in the air. I could smell the fear on myself, and I could smell death—the sweet, sickening smell of death. For those who have never experienced the smell, it's something you won't forget.

I couldn't understand why the enemy had decided to try to breach the wire at that point. Even if they were able to get inside the perimeter, there would have been no cover. The flight line was quite a distance away. The closest thing of any value to that point was the billeting area.

I later found out I'd killed nine people that night. One of them was my hootchmaid, the young girl who had shined my boots, washed my uniforms, and taken care of the area where I lived. We also learned that we'd killed the company barber, several of the people who worked in the mess hall, and four or five more hootchmaids. We had also captured two other hootchmaids. From them, we found out that their mission was to lead the VC through the wire and into the area where the pilots lived. They were to kill as many of the pilots as possible before they made their escape or were killed themselves.

I must have fallen asleep. When I raised my head and looked over the berm, it was just starting to grow light in the eastern part of the sky. Looking at my watch, I saw that it was a few minutes before five. I'd been there for somewhere between two and a half to three hours. The sound of gunfire had slackened off to almost nothing. There were a few scattered shots from time to time, but that was all. The VC didn't like to be engaged in any kind of prolonged fight during the daylight hours because they understood how fast we could react using helicopters and fast-movers (jets).

I headed back to the billeting area to get my flight gear, knowing we still had missions scheduled for the day. Of course, they might have changed due to the severity of the overnight attacks. Regardless of where we were going, I still had to have the aircraft ready to go. As the copilot, it was my job to do the preflight and ensure that the aircraft was flyable.

In fact, it was the crew chiefs who kept the aircraft in the air. The pilots and the copilots were just the drivers. The crew chiefs, along with their door gunners, were the ones who pulled all of the daily inspections and conducted the post-flight inspections after the last flight of the day, although some of the pilots did help. It was also the crew chiefs who made sure that any and all deficiencies found during the day's flight were taken care of before the first flight the next morning.

Then there was the never-ending task of trying to keep the aircraft clean. These men took extreme pride in their helicopters. They didn't seem to care how many hours they had to put in as long as their aircraft were clean, flyable, and mission-ready. It was not unusual for a pilot to arrive at the aircraft well before the sun came up and find the crew chief curled up in the cargo compartment, sound asleep after working all night.

There had been no sleep for the crew chiefs that night. When I reached the aircraft, no one was there. I checked the logbook and found no write-ups that would prohibit the aircraft from flight. Checking the logbook was always the first step in the preflight. The pilot could see what, if anything, the crew chief had found and entered in the logbook.

The crew chief for the aircraft in the next revetment was going over his helicopter. I asked him if he knew where I could find my crew chief. He pointed toward the rearm point and told me that the crew chief and the gunner were helping rearm and refuel the gunships. They'd been there all night. Clearly, with nobody having gotten any sleep the night before, it was going to be a very long day.

I continued with the preflight. After completing the inspection of the bottom of the aircraft, I climbed up on the roof to inspect the rotor head. I could see several other people doing the same thing on neighboring aircraft.

I was up there only a short time when I heard something go by my head. It made a zinging sound, followed closely by the sharp *crack* of a rifle discharge. I shrugged it off and didn't pay any attention to it. I guess my mind wasn't working too well at the time.

A few minutes later it happened again. I noticed then that everyone else had gotten down from the top of their aircraft and was hiding inside the revetments. It finally dawned on me—*sniper!* Some asshole was trying to kill me. I didn't have to think twice about getting off the top of the helicopter.

With everyone else in the revetments, they seemed like the right place to be.

It was somewhat of a joke sitting there in the revetment. Nobody could move, yet we felt safe enough. We were yelling back and forth to each other. No one had been hit. Maybe they should just leave the sniper alone. If they killed him, they might replace him with someone who could shoot better.

After about an hour, word was passed down the line that grunts from the 199th Light Infantry Brigade were going to try to flush out the bad guy. It would take a while before they began, so we would have to stay where we were. That suited the hell out of me. I really didn't have anywhere I needed to go.

I was squatting down, leaning back against the corrugated metal plate of the wall. I'd just bent forward to light a cigarette when I heard something hit the revetment right behind my head. Out of the corner of my eye I saw something shiny spinning on the tarmac a short distance away. It was a bullet. Like a damn fool, I jumped out of the revetment to retrieve it. As soon as I reached the bullet, another round hit by my right foot. I grabbed the spent round and dove back into the revetment. The bullet was still hot.

I moved back to the place I'd been before the shot and found the mark where the bullet had hit. Squatting back down, I put my head back against the revetment and realized that if I hadn't been lighting that damn cigarette, the bullet would have hit me right in the left temple. Maybe it wasn't such a bad idea to get rid of this guy. His aim seemed to be getting better with practice. I carried that bullet on my dog tag chain for two years. It was lost when I was attending the Air Force Jungle Survival School in the Philippines en route to my second tour in Vietnam.

It took close to two hours for the infantry to clear the snipers from around the perimeter and away from the airfield. There had been only a handful of them, but they sure kept us from getting our helicopters into the air. To the best of my knowledge, no one in my unit was hit. However, a lot of people had been pinned down. During the fighting the night before, two guys had climbed the water tank in the company area to get a better view. But they had to stay there all night and the better part of the morning because every time they tried to come down, they were shot at.

We finally got off the ground around ten o'clock in the morning. I was flying copilot with Dick Washburn. We were going to Dong Tam. There were two flights of five slicks, two light fire teams of two gunships each and the C&C aircraft. Elements of the 9th Division had been hit during the night, and we were to give support to those units. The base at Dong Tam hadn't been hit, but a lot of their units were attacked in their NDPs (night defensive positions).

The VC and NVA had attacked cities and military bases all over the country and had called for a general uprising to support them, but it failed to materialize. Now the bad guys were out in force and the fight was on. So much for the holiday truce.

Our day consisted of hauling supplies, ammo, hot food, and replacements to units in the field. Some of them had been hit pretty badly during the night. Luckily for us, the 191st AHC (call sign "Boomerang") stationed at Dong Tam had already removed the dead and wounded, a job nobody liked doing. By the number of replacements we were taking to the field, the 191st had already done a full day's work by the time we arrived on the scene.

We'd been split into one- and two-ship elements. There were a lot of platoon-size units working separately, trying to find the enemy, which had broken contact as soon as the sun came up. When they were located, we quickly moved other troops into the area and attempted to destroy them. The main problem was that the VC/NVA didn't want to be found. There was something about the daylight they just didn't like.

It was an afternoon of continuous flying. Everyone was dead tired, but there was no letup. Our gunships were working with the "Bounty Hunters"—the gun platoon from the 191st—to provide cover for the lift ships. Even so, there were not enough guns to cover us all, and we were taking light small-arms fire on every approach. I guess the bad guys were as tired as we were because they were doing a lot of shooting but not hitting much.

We were all looking forward to being released and returning to Long Binh. I was sure there would be no party that night; that didn't matter because I wanted only to go to sleep. I'd been tired before, but by that time it was hard for me to understand how any of our people could still keep their eyes open, much less fly those damn helicopters.

The sun was starting to set when we were finally told to land, refuel, and shut the aircraft down for the night. We were going to be standing by at Dong Tam for the next few hours. That was the best news I'd heard all day. As soon as we secured the aircraft, I lay down on the ground and watched the setting sun.

I don't remember falling asleep, but when I felt someone kicking my foot, I opened my eyes and it was very dark. There was a lot of movement and noise going on around all of the aircraft. Dick was saying something about a briefing and some town that had just been overrun. I was still half asleep and nothing made any sense to me. He reached down, grabbed my arm, and pulled me to my feet. As we walked toward the lead aircraft, he said something about it being time for me to earn my combat pay for the month. Combat pay, shit! I didn't even know where in the hell I was!

The Old Man was standing by his helicopter when we arrived, but we had to wait a few minutes for the other pilots to get there before the briefing began. There wasn't any of the joking and bullshit that was usual when you got that many pilots together. Everyone was too tired and the mood was too serious. I began to worry; I'd never seen them so subdued before. I wondered what we were going to be getting into.

Once everyone was gathered, the briefing began. The VC/NVA had come out of their holes and were attacking in force. Several of the larger towns were being hit, and at least two had been, or were at that moment, being overrun. The towns of My Tho (pronounced "me toe") and Ben Tre ("ben tray") were under attack. Ben Tre, about twenty miles to the northeast, was already in enemy hands. The ARVN defenders had just folded. The Americans, about thirty of them, were holding out in the MACV compound. Needless to say, they were surrounded and running low on ammunition.

Our job was to reinforce and resupply the compound. However, that would prove difficult to do. We were to move out to the field location of the units we'd been supporting during the day, and pick up people to be inserted directly into the MACV compound. Then we were to return to Dong Tam, onload ammunition, and depart as two flights of five, with the second platoon in the lead.

Dick and I departed Dong Tam for one of the field locations we'd been working that afternoon. Upon landing, we loaded five troops aboard, one lieutenant and four enlisted men. We then headed back to Dong Tam to join the rest of the company and load the ammunition. That part of the operation took only twenty minutes. When we arrived, the rest of the company was already loaded and ready to go. Five minutes later, so were we.

The company commander was flying over the town of Ben Tre in the C&C ship. He was reporting on the situation and condition of the city and the MACV compound as we were departing Dong Tam. From what he was saying, things were going to be difficult; the city was on fire and the compound would be almost impossible to find in the smoke and flames. I was trying to picture this in my mind, but I just could not conceive it. I'd never seen a fire as big as he was describing. I had seen movies of towns burning, but hell, that was Hollywood.

From there on the ground, I could just make out a dull yellow glow in the east. As we followed the second aircraft in the formation of ten into the air, I couldn't shake the feeling of total helplessness that had come over me. Fires glowed almost everywhere I looked. Most of them were small, but several were quite large and clearly out of control. The one we were headed for seemed to be the largest of them all.

As we gained altitude I saw that other aircraft were trying to beat back the VC/NVA. I was watching a pair of gunships from the 191st (the "Bounty Hunters") engaging a target on the ground about three miles away. It was fascinating. One would roll in on his gun run just as the other was completing his pass. That way they were able to cover each other's break.

As the one that had just completed his run made his break, his door guns would be firing. I could see the red tracers from his M-60 hitting in the target area. The other aircraft would start inbound with his miniguns firing three thousand rounds a minute. Every fifth round was a tracer, and it looked like a water hose spitting out a bright red jet of fire. Then the minigun would stop as the rockets were launched. I could see each rocket as it left the tube, and watch the rocket motor as it drove the warhead toward the target.

However, the bad guys on the ground were not just sitting back and taking it. They were putting up one hell of a fight. Every time one of the gunships made its run, I saw muzzle flashes and lines of green tracers coming up from the ground. I got the definite impression that the people on the ground were not VC but NVA troops who were standing and fighting. That was unlike the VC, who would usually fight for a short while, then fade away. The NVA were good, and they seemed to be well disciplined.

As we turned toward the east, I was still watching the two gunships as they continued to place their fire into the enemy positions. One of the gunships began his firing pass. The minigun was firing as the helicopter dove down toward the target. Only this time the minigun didn't stop firing. There were green tracers coming up toward the aircraft. The continuous line of red tracers from the gunship seemed to be following the path of the enemy fire right back to its source as it came up at them.

I kept waiting for the minigun to stop firing, but it didn't. The gunship continued its dive. The rockets never fired. As I watched, the aircraft suddenly flew right into the ground. It seemed as if everything were happening in slow motion. The firing on the ground stopped. The second gunship broke off its gun run and climbed out of the area. Then came the explosion.

There was no fire, just a large, bright flash as the helicopter disintegrated. Afterward there were several smaller secondary explosions as the rockets that had not yet been fired began to cook off.

We would never know what caused the aircraft to crash. It could have been that the ground fire hit the pilot, or he had what is known as target fixation. The only known fact was that four men out of the 191st Assault Helicopter Company's gun platoon had just died.

That was the first aircraft I'd seen crash. I'd seen others take hits from ground fire, but they had all made it back to their bases and landed safely. This was different. It brought the grim reality home to me that I could die out there. Those people were trying to kill me. I could only hope that the aircraft that I'd just witnessed crashing had crashed on top of the people shooting at it.

Christ! Would the night never end? We had our own mission to worry about. We were flying as a flight of ten in a trail formation at two thousand feet. All of the aircraft had their position lights on steady dim. I could barely make out the helicopter in front of me. There were also four gunships and a C&C ship out there somewhere.

Straight line, Ben Tre was about a fifteen-minute flight. However, we were going to overfly the city and try to locate the MACV compound. Then we would have to make a right-hand turn to the northwest, set up our separation, turn back to the southeast, and make single-ship approaches into the one-ship LZ.

But as we gained altitude coming out of Dong Tam, we saw that the city was completely engulfed in flame. Smoke was everywhere. I couldn't see the streets. It was impossible to pick out any particular building, much less the small area that made up the MACV compound.

There was a large canal just east of the compound. Just across that canal was an ARVN outpost. It was one of those triangular affairs where the local militia was stationed, with their families living with them. What a hell of a way to fight a war! Those were not the most reliable or best-trained soldiers in the South Vietnamese Army. In fact, they were what I would consider the last line of defense. There was no sign of life in the ARVN compound. It had to make you wonder why. However, at the time, I was so new in country and so inexperienced that none of this entered my mind.

As we came across the burning city, someone, it may have been Jim Weaver, said over the radio, "Nothing can get us now except a .50 cal." He had just made the comment when a line of *red* tracers came arcing up out of the ARVN compound. The first burst passed just in front of the nose of the lead aircraft. The second burst was between the tail of the lead aircraft and the nose of the number-two aircraft. The third was between the tail of number two and the nose of the helicopter I was flying in, number three in the flight of ten. From that point on I really don't know what the hell happened. Those damn .50 caliber tracers looked like basketballs coming up at us. They lit up the inside of the aircraft like it was daylight.

As soon as we started taking the .50 caliber fire, Dick Washburn reached up and turned off all our navigation and instrument lights; we were completely blacked out. When I looked outside of the aircraft, the two helicopters in front of us had disappeared. They had both turned out their running lights and I had no idea where they were. So now we had a burning city below obscured by heavy smoke; we had fifteen helicopters, including the four guns and the C&C, milling around invisible in the night sky; and some asshole on the ground was trying to shoot us out of the air. What a way to make a living!

Madness, it was total goddamn madness. How in the hell could anyone make heads or tails out of this mess? I was in a state of near panic. There was no doubt in my mind that I was going to die that night. Then a voice came over the radio. It was Major Andrews, the company commander, with emphasis on Commander.

"Kingsman flight, Lancer Six, this is Kingsman Six."

Kingsman One-six, Captain Peterson, the platoon leader of the first platoon; Captain Jack of the second platoon; and Captain Finch of the gun platoon responded in order.

"Kingsman One-six, this is Six. I am to your north at three

thousand feet. I want you to get your people up to six thousand feet over the city, get them sorted out, and get their lights on. The one thing we don't need is to start running into each other."

"Six, One-six. Good copy."

"Kingsman Two-six, this is Six. I want your people at five thousand feet. Same thing. I'll let you know when I want you to start inbound to the MACV compound."

"Six, Two-six. Copy."

"Lancer Six, it's been confirmed that the ARVN compound has been overrun. There are no friendlies in the area. Whoever is down there is dead or the bad guys. You are cleared to roll in hot. I want you to take out that .50 cal and anything else you can find. Do not expend both fire teams. I might need to cover the One-six and the Two-six elements when they begin their approach into the MACV compound."

"Six, this is Lancer Six. I have a good copy. I will use only one fire team on the compound and keep the other one high and dry unless we run into something we can't handle. Give me about two minutes and we'll blow the shit out of whoever and whatever is in the target area."

Kingsman Six acknowledged Lancer Six's transmission. All of this had taken no more than forty-five seconds. As soon as the part pertaining to the second platoon had come over the radio, Dick had begun a five-hundred-foot-a-minute climb. The only thing he told me was to keep my head out of the cockpit and not to let us run into anything. Climbing at the rate of five hundred feet a minute, it would take us six minutes to reach five thousand feet. It was a long six minutes.

Shortly after starting our climb, I heard Captain Finch come over the radio. "Lancer Six is inbound hot." I was supposed to be watching for other aircraft that might be close to us, but I couldn't keep my eyes away from the area where the rockets were exploding. It was quite a show.

I was still watching the gunships putting their rockets into what used to be the ARVN compound and wishing that I was flying one of them. I kept thinking, Man, that's where the action is. Reality caught up to me with a vengeance as Dick racked the helicopter into a sharp left-hand diving turn. Looking up, I could see the outline of a blacked-out helicopter just above us. We had damn near hit him.

Needless to say, Dick was not happy, and he let me know it in no uncertain terms. "Goddamn it, Lieutenant, this isn't some kind of a damn game we're playing out here. This is for real. If you don't get your head out of your ass and start doing your damn job, we're sure as shit going to get killed."

There was nothing I could say. He was right and I knew it. I hadn't been doing my part. Daydreaming was not part of my job description.

I was just beginning to understand that being part of an aircraft crew was a total team effort. Everyone had an assigned area of responsibility, and each of us had to ensure that our area was covered. I hadn't done that.

Dick called the Old Man, Kingsman Six, and told him about our near miss. I was thankful he didn't mention anything about me having my head up my ass and locked in position. He did recommend that everyone above three thousand feet turn on their lights. Six concurred and made the call. Lights came on all around us as the aircraft continued climbing to their assigned altitudes. Some were so close that it looked as though I could reach out and touch them. It scared the hell out of me. I had been in country for thirty days and had damn near died because of my own stupidity. God, would I live long enough to ever learn?

Now it seemed that we were starting to get things sorted out. One helicopter was flying level at five thousand feet with its lights on bright flash. That was Captain Jack. Another aircraft fell in behind him, and we, as the number-three aircraft, moved into position in the trail of number two. I called to let the lead know we had joined up. Four and five called shortly thereafter.

A thousand feet above us I could see the aircraft of the first platoon beginning to join up. Off to the south the two gunships of the second fire team were in an orbit at three thousand feet. The first fire team was still working on the ARVN compound. But I didn't pay any attention to them. They continued to do what they got paid to do—hang their asses out, kill people, and protect us.

Kingsman Six called and informed us he was going to make a run down the main street starting at the small airfield on the east side of the burning town. His run would be from east to west at less than one hundred feet. The MACV compound was located on the left-hand (south) side of the street. Six's plan was to try to pinpoint the compound in all of that smoke and give us some kind of reference point. A few minutes later he was back on the radio.

"Kingsman Two-six, this is Six. The MACV compound is located about a klick and a half down the main drag as you go east to west. There will be a jeep in the compound with its headlights flashing. Don't mistake it for muzzle flashes. Also, there is a large tree on the west end of the compound and a two-niner-two antenna to the south. It is a small LZ. Start your approach from over the airstrip to the east of the town. You'll have to go in low, about fifty feet."

"Two-six. Good copy."

"Also, Two-six, when you get on the ground, I want you to call and let your number-two aircraft know you're in so he can start his approach."

"Six, Two-six. Roger that."

After listening to that exchange on the radio, I finally realized why the company commander made more money than I did; the man definitely had all of his shit in one bucket. I didn't think anyone could have made that mess we had roaming around the sky work, but he did, and it took only a few minutes.

Suddenly, Captain Jack's aircraft disappeared. He had turned off his lights as he headed for the smoke below. The lights on the number-two aircraft changed from steady bright to flashing as he took over the lead position. We continued to fly over the burning city.

I felt someone hitting me on the shoulder. It was the lieutenant we'd picked up. He was yelling at me over the sound of the helicopter, "Where are we going?" I just pointed to the burning city below. The lieutenant looked at me and then collapsed. At first I thought he'd been hit, but after the crew chief checked him and couldn't find any wounds, we realized that the poor son of a bitch had fainted.

Captain Jack called to say he'd landed and was on his way out. He confirmed what the CO had reported on the landing area. The lights on the aircraft in front of us went out as number two turned to the east to begin his approach. As I reached up to turn our lights to the flash position, I thought, We're next. Maybe I should just crawl in the back and join the lieutenant on the floor. I wasn't looking forward to going down into that mess any more than he was.

After about five minutes number two called that he was coming out. I turned our lights out as Dick headed down into the thick smoke. We crossed over the small airstrip on the east side of town and followed the main street to the west. Flying in the smoke at fifty feet above the ground and thirty knots forward airspeed was not my idea of having fun.

Dick had me get on the controls with him, and told me to try to spot the flashing headlights inside the compound. The radio operator in the MACV compound was talking to us and trying to tell us how close we were getting. Just as he said we were almost on top of them, I saw the lights. Dick had seen them at the same time and turned toward the flashing headlights of the jeep. We'd been told that the landing area was small, but what we found was ridiculous—there was absolutely no way to make a normal approach into the place.

Dick brought the aircraft to a fifty-foot, out-of-ground-effect hover and moved it over to the center of the compound. It was just like the man had said. There was a very large tree off our nose and the radio antenna was off to the left. The jeep with its headlights on had been backed up under the tree to give us more room to land. Landing there during daylight would have been a feat; at night . . . All I could think was that I just wanted to go home.

At that point it was very clear to me that Dick Washburn was the aircraft commander and I was just a very scared passenger. We started a vertical descent toward the center of the compound. The tips of the rotor blades were hitting the branches of the tree in front of us. The guy wires of the antennas were just to our left. Those were our biggest worry. We could cut the branches and small limbs, but if we hit the wires, we would end up as a big ball of wreckage on the ground.

I don't know if I kept my eyes open or not, but the next thing I remember, we were on the ground and the troops, including the lieutenant who had passed out, were off-loading the ammo we'd brought in. We had to go out the opposite way we'd come in—straight up. If nothing else, I was getting one hell of an education.

Dick made the radio call that we were coming out of the compound, and I heard the number-four aircraft respond that he was inbound. I kept my eyes inside the aircraft and monitored the instruments as Dick concentrated on getting us out of the compound without hitting anything. I guess we both did our jobs the way we were supposed to because shortly afterward we were climbing up through the smoke and heading back to Dong Tam.

If everything went as planned, it would take about ten minutes for each aircraft to make its approach, off-load, and depart. There were seven helicopters behind us. So it looked like it was going to be close to an hour's wait on the ground while the rest of the company completed its part of reinforcing and resupplying the people inside the compound.

About six minutes after we left, the aircraft that had followed us into the compound hit the guy wires of the radio antenna and was lying on its side in the middle of the landing zone. Everyone got out of the wreckage all right, but the LZ was unusable. Luckily, there was no fire.

We were on short final to the refuel point when the number-five aircraft—I think WO Mike Ware was the copilot—said they would go in and try to pick up the downed crew. They wouldn't be able to land, but they could hover over the wreckage and let the crew members climb up into the cabin over the aircraft skids. It sounded like it might work, so Kingsman Six told them to go ahead and give it a try.

The crew of the number-four aircraft was picked up and

returned to Dong Tam successfully. However, the number-five aircraft grazed the tree coming out of the compound. By the time the aircraft landed at Dong Tam, it was vibrating so badly from blade damage that the blades would have to be changed before it could be flown back to Long Binh. Oh well, so much for the smooth-running, Swiss-made watch!

It had taken a very high degree of skill and a lot of courage to accomplish the recovery of our people. Although the recovery aircraft had been damaged in the process, no one was left behind. That was the standard of dedication our unit would always hold as commonplace. It was reassuring to know that if you did get into trouble, someone would do everything within his power to bring you home.

With the landing zone inside the compound unusable, the remaining aircraft of the first platoon were ordered to return to Dong Tam. The gunships followed not far behind, landing about five minutes later. The last to land was the C&C aircraft. After all of the aircraft had refueled and the gunships had rearmed, we were released for the evening. It was 2230 hours. We had departed Long Binh eleven and a half hours before. It had been a long day, and it wasn't over. We still had an hour's flight time to get home, and then there was the post-flighting of the aircraft and helping the crew chief get it ready for the next day's mission.

Shortly after departing Dong Tam, Dick gave me the controls and let me fly home. The first platoon was in the lead, and what was left of the second platoon was following. I was bringing up the rear of our platoon, and was followed by the guns and the C&C aircraft. It was an easy flight; all I had to do was follow the helicopter in front of me. As we came across Saigon, I saw fires burning all over the city, the most intense in the Cholon district.

The VC/NVA had wanted the people of the South to rise up and join them in their fight against the government troops. But if that was so, why in the hell did they try to burn every town and city in the country? That just didn't seem to make any sense. But as time went on, I was to find out that most of the things about that damn war didn't make any sense.

Chapter Eight

It was an absolutely glorious morning. The sun was shining and the air smelled fresh. It must have rained after I hit the rack earlier that morning. There was a light breeze coming out of the east. There was not even the usual smell of freshly burned shit in the air. If I'd been drinking last night, I could have accepted the headache I had, but the only explanation for it was the stress of the previous day's missions. When we returned to Long Binh the night before, my only resolve had been to go immediately to bed, and I *had* gone to sleep, on my bunk, fully clothed.

I looked at my watch. It was a little after six o'clock. I'd gotten almost five hours of uninterrupted sleep. It seemed like a lifetime ago that we'd landed. I couldn't think of any reason to get up, so I just lay there thinking.

It was February 2, 1968. I'd been in the United States Army for six years, to the day. I'd been an Army aviator for seventy-three days. Of that seventy-three days, I'd been in Vietnam for thirty-one. I had flown 218 flight hours in nine months of flight school; in my thirty-one days in country, I'd flown seventy-three hours in combat.

I'd come to Southeast Asia with the same doubts, fears, and expectations as so many others before me. Some of the doubts still remained. I wondered if and when I got my own aircraft, would I be able to accomplish whatever mission was assigned to me? Would I be able to live up to the standards set by the people with whom I served? Would I be able to keep my crew and myself alive? But what worried me most of all was, when my tour was finally over, would I be able to walk with my head held high and know I'd done what had been expected of me?

I'd had other doubts when I first arrived in country. Some had already been laid to rest. I would no longer have to wonder how I'd react under fire. We'd been fired upon almost every day that I had flown with the unit. The aircraft I'd been flying was hit twice. Fortunately, there was no major damage, nor had anyone been hurt, and I'd done my job as I was supposed to do. Of course, there were a couple of well-deserved ass-chewings from the aircraft commander just to keep me on track. The learning process never stopped.

The taking of another human life had been one of my biggest concerns. Now, I'd seen death up close and personal. My first was the young soldier with the blond hair, looking at me through those dead blue eyes. Then there were the nine VC I'd killed the previous night. God, had it only been the night before? As I lay there thinking about it, there was no emotion. I had taken the lives of nine people and felt absolutely no remorse. I guess that when the time had come, the training took over and I'd done what a soldier had to do.

The fears . . . I guess the fears remained the same. I still feared the thought of going home a cripple. After watching the gunship of the 191st gun platoon fly into the ground and explode, I couldn't think of a better way to die in combat. To go out in a blaze of glory was the only way; it was quick and clean. No pain, or so I'd been told. I couldn't remember who told me that. I had to wonder how in the hell he knew. I didn't know anyone who'd ever returned from the dead.

The expectations; I didn't know what to expect. I guess I had thoughts of Eddie Rickenbacker flying against Baron von Richthofen, the Red Baron, in World War I. Or maybe Joe Voss flying against the Japanese in the Second World War. There were also the men who flew MiG Alley in the early 1950s in Korea.

This wasn't anything like that. This wasn't the glory of taking on an opponent one-to-one. We were supporting the grunts, the infantry. The people who in the end would pay the heaviest price. Up to that point, I'd experienced no personal glory, but the self-satisfaction was indescribable. Watching the old NCOs and the young troopers going out and doing their jobs day after day was truly something to behold. I really didn't know whether I would have wanted to trade my job for anything else. But what the hell, I still had 334 days left in country to figure it out!

By nine o'clock we were on our way back to Dong Tam. The maintenance crew had already recovered the aircraft that crashed in the compound at Ben Tre. This was accomplished with the use of a CH-47 helicopter. They had to sling the wreckage out, and it was now lying in a heap somewhere at the repair facility at Vung Tau. The other damaged aircraft was having its blades changed and would soon be flyable again.

Most of our day was spent flying short resupply missions. There was no heavy contact. Once again the bad guys had elected not to come out into the daylight and play. No wonder; they'd taken a pretty good beating over the previous two nights.

That was evident from the large number of bodies left behind. The NVA/VC normally removed their dead from the battlefield whenever possible. That was done to deny the enemy—us—the knowledge of how badly they'd been hurt. But during Tet they were hurt very badly, and bodies were lying all over the place. I began to wonder what they were going to do with them. Whatever it was, it would have to be soon. Even after two days, they were starting to get ripe.

It was late in the afternoon and we were on our last resupply mission before being released for the day. We were going back into one of the positions we'd been working earlier in the morning. As we approached the field location I could see a CH-47 departing the area. I thought it was kind of strange because he had a sling load under him. We had seen the 47s working all day, carrying supplies to the troops in the field, but that was the first time I saw them *return* hauling anything.

As the CH-47, call sign "Hillclimber," crossed about a thousand yards ahead and five hundred feet above us, I saw that the cargo net was filled with bodies of the VC/NVA soldiers killed the night before. I heard someone ask on the radio, "Hey, Hillclimber, where are you going with all of those dead dinks?"

The reply was somewhat of a shock. "This is Hillclimber, Three-six. Going to take them about five miles out to sea and dump 'em."

When we landed to drop off our supplies, there were no bodies anywhere in sight. What a way to run a war! It made me wonder how the bad guys could keep track and account for their people. If they went out and didn't return, were they simply written off as dead?

On the flight back to Long Binh we once again had to fly over Saigon. If the bad guys were playing hard to find out in the area we'd been working, it was an entirely different story back there. There was still fighting going on all over the place, particularly in the Cholon district. It was just getting dark as we flew across the city, and I could see the firefights in the fading light. Red and green tracers were crisscrossing wide boulevards and narrow alleys. Tracers were coming out of windows and disappearing into other windows not more than thirty feet away. That was a type of fighting I wanted no part of; house-to-house combat is not an easy way to make a living.

The following morning we had a change of scenery. We were sent to support the 199th Light Infantry Brigade. I was glad to get away from the Dong Tam area and its monotonous, flat, open rice paddies. We would be working to the northwest of Long Binh, where the area was heavily wooded.

The 199th rear area was just across the road from our company. Inasmuch as we did not have the long flight to get on station as when we went to Dong Tam, the crews got an extra hour's sleep. The first mission of the day was taking hot food to the units in the field. These were single-ship missions. It looked like it was going to be a nice and easy day.

Well, I was half right. It was a very easy day. As far as being nice, it started off bad on the first resupply run and then got steadily worse. The company we were going to drop off hot chow to had blown an LZ in the woods. Unfortunately, the LZ was too small, so we had to fly around for about thirty minutes while they blew more trees down to make the landing zone large enough to use.

The next resupply run didn't work out a whole lot better. The topper occurred when we landed at one of the brigade's fire support bases. As we approached it, I could see a large stack of logs and small trees about two hundred feet outside the wire. There was a lot of activity around it as more timber was being stacked on top of the pile.

After we landed, I got a closer look at what they were doing. If I'd been shocked at the bodies being dumped at sea yesterday, this was enough to make anyone sick. The logs were stacked about thirty feet high. There was a layer of logs and a layer of dead NVA, a layer of logs and a layer of NVA. There must have been close to three hundred bodies in that pile. Off to one side was a cargo net filled with cans of gas.

We were told to shut down and stand by. Once the aircraft was secured, I got out and walked over to the wire and watched. A short time later a young soldier walked by, and I asked him what they were going to do. His reply was short and to the point: "Gonna burn the bastards."

While we were supporting the 9th Division out of Dong Tam, our sister company, the 95th AHC, had been removing the dead and wounded from the fire support base. Although these men had killed a lot of the NVA who had been trying to overrun them, they also lost a lot of their own people. There was no compassion in the eyes of the young men building the funeral pyre. I couldn't blame them. I just hoped they waited until we were long gone before they put a match to that pile of wood.

We departed a couple of hours later. The pile of logs and bodies was still there. The smell of gasoline grew overpowering as more fuel was added to the growing pyre. I was glad to finally get away from the area. I didn't want to see what was about to come.

Later in the afternoon, as we continued the resupply missions, smoke began to rise from the fire support base.

Although we tried to stay away from the cloud, we could still smell the awful stench of burning bodies. It was something I would not soon forget. Our work ended early and I could truthfully say that I was glad to see the day done.

The next couple of days supporting the 199th Light Infantry Brigade were relatively easy, and I didn't see any more bodies being disposed of. We were flying six to eight hours a day doing resupply missions without an awful lot of enemy action involved. We took some light sniper fire, although for the most part it was ineffective. It seemed that the bad guys just wanted to let us know they were still in the area. If that was the case, I'd rather they had just sent us a letter.

On the evening of February 6, I was informed that the following morning I'd be flying as copilot with Warrant Officer Dean. It would be my first mission in support of Special Forces out of Ho Ngoc Tao.

The official designation was B-56 Detachment, Project Sigma (Special Recon). They were better known as LRPs (Long Range Patrol). The 5th Special Forces Group (Airborne) had formed Project Sigma in late 1966 as an unconventional warfare operations project. The detachment had eight reconnaissance teams, three commando companies, and one camp-defense company. The assigned companies were made up of ethnic Cambodian and Chinese personnel. Because large parts of southern Vietnam had once been Cambodian, and because the Vietnamese almost always mistreated their ethnic Cambodian minority, the Cambodians had a strong dislike for the Vietnamese, North and South. They really didn't care which ones they killed.

We arrived at Ho Ngoc Tao late in the morning. The mission was one I'd been looking forward to. I had no idea what the hell I was getting into, but I had a feeling it was going to be very interesting.

Six aircraft were assigned to that mission: a C&C ship, two gunships, and three insertion aircraft. After landing, I followed the other pilots into the compound for the briefing.

We would insert twenty-four people—six Americans and

eighteen Cambodians—eight per aircraft. Their mission was to set up an ambush and monitor a road. With the Tet offensive still going full swing, they would be watching to see if reinforcements were moving toward Saigon.

The area they would go into was about thirty miles northwest of Bien Hoa Air Base along Highway 15. The landing zone, a one-ship LZ, was located a mile past a blown-out bridge on the north side of a river. The area had been defoliated, and the dirt-road "highway" could be seen very clearly from the air. We would be landing in a small clearing alongside the road.

It was to be a late-afternoon insertion. After putting the troops on the ground, we would return to Ho Ngoc Tao and stand by. Hell, that didn't sound too bad. We'd get about an hour's flight time, then get back in time for chow and a few drinks. Not a bad way to spend a day in a tropical paradise.

The C&C took off at 1545 hours and headed for the area of operation. We departed fifteen minutes later with a flight of five. En route to the LZ, the lift ships went into a trail formation—one behind the other—and picked up the spacing that would allow the lead aircraft to land and depart just as the number-two ship was touching down. I was in the third aircraft. The two gunships were following behind and a little above. They would overfly the second aircraft just as he was landing. The guns would be close enough to react if anyone started taking fire during the insertion.

The first two aircraft made their insertion without a hitch. We landed just as number two lifted off. It was the damnedest thing I'd ever seen. You could look down the road for about a mile and see the dead tree limbs making an arch over the road. It looked like a goddamn tunnel. I couldn't help thinking how beautiful it would have been if all the trees had been alive and green.

As our troops departed the aircraft, the thought suddenly went through my mind, Shit, this is easy. What's all the fuss about working with LRPs? In a short time we were out of the trees and on our way back to a large steak and a cold beer. It was a hell of a way to make a living. I could get used to that without any trouble at all.

The sun had gone down and the movie had just started when I heard the sound of helicopters cranking. Looking over the group of people seated to watch the movie, I could see John Dean and several of the other pilots still sitting in the open-air theater. They didn't seem concerned as the two gunships departed the area to the north. If they aren't concerned, why should I be worried? I thought, and sat back to enjoy the movie.

About fifteen minutes later the siren went off. First there was a noise that sounded like a covey of quail taking flight, and then just dead silence. I looked around; I couldn't see anyone. Everybody had disappeared! I had no idea what the siren had meant. I had paid close attention during the briefing and couldn't recall anything being said about any damn siren. Where had everyone gone?

As I stood there gawking like an idiot, the thought hit me: Oh, Christ, the aircraft! I began running toward the helipad. I'd just started moving when I heard the engines being cranked. By the time I arrived at the aircraft, Dean had it up to 6,400 rpm and was ready to lift off. I was still putting on my helmet and fastening my seat belt as we left the ground. All the other aircraft had already departed. I looked over at John and started to ask what was going on but the look on his face stopped me cold: pure disgust. He didn't say a word as we tried to catch the other two aircraft. I could almost hear the crew chief and gunner laughing at me back in their gun wells. The ass-chewing from John would come later, I was sure of that, but just then he had other things on his mind.

We were leaving the city lights behind as we flew to the northeast. The only lights I could see were the red and green position lights on the two aircraft ahead and above us. God, it was dark out there!

Listening to the traffic on the radio, I finally understood the situation. The team on the ground had made contact with a large number of VC and was requesting an extraction. They were about a thousand meters from the LZ where we'd inserted them, and they would not be able to get back to that area.

The gunships were on station and providing close support with rockets and minigun fire. In the distance steady streams of red tracers from the miniguns poured toward the ground. Three thousand rounds per minute coming out of each of those guns. God, I'd hate to be on the receiving end of them. The guns were attempting to put a ring of fire around the team as the men moved to the road where we would pick them up. The only thing I couldn't figure out was just how we were going to get to them if they were set up on the road and the road was under the trees.

We were still about five minutes out when the lead aircraft told us to pick up our separation. Both the number two and our aircraft slowed to about forty knots. The lead aircraft maintained his ninety knots and quickly pulled away. After close to a minute the number-two aircraft increased its air-speed and moved out ahead of us. I could see the anticollision lights and the navigation lights of the first two helicopters out in front of us. Then they were gone.

Just as the lights of the other two aircraft went out, John reached up and turned our navigation lights to the dim position and the anticollision light off. Then, looking out into the darkness, I could just make out the lights on the aircraft in front of us. The lead aircraft was off to the left in a left-hand descending turn.

Down on top of the trees was a helicopter with all its lights on. It was the C&C ship. Now what in the hell was he doing? Before I had a chance to ask, I heard him talking to the lead aircraft on the radio. "Lead, this is Charlie-Charlie. I'm going to mark the LZ for you as briefed. The exit point is the same as we discussed before. The team is in position on the road at this time. Lancers will provide cover. I'm coming over the LZ . . . now!"

As the C&C ship continued on a straight course, I could just make out the dimmed lights of the lead aircraft approaching what I assumed was the landing zone. The dimmed lights came to a stop and then disappeared. John started a hard left-hand, 180-degree turn, and I saw the lights of number two as it seemed to be on short final. As we rolled out of our turn, his lights disappeared also.

We were on a short final to a lighter spot in the trees, and as we got closer I could make out the landing zone we'd used to insert the team earlier in the day. I still didn't know what the plan was. How had I missed so many details of the mission? My mind was full of questions, and I felt so damn useless just sitting there.

John brought me back to the present. "Okay, Bill, I want you to stay on the controls with me. Our people are about a hundred meters down the road on the right-hand side. All we have to do is follow the guy in front of us. As soon as all of the people are on board, lead will head down the road to an area that has a break in the overhead branches that will let us get out of these damn trees." It was good to hear him talking to me; those were the first words he'd spoken to me since we took off.

We were now in the LZ. The mission had turned into something I'd heard about in flight school but hadn't really believed. Making a blacked-out approach at night to an unmarked LZ was simply unbelievable, but making it to a confined area with overhead trees was insane.

John hovered the aircraft sideways to the left, and all of a sudden we were on the road. I could see the number-two aircraft in front of us. We were inside the long tunnel I'd seen during the daylight. However, in the dark it looked like a very short tunnel. I kept looking to see if there was a light at the end, but couldn't see one. It was crazy! What if the bad guys opened up on us? There was no way to take evasive action. What if the helicopter in front of us was hit or crashed? There was no way to turn around or go over him, as the tree limbs were too low. The "what ifs" kept coming, and there were no answers to any of them.

We followed the two lead helicopters as they moved down the road. Luckily, the road was hard-packed and there was little dust. After a short time, which seemed like a lifetime, I saw what at first I thought were muzzle flashes coming from the right side of the road. That in itself was enough to put my heart all the way up in my throat. But the light flashes were coming from the strobe lights that each of the three groups of LRPs was using to mark its position.

All three aircraft came abreast of their troops at the same time and sat down. The troops loaded damn near as fast they'd unloaded during the insertion. Their spacing was perfect. I heard the radio call, "Two's up."

John keyed the transmit switch and reported, "Three's up." The next call was, "Lead's lifting now." With that, all three aircraft came off of the ground and started hovering down the road.

To that point, no one had fired at us. Maybe they'd taken enough of a beating for one night. With the gunships overhead, any muzzle flashes or tracers would be easily seen, even through the defoliated trees. Whatever the reason, it suited the hell out of me.

We continued down the road for close to two hundred meters when the lead aircraft called, "Lead's coming out with a left break." Ten seconds later number two made the same call, and I watched him climb up into an opening in the trees. Then it was our turn. I could see the break in the overhead tree limbs as we got closer. I focused my attention on the instrument panel, knowing that John would be concentrating on trying to get us out through the hole without hitting something.

We moved into a position directly under the opening and came to a hover. As John pulled in power and started to rise, I watched the torque gauge climb. When it reached forty-five percent, I began calling out the power setting, "Forty-six . . . forty-seven . . . forty-eight . . . forty-nine pounds. Hold it." John held the power right on forty-nine pounds of torque and we continued to climb straight up through the trees.

The crew chief finally announced that we were clear. John called the C&C ship to let him know that the LZ was clear, then lowered the nose of the aircraft to pick up forward airspeed. As soon as we had enough airspeed, we initiated a left-hand turn and began to climb.

It's funny the way things intrude into your thoughts. As we

climbed into the darkness, I slowly let out my breath. We had to have been down in that hole for at least three minutes. For the entire time we'd been on the ground, I couldn't remember breathing.

Sitting there, I reached down to the radio console, picked up my cigarettes, lit one, and tried to relax. As the flame of my lighter went out, I looked out the window and saw the stars. I didn't recall seeing any stars before we had entered the trees. Now they were everywhere. Why hadn't I noticed them before? There was no moon, but from fifteen hundred feet I could make out the trees below just from the light of the stars. The outside air temperature was in the mid-seventies, but for some reason I was freezing. Why was I so cold? I took off my gloves and was surprised to find they were wringing wet. So was my flight suit. It wasn't hot enough to make me sweat, so what could have caused it? Fear! I couldn't remember being scared. But if I hadn't been, then why was I so wet?

As we flew back to Ho Ngoc Tao, I could see the city lights coming into view. I asked John what would happen now that the mission was coming to an end. He told me we'd drop the troops off, shut down, go to the debriefing, then return to Long Binh. I also asked about what had happened when we were called out for the extraction. I was concerned about why I hadn't known about the alert siren and why I hadn't been briefed on the extraction procedure of going under the trees. It seemed I was the only new guy on this mission, and he'd assumed someone would tell me about it. No one had. As for the extraction, the air-mission commander (AMC) and the other aircraft commanders had a separate briefing after the insertion, and they didn't think it necessary for the copilots to be there.

I was dumbfounded. That was the biggest line of bullshit I'd ever heard. It violated everything I'd been taught in the five years I was in the infantry and in OCS. One of the most important things you learned was to keep the troops informed. You never knew when the officers or NCOs would be taken out of action and the next highest ranking man would have to take over and continue the mission.

Sitting on my bunk after returning to Long Binh, I went over the lessons learned on my first LRP mission. There were many, but the one that had the most impact on me was the lack of briefings. I made a promise to myself that from then on, I would be fully briefed on any mission I was on, whether "they"—whoever they might be—thought it necessary or not. In addition, when I was made aircraft commander, my crew would know as much about any current mission as I did.

It was a little after midnight when I finally lay down to go to sleep. As I was dozing off, two thoughts entered my mind. First, I liked the LRP missions and would try to stay on them as often as I could. Second, I wondered what the next day would bring.

Chapter Nine

The Tet offensive continued. The fighting was slacking off, but the VC/NVA were still a force to reckon with even though the general uprising they'd hoped for had failed to materialize.

Along with the fighting came the rumors. One was that, with the beating the VC/NVA had taken, the war would soon end. No one took that rumor seriously.

There was also the story that the bad guys were regrouping for another assault on the populated areas. That rumor we could almost believe. However, no one had any idea where the VC/NVA would get the troops to mount the assault, since they'd lost a tremendous number of people. We would hear later that just in the month of February, during the Tet offensive, the North Vietnamese Army and the Viet Cong lost forty thousand people.

Another tale being told was that the U.S. troops would pull back and let the South Vietnamese Army do its own fighting. We knew that had to be a damn joke. I'd been there for only a short time, and even I could see that those bastards could not or would not fight.

There were so many rumors going around that we paid little attention to most of them. However, one had everyone's interest: Our unit was to be transferred to another area. No one seemed to know how that story started or where we were supposed to be moving. Needless to say, there was a lot of conversation about it.

We had a warrant officer by the name of Craig Smith infused into our unit from the 101st Airborne Division, which was stationed at a place called Phu Bai up in I ("eye") Corps, located in the very northern part of South Vietnam. Craig kept telling us how lucky we were to be flying in the Delta, and not having to worry about flying in the mountains closer to North Vietnam. He thought we were fortunate because we had to contend mostly with the VC and not the hardcore NVA. He also commented on how good our living conditions were.

I found that hard to believe. We were living in tents with dirt floors. We did not have showers. We were flying our asses off from before sunrise until well after sunset. But even so, he kept telling us how good we had it. If that was having it good, then God help us if we ever had it bad.

As rumors continued to circulate, missions kept coming down. We were working with the 199th Light Infantry Brigade almost every day, a big help to us since their headquarters and brigade rear were located just across the road. This meant that the units we were supporting would not be more than twenty to thirty minutes' flight time from our home base. We would not have to fly for an hour and a half, refuel, and then report to a unit in the field. It also gave us that extra hour of much-needed sleep.

Brigadier General Robert C. Forbes, Commanding General, 199th Light Infantry Brigade, had been using our aircraft as his command and control aircraft off and on since the beginning of Tet, and our helicopters had been supporting his brigade in some of the heaviest fighting in the area. That included the heliborne assault into the Phu Tho racetrack, which the enemy had been using as a command post. We inserted part of the 3d Battalion, 7th Infantry into the infield of the racetrack. It took eight hours of fighting before the NVA had been killed or driven out.

One evening around the middle of February 1968, Dick Washburn and I returned from flying C&C with General Forbes. After we landed, the general asked if we would like to join him at the 199th Infantry Brigade's Officers' Club later that evening. We accepted without hesitation. He also told us the invitation included the other pilots in our platoon.

That evening, after we completed the postflight on the aircraft, the afteraction report on the day's mission, and gotten something to eat, eight of us headed across the road to the Officers' Club, the first time any of us had been there. Although I'd been in country for only forty-five days or so, the place already seemed to be something from another world. There were tables with tablecloths and candles. The chairs were padded and had armrests. One of the first things that caught my attention was the smell of the food being served. It also had a jukebox, which was going loud and strong. It looked just like an Officers' Club back in the States. How soon we forgot about the comforts of home!

The main room was crowded and very noisy. As we entered, the noise died down and just about everyone turned to look at us. We were, without a doubt, out of place. Everyone in the club wore clean, starched uniforms with spit-shined boots. We still had on our dirty flight suits, and our boots hadn't seen polish in at least two weeks. One look was all it took to know that most of the people there were REMFs. And that one look also told us that our visit could make for a very interesting evening.

A captain came up and introduced himself as the general's aide. He asked us to join the general at his table in the rear of the club. After we were seated and the introductions made, General Forbes ordered the first round of drinks and said that after that we were on our own.

The first round served to break the ice. The conversations were mostly about the actions in which we had supported the brigade. I bought the next round, and then, I think, Jerry Seevers got the round after that. The drinks kept coming. The more we drank, the louder we became. After a while we started rolling dice to see who would pay for the next round of drinks. When someone lost, a roar would sound from our table. The noise seemed to bother a lot of people in the club. Shit, we were with the general, so who cared what a bunch of REMFs thought?

After the general bought the first round, he never had to buy another because once we started rolling the dice, he never lost. He must have had a much better meal than we'd had. The more we drank, the more the alcohol affected us, but the drinks did not seem to bother the general at all. And he really seemed to be enjoying himself. Maybe it was his way to show his appreciation for the work we'd done for him. It also gave him a chance to relax.

It was getting late and about time for us to head back to our company area when Washburn lost a roll of the dice. He stood up and hit the table as hard as he could with the palms of his hands. It sounded like a pistol shot. The club became deathly quiet. Dick looked down at the general and said, in a voice loud enough for everyone still in the club to hear, "General, there ain't never been a commissioned officer able to beat a warrant officer at nothing. So, evidently, you cheated. I'm going to whip your damn ass." The room was deathly quiet. Everyone seemed to be holding their breath.

I just sat there with my mouth open. As a first lieutenant, I was the ranking person in our group. I thought we were all going to the stockade. You just don't threaten a general— even one with just one star—with bodily harm and get away with it. Oh, well, they wouldn't have to move us very far, as LBJ (Long Binh Jail) was only five miles or so down the road.

The general sat there for a few seconds staring at Washburn, then burst out laughing. I leaned back in my chair before letting out a long sigh of relief as I watched the tears begin rolling down the general's cheeks. Still laughing, he looked at Dick and said, "Mr. Washburn, if I were cheating, which I am not admitting to, you would never be able to figure out how I did it." With that, everyone at the table started laughing, cheering, and raising hell. That also brought more dirty looks from the other people in the club.

After a few minutes, the general stood up, which brought the noise level down to absolute quiet. Still laughing, he said that the call of nature was getting the best of him. He had to leave and use the latrine. However, he wanted all of us to be there when he returned. As he departed, the noise level began to rise. It was turning into one hell of a party.

No sooner had the door closed behind the general than we were besieged by most of the other people in the club. Officers ranging from second lieutenants to full colonels were demanding that the eight of us get the hell out of their club or they would throw us out. Well, that created a few new problems for us: We were just intoxicated enough that we didn't believe that a bunch of rear-echelon straphangers would be able to make us leave. Hell, we were combat pilots. We went out, defied the law of gravity, cheated death, and did battle with the bad guys on a daily basis. Most of these people had never been on the outside of the wire. In our drunken state, we did not take into account that we were outnumbered about four to one. Even if we'd considered that fact, we would have thought those were very good odds.

Also, we'd been instructed by the general *not* to leave. It looked as though the party was going to get very lively, not so much because we'd been instructed to stay, but because we didn't take too kindly to having someone tell us to either leave or be thrown out.

Fortunately for everyone concerned, the general returned. As he walked back to the table, everything quieted down. Looking around, he asked what the problem was. I explained that he'd told us to stay and "these people" were insisting that we leave. At that point, the general gazed around the room and said, "Gentlemen, we have a staff meeting at 0700 hours. I think it would be advisable if you were to retire for the evening." The "suggestion" left no doubt in anyone's mind that it was an order. People quietly departed the area.

It had been one hell of a party. Everyone in our group seemed to have had a good time. But it was late and all of us still had to stop by Operations to receive our missions for the next day. After thanking the general for the invitation, we headed back to our company area.

We didn't have much of a chance to visit the Officers' Club again after that night; we'd just received a change of mission. We were once again supporting the 9th Division, and the flying never let up. We were in the air before the sun came up each morning, and returning from Dong Tam well after it went down.

The VC/NVA had decided that enough was enough. They

no longer wanted to stand and fight. They had crawled back into their holes. The war had become a case of "find me if you can." And finding them took a lot of time and effort. We went back to moving troops over our entire area of operation. It was not uncommon to make thirty to forty landings in one day.

At the end of February we were told that one of the rumors we'd heard was true: We would be moving within two to three weeks. We were not told where we were going, only that the advance party would be leaving the next day.

Over the next two weeks, every time we returned to the company area, it seemed to have grown smaller. Most of our equipment had been packed in conex containers and was ready for shipment. The last things left standing were the mess tent and the tents we slept in. We still had no idea where we were going.

On March 17 most of the company pulled out and headed north. I was to follow two days later with the last flight of five aircraft. We were on our way to I Corps, with our final destination Hue/Phu Bai. We were going to support the 101st Airborne Division. We would not be part of the 101st, but op-con (under operational control) to them. No one else seemed to care one way or another, but I was happy as hell. The only thing better would have been assignment to the Screaming Eagles. The one thing I didn't like about the move was that over the last two and a half months I'd gotten to know the III and IV Corps area fairly well. I did not get lost nearly as much as I used to.

Late in the morning of March 19 we departed Long Binh for the last time. I was flying with Dick Washburn. I guess they figured he would be able to keep me out of trouble, or at least from getting completely lost.

The trip would take two days, with our first refueling stop at Phan Thiet. Once we topped off, we headed north along the coast, passing to the west of Cam Ranh Bay, one of the largest deep-water ports in Southeast Asia. It had six piers capable of off-loading four thousand tons of cargo per day. The storage area could hold seventy-five thousand barrels of petroleum products, and the two-thousand-bed hospital was the largest in Vietnam. It was one hell of a large complex.

At 1630 hours we landed at an Army airfield at Dong Ba Thin, where we spent the night. A lot of helicopter units were stationed there, as well as several fixed-wing units, and the living conditions were a lot better than what we'd just left. Apparently, we were back in the middle of civilization.

After we tied the aircraft down, refueled, and made arrangements for the crews, I headed for the Officers' Club, called "The Sands." It was like being back in the States, only the prices were a lot better. The steak and lobster dinner was less than five dollars. I ordered a bottle of rum and two orders of steak and lobster. As far as I was concerned, they could simply throw me out when they closed. A little after midnight that's exactly what happened.

Daylight arrived way too soon. We were once again airborne and headed north. We followed Highway 1 as it ran along the coast, observing mile after mile of some of the prettiest beaches I'd ever seen, with not a footprint in the sand. If there hadn't been a war going on at the time, it would have been a vacationer's paradise.

There was one more refueling stop, at Chu Lai, before we reached Hue/Phu Bai. Chu Lai was another garden spot along the coast. From the refueling area, you could see the beach. It was damn near within walking distance. If that were an indication of things to come, I thought, maybe it wouldn't be so bad after all.

The last leg of the trip was nearly a two-hour flight. We flew low-level along the beach past Da Nang in order to stay out of the heavy jet traffic at Da Nang Air Force Base. Once we were out over the bay, we began climbing. As we gained altitude, we could see where Highway 1 snaked its way up the mountain and over the Hai Van Pass. There, the mountains came right out to the water's edge, a sheer cliff rising two thousand feet straight up from the water. Looking at the way the road twisted and turned, I could understand how the VC could easily set up an ambush there wherever or whenever they wanted. I was glad I didn't have to drive Highway 1.

After an hour I could just make out Phu Bai in the distance.

"Phu Bai Tower, this is Kingsman Two-five."

"Kingsman Two-five, Phu Bai Tower. Go ahead."

"This is Two-five with a flight of five. Five miles to the south for landing."

"Roger, Two-five. The winds are 085 at twelve. Be advised we have artillery impacting five miles to the west."

"This is Two-five. Good copy. Do you have any other Kingsman elements at your location?"

"This is Phu Bai Tower. That's affirm. Your people are on the west side of the airfield. You are cleared from your present position direct. Call short final."

We landed behind the last aircraft that was parked beside the dirt road. After we shut down, I went looking for Captain Schlater. I found him standing by his aircraft talking to two or three of the other aircraft commanders. I reported to him that the last element had arrived intact. This wasn't really necessary as he would have seen the flight land. However, it seemed the proper thing to do.

After we'd talked for a while, I asked, "Where are we going to be staying?"

His reply was, "See where the artillery is breaking?" I nodded. "As soon as they stop, that's home."

Shit! So much for civilization. It looked as if we were going to be a hell of a lot worse off than we'd been down south. Our "new home" was to be located among some low, grassy, rolling hills five miles west of Phu Bai and eight miles from the beach, definitely not within walking distance of rest and recreation. The hills themselves were covered with huge concrete graves.

As soon as the artillery lifted, two aircraft—one belonging to the company commander—departed the airfield and flew out to our new area. The rest of us followed in flights of five at ten-minute intervals. As we made our approach we were told to pick a spot to land. Some of the aircraft were landing on the hilltops, while others were setting down in the small valleys. There was no order to it at all. That would not last for long.

The engineers were already on site with bulldozers and

road scrapers, carving out the sides of the hills for our helicopters. They must have begun moving before the artillery even stopped.

Over the next six days there was very little flying. On the ground there seemed to be mass confusion everywhere. Tents were to be erected, perimeter wire to be strung, and truckloads of sandbags to be delivered for building revetments and bunkers. Our equipment had already arrived in the conex containers sent ahead by ship. Slowly, out of the utter confusion, my home for the next nine months emerged. Our grass-covered hills were slowly turned into an upside-down red dust bowl.

Ours was not the only unit located there. The 101st Airborne Division was also setting up housekeeping. We soon discovered that the area was to be known as Camp Eagle.

Next came the task of learning our new area of operation. We were given orientation rides with Alpha Company of the 101st Aviation Battalion, men flying the area for some time. The rides consisted of flying as copilot on their missions.

I Corps called for an entirely different type of flying than we'd done down south. We still had the low-lying areas with the rice paddies to the east. However, five miles to the west the mountains began. Up to that time there hadn't been many flights deep into the mountains. The NVA owned it all.

The division had already established a fire support base named Birmingham, six miles west of Camp Eagle along Highway 547, a narrow one-lane dirt road. The engineers were widening it to two wide lanes.

On the twenty-fifth, I was given my aircraft-commander check ride. It proved to be an all-day affair. Later that evening I was told we were going to be supporting the 101st LRPs, and that was going to be a continuing mission. When asked if I'd be interested in flying for them, I jumped at the chance. The next morning I landed at the LRP pad.

Probably no soldiers were more hated by the NVA/VC than LRPs. Those silent searchers sprang quick, lethal ambushes on small enemy units. When larger enemy groups confronted them, they simply sat quietly, or called in artillery and air strikes. The LRPs pinpointed communist base camps, supply depots, infiltration routes, and troop movements. And most galling of all to the NVA and VC, they were masters of the quiet, shadow war originally pioneered by the enemy.

The small LRP teams were elite units, with much more freedom than the infantrymen of company-size units. But along with that freedom came additional responsibility. Because the LRP teams were reconnaissance teams that had to move silently and be able to insert and extract quickly, they generally worked in groups of six, so the enemy almost always outnumbered them. The LRPs knew that if they were detected and surrounded, their lives would last no longer than a candle flame would in a gale.

Yet the LRP team was not alone. The PRC-25 radio strapped on the back of the radioman allowed the team to call for the support of howitzer batteries, F-4 Phantom jets, Cobra gunships, and quick reaction forces that were kept waiting in reserve. Because they were few and well trained, they also had another ally, one usually considered by others to be the most hostile of enemies: the jungle.

Captain Peter Fitts had formed the division LRP company back at Fort Campbell and brought it to Vietnam, where, after a month or two, it became F Company, 58th Infantry (LRP). First Sergeant Darol Walker had also come over with the unit, along with Platoon Sergeants John Brubaker, Owen "Rocky" Bigelon, Richard Burnell, and Harold Beck. All of those men were professional airborne soldiers. When the company arrived in country in mid-November 1967, there had been less than seventy men. They had been receiving and training volunteers who were arriving from other units, as well as from SERTS (Screaming Eagle Replacement Training School), which was located at Bien Hoa.

After joining the division, every lieutenant and junior enlisted man stopped at SERTS, a single five-day course more important than college to the education of a combat soldier. Lessons learned at SERTS would save many lives before the war ended.

The Long Range Reconnaissance Patrol Detachment of

the 1st Brigade of the 101st Airborne Division preceded the
division to Vietnam and had already been in the field for more
than two years. The legendary unit, better known as the Old
Foul Dudes, was being disbanded. They'd worked and lived
like nomads, going wherever they were needed. Some of its
LRPs went to line units, while others went to the Special
Forces, but a few decided to transfer to the newly arrived division LRP company. They were not happy to be part of what
they felt was a Stateside LRP unit, but it beat most of their al-
ternatives. Slowly, but surely, the company filled up. It was
even running some missions.

During the first week of April 1968, I inserted my first LRP
team as an aircraft commander. Sergeant McKinnon went in
with a five-man recon team. We made a first-light insertion
into a large grassy LZ that went off without a hitch. The team
moved off the LZ to wait and listen for sounds of movement
or any other indication that it had been compromised. We
circled a few miles away, and after twenty minutes headed
back to Camp Eagle.

Once we landed, we remained on standby. At 1245 hours
Sergeant McKinnon called in a spot report to record that his
team had found a trail network and was reconning the area.
Shortly afterward he radioed that they had found a base
camp. They reported that they could see the NVA stacking
ammo crates large enough to be 122mm rockets, which was
what they were looking for. Operations decided that the team
should be extracted immediately.

The mission was getting more interesting; the base camp
was not that far from the LZ. Sergeant McKinnon's team had
started moving back to the clearing just as we departed Camp
Eagle so they could be ready for pickup by the time we got
there.

The C&C aircraft had climbed to two thousand feet, and
the gunships were at fifteen hundred. I stayed at five hundred
feet with the chase ship, which trailed about half a mile behind me.

As the LZ came into view, as usual I called for the team to
pop smoke to pinpoint its position. Instead of one smoke, I

saw three. When I radioed that I had a red, yellow, and a purple smoke, the RTO said he'd put out grape (purple). I told the guns to hit the red and yellow smoke, and headed to where the purple smoke was still coming up.

With the gunships putting rocket and minigun fire all around the LZ, and both of my door guns firing into the tree lines, I didn't know if we were taking any fire or not. If we were, we didn't take any hits. But we got in and picked the team up without any difficulty.

When we landed at Camp Eagle a short time later, the LRP team was rushed into the debriefing tent to be interviewed first as a group and then individually. Usually, each man on the ground sees things differently, so it was important that each describe what he'd seen or heard while on the mission, independently of the others. All of the little pieces would then come together as one complete picture.

The debriefing had just ended when we were notified that air strikes had been put in on the base camp, resulting in two very large secondary explosions and a number of smaller ones. Now *that* was the way it was supposed to happen. There had been too many times that Division had gotten good information and, for whatever reason, just sat on it. That day was different; the LRPs had found the bad guys' base, reported it, and gotten out without losing anyone. It had really ruined the day for the NVA. It was a damn good day's work.

At the beginning of the second week in April, the division began moving west of Fire Support Base Birmingham. A little more than five miles along Highway 547, the valley floor ended and the mountains began. The next fire support base, which was going to be called Bastogne, was being constructed in an area about a mile farther back into the mountains. It was named after the little town in Belgium where the 101st had fought the Germans to a standstill in the Battle of the Bulge during World War II.

It was to be a company-size operation, our first since moving north. It would also be an entirely new type of operation. We would be going in as flights of five. There would be no large open rice paddies in which to land. We'd have to pick a spot on the top or side of a mountain, or wherever there was a bomb crater large enough in which to get a helicopter.

I was told I'd be flying the lead aircraft. I didn't have the faintest idea why I was chosen to lead the flight. It seemed to me they would have wanted someone with more experience in the lead. However, mine was not to reason why, mine was just to do it, damn it.

We were ordered to pick up troops at a rock quarry between Camp Eagle and Fire Support Base Birmingham at 0700 hours. We landed on a one-lane dirt road and sat, patiently waiting. The troops finally came out of the quarry in single file and made their way to the aircraft.

In the gray early morning light, even before I could see his face, I recognized the man leading the file. I would have recognized that walk anywhere. It was Platoon Sergeant Richard Clary, one of my instructors in jump school in 1962. Clary had also been my platoon sergeant for three years while I was with the 504th Airborne Infantry in Germany, from 1962 to 1965. I hadn't seen him in three years, but I couldn't help thinking how glad I was not to be getting off the helicopter with him on the LZ.

The area had been heavily hit by artillery and tac air, and most of the foliage had been blown off the trees. The trunks were still standing anywhere from two to 150 feet in the air. But where some of the heavier bombs had hit, the trees had been taken completely out, leaving only large bomb craters. Those were the areas where we were to try to land.

That was a type of flying that I hadn't before done. I doubted if any of us had. For a brand-new aircraft commander, it was a challenge. Although we didn't know it at the time, it was to become common practice. The crew chief and gunner were busy putting out suppressive fire while I tried to figure out how to land. I finally told the crew chief and gunner that they had to talk me down through the vegetation. They did, keeping the tail rotor clear of the jagged tree trunks and fallen timber.

After we had the first lift on the ground, things went a little better. The troops secured and began enlarging the LZ. They had met only light resistance on the ground. I guess the air strikes and artillery had done their job as advertised.

We made three more trips into the landing zone. Then CH-47s (heavy-lift helicopters) began bringing in the engineers with their equipment. Among the first items were the bulldozers. They immediately began clearing the downed trees and leveling the area. Before nightfall Bastogne was starting to take shape. The artillery battery had been brought in, bunkers dug, and fighting positions established. The line companies had patrols out to see if NVA were lurking out and about in the nearby jungle.

A week later I was assigned to fly what was known as a "sniffer" mission. I had no idea what I'd be doing. When I asked what the mission entailed, I was simply told that I'd be briefed sometime before we took off.

Two captains from Division G-2 (Intelligence Section) met me at my aircraft and quickly went about installing equipment in the cargo compartment that was designed to detect the trace amounts of ammonia given off by the human body. After brief introductions were made, I once again asked what in the hell we were going to be doing.

One of the captains told me four aircraft were involved: a C&C, two gunships, and my slick. The G-2 personnel would be on my aircraft and would operate the equipment. We would depart Camp Eagle as a flight of four and proceed to the target area, a valley six miles west of Bastogne. Upon our arrival, the C&C would remain fifteen hundred feet above me. The gunships would orbit five hundred feet above my aircraft, and I would drop down to fifty feet over the trees. The C&C would then vector me in a grid pattern at thirty knots forward airspeed. We would fly the grid pattern from north to south, then from east to west, until we'd covered every square yard of the valley.

The man in the back, who was monitoring the equipment, would have his own radio communications with the C&C aircraft. Whenever the needle on his equipment showed a high ammonia reading, he would radio the word "hot" to the C&C. The copilot of the C&C would be following my position on his map. When he heard the word "hot," he would make a dot on the map. When we were through with the flight and had returned to Camp Eagle, they would take a pen and connect the dots, just like a kid's game. By doing that they could, and sometimes did, show where a trail was located under the jungle canopy.

That type of mission could be fun, or if not fun, at least interesting. The one thing I didn't like about it was the altitude and airspeed at which we'd be flying. It was definitely in what was known as the "dead man's curve." If we got shot down, or if the damn engine just decided to quit, we would not be high enough or going fast enough to enter an autorotation. We would just crash into the trees fifty feet below us. Oh, well, what the hell! I guess that's what they gave us flight pay for.

In fact, we flew the mission and returned without any problems. Flying around in circles for two hours had to be boring for the guns. Still, I was glad they were there watching over us.

We were back in the same general area the next day. We rechecked the valley we'd done the previous day, then moved over the ridge line to the next valley to the west. When we dropped down into the north end of the valley to begin our grid pattern, we immediately started getting hot readings. A few seconds later, out of the corner of my eye, I saw a green flash. Then there was another one, off the nose. While I was trying to figure out what it was, the crew chief began firing, and yelling that we were taking fire.

What I'd seen were the green tracers used by the NVA. I told the C&C and the guns that we were taking fire and that I was breaking left. I wasted no time getting the hell out of there. I could not believe I hadn't recognized those green lights as tracers. A mistake like that could have gotten me killed in one hell of a hurry.

As soon as I called, saying I was receiving fire, the guns started putting rockets right under me. Luckily, they hadn't gotten complacent after the previous day's uneventful flight. We climbed to fifteen hundred feet and headed to the south end of the valley, planning to start there and work our way northward. But as soon as I descended to my working altitude and began the first leg of the grid, we received heavy automatic weapons fire from the trees below. As I was climbing out, I called the C&C and said, "That's enough of this shit. Those guys are really pissed off. I'm going home." I didn't get any argument from anyone.

Over the next couple of days the weather steadily deteriorated. We were able to get into FSB Bastogne, but the mountains beyond were pretty well socked in. The LRPs were still trying to get some teams in there, but with the weather the way it was, they were unable to do so. To try it would have been suicide. Our missions during that period were mostly just ash-and-trash flights to units working to the east of the mountains.

At 1900 hours on April 20 we were informed that the following morning we would be making a combat assault into the mountains west of FSB Bastogne, a platoon-size operation. Two flights of five would move the troops, and two light fire teams would provide gun support. There would also be a C&C aircraft plus a maintenance ship. We would be putting in the 1st Battalion, 501st Airborne Infantry. They would be taking a ridge line on which to establish another fire support base, to be named Vehgel, six miles west of Bastogne. The LZ was to be a small valley that ran south to north and was on the east side of the ridge line.

As I listened to the briefing, there was no doubt in my mind that we were going to the first valley I'd flown the sniffer mission in, and I knew that the bad guys were there. As the briefing continued, we were told that under no circumstances were we to go west of the ridge line.

Kingsman Five (our XO, Major Tuttle) would be flying the C&C aircraft as the air mission commander, with Captain Peterson as his copilot. Captain Schlater would lead the first flight of five, and Lieutenant Greenlee would lead the second. I would be flying the number-five slot in the second group. Captain Floyd Olsen, with WO1 Robert "Smitty" Link as his copilot, flew the maintenance aircraft. Their call sign was "Fosdick Five."

At 0800 hours the next morning, the first flight of five with one light fire team (two gunships) departed Camp Eagle to stand by at FSB Bastogne. The weather was bad. The second flight was to remain at Eagle until called. The call came at approximately 1100 hours.

The weather was marginal at best, and clouds obscured the mountaintops, forcing us to fly at low level through the mountains, in a misting rain, to reach our target area. Our section was in a trail formation behind the first flight of five. We headed south and then turned to the west, following some small valleys. As we turned back to the north again, ahead of us lay the valley where I'd been a week earlier.

Captain Schlater's flight was about a quarter of a mile ahead of us and had already started its approach. I heard several aircraft call that they were taking fire. Then I saw those damn green tracers coming up from the valley floor again. I watched as the aircraft in front of me, flown by Butch Meola, started taking hits. It wasn't like in the movies. There were no parts flying off, it didn't burst into flames, nor did the aircraft stagger in the air as if hit with a giant fist. It just seemed to lose power.

When the enemy fire first struck the aircraft, the master caution panel had lit up like a Christmas tree, and the power began to bleed off. Butch did as he'd been taught, and entered an autorotoration while making his radio call. "Kingsman Two-nine has been hit. We are going down a mile south of the LZ."

As soon as I saw the aircraft start to go down, I followed him, then I called lead. "Two-six . . . Two-five. I'm following Two-nine down. I'll pick up the crew. The troops on both aircraft can secure the downed aircraft."

"Two-five . . . Two-six. Roger. Marry up with us at Bastogne."

"This is Two-five. Roger that."

Butch's autorotation was picture-perfect. His flight school instructor would have been proud of him. He landed on the valley floor in some tall elephant grass. I saw that there were fallen trees as well as a lot of tree stumps in the grass. While I was trying to pick a spot in which to set down, I heard him talking to his crew.

Evidently, a bullet had penetrated one of the wiring bundles in Butch's aircraft and shorted out the radio. Everything that was said on the intercom was being transmitted over the air. I could hear him asking, "Is anybody hit? Is anybody hit?" Then his crew chief answered, "I'm hit."

"Oh, no. Where?"

"I'm hit in the head."

"Oh, God, no! Not the head."

"No . . . no, I'm hit in the leg."

"Well, you dumb son of a bitch, make up your goddamn mind."

While that was taking place, I was still trying to get my aircraft on the ground, but I was laughing so hard that the aircraft was wobbling all over the place. Everyone on board must have thought I'd finally gone completely crazy. My co-pilot, Ed Ragan, took the controls and landed the aircraft.

Ed had been with the company only a short time, but he'd come right out of flight school into one of the hottest areas in Vietnam. Now he sat there looking at me with an expression on his face that said, "What in the hell kind of loony bin have I gotten into? Here we are with an aircraft being shot out of the sky, a crew chief shot, and this crazy fool is sitting here laughing his damn fool head off."

As soon as we touched down, the grunts on my aircraft got off and joined the ones who had been on Butch Meola's bird. They immediately set up a perimeter to secure the downed aircraft. Butch and his gunner helped his crew chief back to where we were and loaded him on board. The crew chief had taken a round dead center in his rectum. I'd heard of people getting shot in the ass, but this was the first time I'd ever seen it in living color.

After dropping off the crew of the downed aircraft at Bastogne, we rejoined the flight and headed back to the LZ with another load of troops. The insertion went just as planned for the second lift. But then the weather really turned to shit. We were directed to return to Camp Eagle and stand by. The time was around 1230 hours.

At 1420 hours we were back in the air again. We made two more lifts into the LZ in the valley. We were released from our mission at 1730 hours due to the weather and told to go to LZ Sally.

We arrived back at the LZ around 1800 hours and worked for the 2d Brigade until 1945 hours, when we were released for the day. Returning to Camp Eagle at 2020 hours, we were told that the maintenance aircraft, Fosdick Five, had not been heard from since 1515 hours.

Around 1830 hours the battalion had been notified that we had an aircraft missing. They'd sent out an alert to Phu Bai, Red Beach, Marble Mountain, 101st Aviation Battalion, FSB Bastogne, and Da Nang to see if Fosdick Five was sitting on the ground at any of those locations due to the weather. The reports were all negative. No immediate search-and-rescue mission could be initiated due to the darkness.

During the night, our Operations officer, Captain Kenneth Fitch, formulated the plan for a search-and-rescue mission. The next morning, April 22, we put eleven UH-1Hs and five gunships in the air for an all-day search.

The entire area where Fosdick Five might have gone down was broken up into sections, and areas were assigned to each platoon. The search continued from dawn to dusk. However, there were no sightings of the missing aircraft. There were also no emergency radio signals from Fosdick Five. The search was terminated at 1830 hours due to darkness.

I flew over ten hours that day with negative results. There had been six people on board Fosdick Five: the aircraft commander, Capt. Floyd Olsen; copilot, WO1 Robert Link; crew chief, Sp5. Frankie B. Johnson; gunner, Sp5. Larry C. Jamerson; technical inspector, S.Sgt. Lyle Everett Mackedanz; and one passenger, Sp4. James E. Cramer. They had simply disappeared. Six more young men had joined the rolls of those listed as missing in action (MIA).

For the next two days we were kept out of the mountains by

the weather. We were restricted to working along the ten-mile stretch of flatland between the mountains and the ocean.

On April 25 we supported the 2d Brigade out of LZ Sally. We put in eight hours of flight time before being released for the day. All in all, it was a good day's work. We had made thirty-eight takeoffs and landings. Mostly it was just general ash and trash; we moved a lot of troops around from one place to another, and did a lot of resupplying. Just before we called it a day, we took mermite cans of hot food to as many of the units as we could reach.

We arrived back at Camp Eagle at around 1600 hours. After getting the aircraft taken care of and filling out the af-teraction report, it was time for a cold beer or three. Thirty minutes later Dave Greenlee came into the club and said, "We've got a Tac E [Tactical Emergency] west of Bastogne. I need somebody to go with me."

Looking around, I didn't see a crowd making a mad dash for the door. In fact, I didn't see anyone moving at all. I looked at Dave for a few seconds, then stood up and replied, "Hell, why not!"

Ten minutes later we were in the air en route to FSB Bastogne. The weather was awful. The bottoms of the clouds were down to under a thousand feet. There was a light rain and heavy fog. The visibility had to be under half a mile, and it was getting worse as we approached the mountains.

Upon arrival at Bastogne, we landed at the log pad and got our briefing. A company was in contact with the NVA and needed a resupply of ammunition and medical supplies. They were located about a thousand meters to the northwest. We would have to follow Highway 547, which from there was nothing but a wide footpath under the jungle canopy. When the ground unit was able to hear us, they would try to talk us in to their location. Damn, but that sounded like it was going to be fun. Right then I would much rather have been back in the club with my cold beer.

After loading the supplies on board, we took off. Staying low over the trees, we followed the trail farther into the mountains. The visibility had gotten worse, at best less than a quarter mile. At times we flew into patches of dense, low-lying fog. Man, I didn't like that at all!

After what seemed a lifetime, the RTO of the infantry company in contact came up on the radio. He said he could hear us, and asked if we could tell him where we were. We told him we were low over 547. He said they were located about three hundred meters up the mountain to the north. As I looked at the mountainside, I could see where the mountain disappeared into the overcast.

We turned to the north, keeping visual contact with the trees through the chin bubble. We started a slow climb, which actually was more of an out-of-ground-effect hover. The RTO told us we were getting louder and sounded as though we were coming right at him. I told him to pop a smoke grenade. A few minutes later I saw a cloud of red smoke hanging over the trees.

I identified the color as red, and the RTO confirmed it. When I asked where they wanted their supplies, I was told to drop them right in the middle of the smoke. As we hovered to the center of the cloud of smoke, I told the crew chief and gunner to kick the supplies out.

I then asked the guy on the ground, "Did you get it?"

His reply was, "Get what?"

I started to ask, "What the hell do you mean, get what?" when I realized that the smoke was drifting across the tree-tops and I hadn't taken that into account. I keyed the mike and said, "Shit! We just resupplied the bad guys. Okay, guys, don't go anywhere. We'll be right back." Christ, as if once weren't bad enough, we had to do it all over again. I called Bastogne and told them we would be back there in ten minutes and to get another load ready. They said it would be waiting for us when we landed. I was really glad they didn't ask any embarrassing questions, such as, "Why?"

After picking up the second load of supplies, we went back into the fog. We found the ground unit the same way we had the first time, only now I went to the far side of the red cloud and saw where the smoke was coming up through the trees.

As I looked through the chin bubble, I could see a man

with a handset up to his ear, and he was talking to me. When I asked him where he wanted me to drop the supplies this time, he said to put them right in his arms, and then he opened his arms wide.

We must have awakened the NVA on our first trip. While the crew chief and gunner were busy throwing the cases of supplies out of the aircraft, several lines of green tracers darted out of the fog. This time I didn't have any trouble recognizing them for what they were, but I couldn't go anywhere. The people on the ground needed those supplies, so we had to sit there until the off-loading was completed.

It was weird, hovering, watching those pale green lines searching for us and not being able to do anything about it. Each time I felt a few of the rounds hit the aircraft, my eyes automatically went to the instrument panel. Everything was right where it was supposed to be. I wished they would hurry up and get those goddamn supplies unloaded.

When a few more rounds hit the aircraft, I started yelling for the crew to get the lead out. At that moment, a bullet came through my chin bubble and hit the leading edge of my armored seat. A quarter of an inch higher and I would have been gut-shot. More than likely, I would have just been a dead man waiting to die. Not a pleasant thought.

I was in the process of pulling in power to leave when I heard the crew chief yell, "We are up. Let's get the hell out of here." No shit, cowboy. By that time nothing could have kept me anywhere around that area for any price.

As we passed over Bastogne, I called, "Bastogne Control, Kingsman Two-five."

"Two-five, this is Bastogne Control."

"Yeah, Bastogne. We got your people what they needed. We took some hits in the process. They said that they would be okay. We're going to try to get this thing back to Camp Eagle. See you in the morning."

"Roger, Two-five. Thanks a lot. We owe you."

We proceeded to Camp Eagle and landed in our maintenance area. After we checked over the aircraft, and counted the bullet holes—and there were a lot of them to count—we turned it over to the maintenance section. I headed back to the club.

The guy tending bar saw me as I walked in. He reached over, pulled a cold beer out of the cooler, and held it up to me. I shook my head and pointed at a full bottle of rum. "That's what I want." It was going to take a hell of a lot more than beer to get me to stop shaking. Outside, the rain started to come down harder. I sat in the corner of my little world and drank my rum. I just wanted to be left alone.

The next morning, when I woke up at about 0600 hours, the fog was right down to the ground, so there was no way that we would be flying. I went back to bed.

The weather eventually cleared enough so that by a little after noon a few of us were able to proceed with our missions. Ed Ragan and I would be going back to Bastogne. All we'd be doing was hauling people and supplies from Camp Eagle to Bastogne. It was going to be a short day of ash and trash.

The weather at Bastogne was about the same as the day before, but as the afternoon wore on, the weather worsened. Somewhere around 1700 hours we were told by the Tactical Operations Center that we were released and could return to Camp Eagle. As we were preparing to depart, the TOC called and asked if we could do them a favor. Would we take several cases of cold beer and Cokes to the unit I'd resupplied the day before?

Looking at the low-hanging clouds and the fog that obscured the mountains, I could not justify risking my aircraft and crew to deliver cold drinks. I informed the TOC that if the weather cleared in the morning, I would be glad to do it. However, I did not think that it was a good idea to try it now. With that, we departed and headed home.

I don't know why, but as soon as we cleared the fire base I reached over and dialed in the radio frequency of the unit up on the mountain. I heard the radio operator in the TOC say, "It's a no go. Those goddamn chickenshit pilots won't do it." As soon as I heard that, I made a 180-degree turn and headed back to the log pad. I had damn near died yesterday resupplying those people, and some son of a bitch was calling us chickenshit! Somebody had an ass-whipping coming, and I was going to deliver it myself.

I was out of the aircraft as soon as we got the skids on the ground. As I headed toward the TOC, a man came out and walked toward me. When he got closer, he asked, "Are you Kingsman Two-five?" When I said yes, he smiled and said, "Don't worry about that idiot who was on the radio. He is being talked to now." I looked to where he was pointing and saw four people. Two were just standing there watching, while the third was beating the hell out of the man who must have been the radio operator. I guess someone figured out you just didn't insult and piss off the people who were your life-line to survival.

The man shook my hand and said, "Thanks again for yesterday. Those guys were in a real bad way. If you hadn't gotten them resupplied, God only knows what would have happened to them."

The tone of his voice made a big impression on me. There was honesty and gratitude in it. As I walked back toward the aircraft, I thought that maybe all of the bullshit might just be worthwhile.

Chapter
Ten

On the morning of April 28, I was assigned to work with the 2d Brigade out of LZ Sally. It was a relief to get away from the mountains for a while. We were supporting the 2/502 Airborne Infantry, which had been my unit when I was at Fort Campbell. The weather had not improved much, but it was good enough to work out in the coastal plains and the rolling piedmont area at the foot of the mountains.

We started out by hauling back all the mermite and water cans that had been delivered the evening before. Then we began ferrying troops from one location to another as they continued to search for the enemy.

Not very much happened until shortly after noon, when one of the platoons from Alpha Company was conducting a sweep near the village of Phuoc Yen, on the Bo River (Song Bo). The river made a complete 180-degree turn, forming an area that looked something like a stocking. The stocking was about two hundred meters wide across the top, which opened to the north, and ran about five hundred meters down each side. The toe of the stocking curved around to the east.

As the platoon approached the northern end of the village, it began to receive scattered rifle fire. As the infantry tried to move against the enemy, it became apparent they'd run into a hell of a lot more than just a few snipers. Another platoon was picked up from its field location and flown in to reinforce the platoon in contact. As they tried to develop the situation, the enemy fire intensified.

After the initial contact had been made, and it was clear this could be more than a few isolated snipers, the battalion commander had me pick him up, and I became the part-time C&C aircraft. Whenever the BC was not on the ground, he was in my aircraft. As it turned out, he spent most of his time with the ground units, but he still wanted me to stay close by. I asked him if I could continue to fly support as long as I could get to him within ten minutes, and he said it would be all right. Boy, was I glad. With things starting to heat up, I didn't want to spend most of the day sitting on the ground, waiting.

With the situation then developing around Phuoc Yen village, the BC wanted to take a look at it from the air. The cloud base was only about a thousand feet, and I didn't want to fly over the village at that altitude, so I asked if a high-speed, low-level pass would be all right with him. He said he just wanted to get a good look at what we were up against.

We flew about a mile to the north, letting down to treetop level. Turning back to the south, we started our run. I wanted to go down the center of the long axis of the stocking. It was only five or six hundred meters from the tree line to where the village ended at the river's edge, and we would not be exposed to enemy fire for long.

We were doing close to 120 knots as we approached the tree line. If everything had gone as planned, I knew the village would be just on the other side of the trees. I keyed the intercom and said, "Okay, boss, here we go."

As we cleared the tree line, there were people all over the damn place, and the most amazing thing was that they were all in khaki uniforms. Most of them seemed to be digging fighting positions. A few stopped to look up at us as we flew over, but most of them simply kept right on digging. With the river on three sides, and the two platoons coming from the north, they did not have anyplace else to go.

The farther down the stocking we went, the more people we saw, and they were not your local everyday Viet Cong; they were North Vietnamese Army Regulars, exactly what we'd been looking for. I could hear the battalion commander in the back of the aircraft saying, "We got 'em. This time we've really got the bastards."

Now that he had them, he had to keep them. The ensuing operation was to be a classic cordon. The BC would maneuver his units until he physically surrounded the enemy. Then they'd have no choice but to fight or surrender.

A call went out for helicopter support. The lift aircraft were to move the troops, while the gunships were to make sure that the NVA didn't try to cross the river. The BC coordinated with the artillery batteries out of LZ Sally to start putting fire into the village.

Two companies from the 1st Battalion of the 501st and two from the 2d Battalion would be involved in the operation. There would also be one company, the Black Panther or Hoc Bao, from the 1st ARVN Division, plus three platoons of Popular Forces (PFs). We called them "Ruff Puffs." These were your local, homegrown Vietnamese militia troops. They were trained primarily for village defense. In most cases the training had been a waste of time.

The Black Panthers, A/2/501 and D/2/501, were deployed across the north end of the stocking. A/1/501 was on the west side of the stocking, on the far side of the river. The three platoons of Ruff Puffs had the east side.

By nightfall all of our units were in place. The most likely escape route would be to the north. If the NVA tried to break out by crossing the river, they would be committing mass suicide. Although the NVA were dedicated and well trained, they were not fanatical like the Japanese of World War II. The Japanese would launch a banzai charge and fight until the last man was dead. The NVA would much rather slip away and live to fight another day. It was something they were very good at. That time, though, their commander had made a very serious mistake. He'd let his soldiers get into a box with no way out.

We had reported to the 2d Brigade log pad at 0600 hours and returned to Camp Eagle a little after 2200. It had been a long eighteen-hour day, and I'd flown for over thirteen hours. Not a bad day's work.

The next morning the weather cleared and we were back with the 2d Brigade. The artillery had pounded the village throughout the night. Trying to find a weak spot in our lines, the NVA had made a few probing attacks toward the north end of the stocking during the night. The bodies of the dead NVA lying in the open told the story; there were no weak spots. A few NVA had tried to escape by swimming across the river, and they also died in the attempt.

During brief firefights, two of the NVA had been taken prisoner, and we learned that the trapped unit was the 90th NVA Regiment's 8th Battalion, approximately six hundred men.

With the weather finally clearing, a steady stream of helicopter gunships was hitting the target area, and flight after flight of F-4 fighter-bombers out of Da Nang were adding five-hundred-pound bombs and canisters of napalm to the destruction. It was beyond me how anyone inside that village could take such a beating and still be able to fight.

Over the next three days the pounding never stopped. The NVA made two more attempts to break out to the north. Both failed. On the morning of the fifth day, May 2, the NVA who were still alive finally gave up: 107 men of the 8th Battalion, 90th NVA Regiment, surrendered en masse. A sweep of the village revealed 419 bodies. Well, nobody could say that the month of May had not started off without one hell of a bang.

A few days later I was told to report for a briefing to the Forward Observation Base (FOB) located at Phu Bai. The Special Forces had a mission coming, and we were supplying one aircraft and crew. It would be my first mission with them since moving north.

The briefing I got was nothing like the ones I'd received before. We were taken into a large room where ten other air crews were assembled. I knew only a few of the other pilots. The room reminded me of a World War II film where the bomber crews were briefed on their mission for the day. The chairs were set in rows opposite a small stage. On the rear of the stage was a large board covered with an Army blanket. The colonel who stood alongside it was not wearing a hat with a fifty-mission crush, but there was no doubt in any-body's mind that he was in charge.

It was very quiet as he introduced himself. He said that it was the only briefing he would give, so it would behoove us to pay close attention. He made it clear that if any of us were having second thoughts, we were free to leave. Once the briefing started, no one would be allowed to leave the com-pound until the mission was completed. If the mission lasted six hours or six weeks, we would be required to remain there. There would be plenty of booze to drink and all of the food we wanted. He even assured us that there would be hot and cold running hootchmaids. Damn, that sounded like the only way to go—just volunteer for the mission and then refuse to fly.

No one got up to leave, so the colonel continued. Only five aircraft would be involved in the coming mission; the other five would be on standby until the first group completed the insertion. The colonel talked to us a little longer before turning the briefing over to his Operations officer.

Once again we were asked if anyone wanted to leave. I wondered why they kept asking that question. Then they took the blanket off the map, and I wished I'd left when I had the chance. We were only five miles from the South China Sea, but there was no water on the map. That meant we were going into North Vietnam or Laos.

Thank God it was not North Vietnam. We were soon told that our destination was to be Laos. We would be staging out of a Special Forces camp called Mai Loc, located two klicks south of the Demilitarized Zone (DMZ). We were to insert a six-man Special Forces team, then stand by at Mai Loc and wait for it to call for extraction. The men were expected to be on the ground no more than three days.

There was a captain from one of the other flight crews whom I assumed would be in charge of the aviation assets. He stood up and wanted to know why the people were going into Laos. What were they after? The Operations officer looked at him for what seemed like a couple of minutes, then said, "Captain, that is about the dumbest damn question you could have asked. You do not have a need to know that kind of information. Your only concern is getting them in and getting them out. Now sit down."

The next item covered what we could have with us while we were on the mission. We wouldn't be allowed to take any personal items; all billfolds, rings, watches, even our dog tags, were to be turned in before we left the briefing room. We would be given a plain flight suit shirt with nothing sewn on it.

After all of that bullshit, we were told that if we were shot down and they could not get us out, we were not to try to get back into Vietnam! We were to head due west and try to get to Thailand. If we were caught, our military records would show that we'd never served in Vietnam. The government of the United States would claim not to have any idea what we were doing or why we were there.

Then the Operations officer read off the air crews that would be making the insertion. There would be a C&C aircraft, two lift ships, and two gunships. The captain who'd wanted to know "why" was not on the list. I was to be the officer in charge (OIC) of the aviation assets for the mission. We were to fly to Mai Loc and report to a Maj. Clyde Sincere for a final and more detailed briefing.

After we landed, I walked to the gate that led into the Special Forces compound. A guy was standing just inside the gate. He was not wearing a hat or a shirt. When I asked him if the boss was around, he said, "Sure, follow me," and headed toward a small building. When we walked in, he went over to a small refrigerator, opened it, and took out two cans of beer. He handed me one and said, "I'm Clyde. I'm the boss." I got the impression right from the start that it was going to be a good assignment. Major Sincere was the type of person who would be easy to work for. I could also tell he wouldn't take any shit from anyone.

The FOB missions were different from the 101st LRP missions in that we were given very little information. When working with the LRPs, we would fly them on their visual reconnaissance (VR) to select an LZ, and we were allowed to sit in on their mission briefing so we'd have the same information as the team we were supporting.

Working with FOB, mission information was distributed strictly "need to know." We were normally led to the LZ or PZ (pickup zone) by an Air Force FAC. The people we were supporting sometimes wore U.S. uniforms, and sometimes would dress in the same kind of black pajamas the VC wore. There were also times when we took one or two people in civilian clothes, dropped them in a jungle clearing, and never saw them again.

On other missions, we resupplied or extracted large numbers of troops, mainly indigenous personnel with a few Americans interspersed among their ranks. We did not know how they'd gotten there, and knew it wouldn't do any good to ask. Although the FOB personnel made us feel welcome, we never felt we were really part of the team. However, that did not interfere with our doing our job, and doing it well.

During the second week in May the company had to turn in three aircraft that were getting too many hours on them. Three new helicopters were needed to replace them. That meant we had to fly the old birds to Hotel Three, which was a maintenance depot located down in Saigon. I was assigned to fly one of the aircraft.

We made the trip in one day. The following day we turned in the old aircraft, and our maintenance people went over the paperwork and test-flew the new ones. We signed for them and were ready to head north the next morning. The aircraft I was to fly back was a UH-1H with the tail number 66-16121. It flew like a dream and smelled just like a new car. I was in love all over again. I knew when we got back to Camp Eagle, someone else would get 121, but at least for the next eight hours she was all mine.

Two days later I was called into Operations and handed a logbook. I'd been assigned my own aircraft. Until then I'd been flying whatever aircraft was available. I now had my own helicopter and crew chief. The aircraft was 121, and the crew chief was Sp4. Tom Turck. My God, I thought I'd died and gone to Heaven. I took the logbook and walked to the revetment to meet my new crew chief.

Tom had crewed on the company commander's aircraft until Major Addiss took command. The major had brought his own crew chief and gunner with him. I'd flown with Tom a couple of times but hadn't really talked to him. He was about five-foot-eight and thin, and weighed only 140 pounds. He had jet-black hair and a full mustache. I'd tried to grow a mustache when I first arrived in country, but succeeded only in looking like I'd forgotten to wash my upper lip.

Tom had been working on the aircraft ever since I flew it back from Saigon. He had a black spade painted on the avionics compartment door. The skid toes, as well as the tail stinger, were painted white to indicate that it was a second platoon aircraft. There was also a large white diamond, with two smaller blue diamonds inside, to identify it as a 17th AHC aircraft.

As we walked around looking at 121, we talked awhile, trying to get a feel for each other. I decided it was as good a time as any to set the ground rules, and let him know I didn't know anything about maintenance and that I didn't have any interest in it. The helicopter was his, along with any maintenance problems that came up. I would help him as best I could, but it would not be very much.

I also told him that while the aircraft was his on the ground, once we were in the air it was mine. I was the aircraft commander and it was my responsibility to accomplish whatever mission we were assigned. Under no circumstances would I tolerate any of my decisions being questioned. Once the mission was completed and we returned to the Castle, we could talk about it.

The two of us would be the only permanent crew for 121. The copilots and gunners would be rotated. If he could not now or at some later date live with those rules, I told him, he was free to ask for another aircraft or pilot. Tom didn't seem to have a problem with what I said.

It was pitch-black at 0500 hours the next morning. I was using a flashlight to preflight 121. Tom was there before I arrived and already had the cowlings open so I could get to the engine. He went around the aircraft with me as I looked it over. All of the big pieces were connected to the airframe, and all of the small pieces seemed to be in order. After I finished the preflight, we headed to the mess tent for breakfast and to wait for our departure time.

The day's mission promised to be an easy one, and we hoped a lot of fun. We were going to the LRP pad to train with them. We'd had been working with the LRP company for only a short time, and there was still a lot of coordination that needed to be accomplished. At the time, they did not have dedicated air crews. Their air support was whoever within the battalion happened to be assigned the mission that day. The missions were getting accomplished, but they could have gone more smoothly.

That day, we would be training in all phases of their operation. We worked first with the Jacob's ladder. It was made of rope, was thirty feet long and two and a half feet wide, and it was a bitch to climb. It was hooked to the tie-down rings on the floor of the aircraft.

Next was the McGuire rig, a nylon seat attached to the end of a 120-foot rope. A sandbag was tied to the nylon seat to help get it through the trees. The other end was tied to the floor of the aircraft. The McGuire rig was used when there was no LZ for the helicopter and the ladder would not reach the ground. The main problem with it was that once the people were in the seat, we had to pull them up through the trees, and we could pick up only three people at a time. Other than the aircraft making one hell of a big target, the McGuire rig worked fine.

We talked about the different ways of signaling from the ground. Smoke was used more than anything else, but we were sure that the NVA were monitoring our radio frequencies because of what happened on the extraction a week or so earlier, when we threw out "grape" and they threw red and yellow. We decided that the team on the ground would say over the radio that it was popping red smoke then put out a yellow smoke. If red smoke came up, the gunships would shoot the shit out of it.

We also signaled with panel markers. They were four feet long and two feet wide. Each panel was silver on one side and international orange on the other. We also knew that the bad guys had them. So our plan was, if I called for a panel marker, the team would flash it three times on one side and then three times on the other. If we saw a panel marker just lying there, the guns would do their thing.

The strobe light was another signaling device we often used, mainly at night. Its drawback was that if a pilot could see it, more than likely the bad guys could see it too.

We also practiced loading and unloading the aircraft. On an insertion, it was unacceptable if I had to remain in the LZ for more than seven seconds.

The extraction was an entirely different situation. During that time, I would stay on the ground until the last man was on board the aircraft. I made it clear to the LRPs that if I put them in, I would bring them out. All of them. Nobody would be left behind. When I said that, I received some very strange looks. I knew they lived by the saying, "LRPs don't leave LRPs behind." I couldn't say I blamed them for doubting me, but those people didn't know me. I hadn't proven myself, and they'd heard tough talk before; talk was cheap.

The next thing was the visual reconnaissance (VR), performed when a team was to be inserted and the team leader wanted to pick out an LZ within his recon zone. I took some of the platoon sergeants and team leaders on a flight so they could give me pointers on what *they* were looking for when selecting an LZ. At the same time I let them know some of the things I needed to make the insertion go more smoothly.

One of the things I brought up was the excessive amount of radio traffic when making an insertion. All of the coordination between the C&C, the gunships, the insert, and the chase ship should be taken care of before we took off. I did not need anyone telling me the shape of the LZ, or where a large tree was located. All of that information I already knew from the VR. All I needed when I was above the treetops doing 120 knots was for the C&C to tell me the heading and distance.

The radio traffic would be something like this: "Two-five, turn right . . . stop . . . turn . . . five hundred meters . . . two hundred meters." At that time I would begin deceleration in order to arrive with enough forward air speed to be able to settle into the LZ. The next thing would be: "Two-five's coming out." That was all that needed to be said over the radio.

After we completed the flight and discussed the VR procedures, I told the LRPs that I wanted to talk about who was in charge of what. I said, "Okay, guys. This is going to be a one-sided conversation. I first want to give you a little background on myself. Then we're going to talk about the chain of command and responsibilities." That seemed to get their attention.

"As you can see, I'm a lieutenant. I haven't always been one. I started out as a private and spent three years with the 504th Airborne in Europe. I reached the rank of sergeant before going to OCS. While I was with the 504th, I became a well-trained 11-Bush-4-Papa. Although I was an 11 Bush, I'm sure you've noticed I don't have a CIB. I have no combat experience as a grunt. I'm a helicopter driver, an aircraft commander. As such, I am like the captain of a ship. It might be a damn small ship, but it's my ship, and my word is law.

"From the time we take off until we bring you back to your company area, I'm the boss wherever the aircraft is concerned. The C&C or the team leader can abort the mission at any time. If I become incapacitated—that's just a nice word for getting my shit blown away—the copilot will take over, abort the mission, and get my young ass to a hospital. If we go down, for whatever reason—combat damage, mechanical failure, or if I just fly into a damn tree—once we're on the ground, the team leader or the ranking team member, regardless of rank, will be in charge.

"Gentlemen, I know some people right now who think that

just because they have the rank sewn on their collars, they know more than a person of lesser rank. I personally think they must have slept through the classes on survival. I do not want those people flying as my copilot or being involved in the mission in any way. This is not a game. However, for lack of a better word, survival is the name of the game. Survival for everyone. And I think that the best chance for myself, as well as for my crew, is to let someone who knows what in the hell they're doing lead the way."

As I talked, I was watching the faces of the people in front of me. Mostly there were surprised looks. I don't think they expected me to be so blunt. In the rear of the group were several of the senior NCOs: Platoon Sergeants John (Doc) Brubaker and Willie Champion, Staff Sergeants Richard Burnell and Al Contreros, and a few others. They all seemed to be nodding in approval. Captain Fitts, the LRP company commander, and First Sergeant Darol Walker appeared to be in agreement. Our time together was going to be a positive learning experience for all of us. I thought we'd gotten off to a damn good start.

During the next week we continued to fly. Every morning I was out there with my trusty flashlight, preflighting the aircraft. Then one morning I said to hell with it and didn't get up. About a half hour later Tom was there shaking the hell out of me. He was yelling, "Get up, Lieutenant. We're going to be late. You've got to preflight. We're going to miss our takeoff time." I told him to go on back to the aircraft and that I would be there in a few minutes.

I went to the mess tent, got a cup of coffee, then headed to the aircraft. When I got there, the engine cowlings were open as usual. I told Tom to close them and get in. The copilot and gunner were looking at me as if I'd lost my mind. I looked at them and said, "What in the hell are you waiting for? Get in."

As I climbed into the aircraft and began strapping in, Tom still stood there, looking at me. He asked, "Aren't you going to do a preflight?"

I said, "Tom, let me ask you a couple of questions. Number one, is this aircraft ready to fly?"

His reply was, "Yes, sir."

"Number two, are you going with it?"

Again his reply was, "Yes, sir."

I shook my head and said, "Good, because if this son of a bitch goes down, you're going to be in it. Now, close the damn engine cowlings and let's go fly."

With one more dejected "Yes, sir," he started to turn away.

I stopped him and said, "Tom, there is one more thing. My name isn't 'sir.' It's Bill."

He was grinning like mad when he responded with a loud, *"Yes, sir,"* and disappeared to the rear of the helicopter.

We had never stopped looking for Fosdick Five. Whenever we were flying, everyone on board scanned the jungle below for some sign of the aircraft. On May 26 one of the Lancer gunships spotted and identified a tail boom in the jungle west of FSB Vehgel. The tail boom was that of Fosdick Five. The next day A/1/327 Airborne Infantry found the main rotor blades in a riverbed two hundred meters from the tail boom.

On May 31, members of the accident investigation board flew to the vicinity of the crash site. After walking for thirty minutes, escorted by a platoon of infantry for security, they arrived at the tail boom. The search party was on the ground for two hours and received enemy fire twice. Due to the enemy activity in the area, the search team could not stay on the ground any longer. The helicopters that extracted them received antiaircraft fire, and one of the aircraft was hit.

Based on the location of the tail boom, the main rotor blades, and the absence of the cockpit and main cabin area, it was determined that the aircraft had come apart in the air after being hit by antiaircraft fire. The tail boom and the main rotor blades were located in the valley I'd been shot out of while on the sniffer mission. We'd been briefed not to go west of the ridge line where we were putting in the fire support base.

Due to the weather, Fosdick Five had apparently flown into

the wrong valley, a single ship with no gun cover, low and slow over the trees. It was probably one of the most inviting targets the NVA gunners could have wished for. No bodies or graves were found. The six men who had been on board would be carried as missing, presumed dead.

Chapter
Eleven

The next four days we were flying for FOB-1, running a mission "across the fence" into Laos. Then it was back to work with the LRPs. We were coming back from a VR west of Vehgel on the second of June. Just to the northeast of the fire base were the burned-out remains of a CH-47 that had been shot down. The only thing left intact was a sixty-foot aluminum ladder. It must have been thrown clear when the aircraft crashed.

I had been thinking about that ladder for some time. I thought that if we took it and cut it in half, it would give us two good ladders we could use instead of the rope Jacob's ladder. It would sure as hell be a lot easier to climb. We landed and picked it up. When rolled up, the ladder filled the entire cargo compartment of the aircraft. I thought about that as I flew back to Camp Eagle. If we used only half of it, it would take up only half as much space. It would be used only for extractions, and then it would be hanging outside of the aircraft. That could work, and work it did. In the months that followed, those ladders were lifesavers for the LRPs.

The infusion process was in full swing. We were losing some of the pilots who had come over with the company to other units, and getting in replacements to ensure that the company would not have all of its experienced pilots DEROS (date of estimated return from overseas), that is, return home, at one time. It bothered me that Dick Washburn was transferred to C Company at LZ Sally. I'd learned a lot from Dick. LZ Sally was not that far away, but I wouldn't have the opportunity to fly with him anymore. I knew I'd miss that; he was one hell of a good teacher.

Most of the replacement pilots, like Ed Ragan, were right out of flight school. A few had been in country two or three months before they came to us. They were all WO1s, and to me they all looked like kids. It was strange. We were losing our experienced pilots, our teachers, and getting inexperienced pilots in return. Now we would become the teachers. That was a sobering thought. Me, a teacher? They had to be shitting me!

Gene Gillenwater, Lou Pulver, and Bill (W.T.) Grant had all come from the 282d AHC (the Black Cats) stationed at Marble Mountain, just outside of Da Nang. Another replacement pilot was Phillip G. "Rod" Heim. He'd come from the 62d Aviation Company (the Coachmen) just down the road at Phu Bai. Gillenwater and Grant went to the first platoon. Pulver and Heim came to the second platoon, my platoon.

Grant and Heim had gone to high school together, and Rod had been the best man at Bill's wedding less than a year before. And there they were, in the same unit. I guess sometimes even the Army does something right.

On the evening of June 5, I was sitting in the tent that served as our Officers' Club. I was watching as one of the new pilots, W. T. Grant, was getting harassed for having been in country for two months and not, as yet, taken any hits. I could see he was beginning to get a little tired of the harassment. The other people at his table could also sense that, and they moved to another table.

I picked up two cold beers from the bar and walked over to his table. I handed him one and, after introducing myself, sat down. Without waiting to get a feel for his mood, I told him, "Mr. Grant, don't let those guys get to you. They're just jealous. Hell, they all wish they were lucky enough not to get shot up."

He said, "Yeah, Lieutenant, I know, but it was getting a little old. By the way, I go by W.T."

"Good. And my name isn't 'Lieutenant.' It's Bill."

We talked for a while and then I said, "I understand that you came from the 282d. How long were you with them?"

"Two months."

"Two months? Then you're not really an FNG. How much flight time did you get with them?"

"Sixty-seven hours. How about you? How long have you been with the Kingsmen?"

"I've been in country for five months."

"How many hours do you have?"

"Six hundred, more or less."

He sat there with his mouth open, then said, "Six hundred?"

I thought for a minute before replying, "Well, I think I'm on the low end of the totem pole on hours flown. I've been flying a lot of LRP and FOB-1 missions. With those, there's a lot of standby time."

Rod Heim came over to join us then. As he started to sit down, I told him that since he was the last person to sit at our table, it was his turn to buy. Off he went to get a round of beer.

As we sat talking, two or three of the other new guys came over and joined us. That was great because, as each one sat down, he had to buy a round of drinks. There were a lot of questions about how the company operated and the different types of missions we flew. Unlike when I'd joined the unit and just sat and listened, those guys were coming right out and asking. In one sense, that was good. However, they were getting only one person's opinion, mine, and there were some people who considered me very opinionated.

W. T. Grant appeared very interested in the LRP missions. Without getting into a lot of war stories, I tried to explain what the LRPs did and how they operated. I went into the training, and the policies we'd established. I also told all of them in no uncertain terms what my commitment was to the LRPs. If I put them in, I would bring them out. No one would ever be left behind. I made it clear that if any of them could not live up to that same kind of commitment, they should never even consider flying on that type of mission.

W.T. wanted to know how he could get assigned to fly with the LRPs. I told him he should talk to either Jim Riden or

Dave Poley, aircraft commanders in the first platoon. They were the only other ACs who were flying LRP missions regularly. When they thought he was ready, they could ask Operations to assign him to fly as copilot.

Needless to say, while we were talking—and I'd been doing most of it—we had continued to drink. All of us were becoming more relaxed. I should have known it was coming, but I didn't know who would be the one. Finally, Rod Heim opened his mouth and inserted both feet. He started telling us what a great job he was going to do while he was with the Kingsmen, how dedicated and dependable he would be. I didn't say anything until he told everyone at the table about all of the medals he was going to get. By then I'd listened to about as much of that bullshit as I could take. I did not know of anyone in the company who went out looking for medals. All of us went out just to do our jobs.

John Dean and Dick Washburn had both been awarded Silver Stars for actions they'd been involved in just before I joined the company. There had been several Distinguished Flying Crosses and a large number of Air Medals for Valor awarded since I'd arrived. We'd just lost six people, and the only thing their families would receive would be the Purple Heart. No, I definitely didn't need to hear any more shit about medals.

Rod stopped talking. Looking at him as I took another sip of my drink, I said, "Boy, don't tell me what in the hell you're going to do. Goddamn it, just show me." It was as if I'd reached over and slapped him across the face. He got quiet and started to turn red. I couldn't tell if he was embarrassed or just getting mad. Probably a little of both.

In the months that followed, Rod did just what I'd told him to do. He showed me. He became a damn fine and very dependable pilot. Three months later this scene would repeat itself. However, it would not be me doing the talking. It would be Rod Heim jumping all over some poor rookie warrant officer who had put his foot in his mouth.

Grant came into the club a couple nights later with his flight helmet in his hands. On the back of it he'd painted WT in big Gothic letters. Under the letters was a huge, bright red cherry. On the front of the visor were the words HAPPINESS IS GETTING SHORT. It looked pretty good, but his grin faded when I told him he hadn't been in country long enough to know what "getting short" meant.

After a lot of good-natured ribbing, I asked him if he could do something similar with my helmet. He said, "Sure," and left the club. About an hour later he returned with my helmet in his hand. On the back of it he'd painted a black spade. Over the spade was my call sign KINGSMAN 25, and under it were the words WILD BILL.

My helmet was not as gaudy as his, but it suited me just fine. I asked him where he'd come up with the "Wild Bill," and he said, "Well, from the one time that I flew with you, and everything that I've heard, it's a proven fact that you aren't playing with a full deck. You are as bad, if not worse, than Poley. I think the name 'Wild Bill' fits you to a tee." I guess it did. From that day forward Wild Bill was my nickname.

The next few days consisted of logistical missions, that is, ash and trash. They were the most versatile missions we could fly. We were assigned to a battalion and supported their every need, anything from taking a man to the rear to moving an entire company of infantry, eight men at a time, from one location to another. Sick, injured, or slightly wounded troops would be taken to the hospital from their field locations, and food and ammunition were sent out from the battalion rear.

We always tried to have a full aircraft load when we flew from one site to another. However, it was not always the case, and we would often be required to make multiple trips to the same unit. It could prove very frustrating.

The battalion commander would sometimes use the aircraft to visit his units in the field. If one of his units came in contact with the enemy, we would become his C&C aircraft for as long as needed. And then there were the battalion staff officers who also needed to use us for one reason or another. On one ash-and-trash mission during the second week in June, I flew for eight and a half hours and made 126 takeoffs and landings.

During that same week, while flying an ash-and-trash mission, I received a radio call from Kingsmen Operations and was told to report to the LRP pad immediately. When I arrived, Sergeant First Class Champion was waiting on the pad. He said he was going along as the belly man. A team needed to be extracted, and for some reason the aircraft that had inserted the team was not available to extract them.

I contacted the C&C aircraft as soon as I departed the pad, and was briefed as we flew west. The team had been in for two days and was moving back to its original LZ for extraction. They were not in contact, but the area they'd been reconning was heavily used by the NVA.

The C&C vectored us in to the LZ, and we arrived just as the members of the team broke into the open. I was not able to land because tree stumps were covering the landing zone, so I held the aircraft at a two-foot hover while the team made its way across the small clearing. They were approaching from the right side of the helicopter and had almost reached us when a line of green tracers came in through one of the open cargo doors and out the other side. The NVA fire had gone about three feet behind me and missed Sergeant Champion by just inches. The enemy fire continued, but Sergeant Champion ignored it as he reached down, grabbed each man, and hauled him into the aircraft.

When all of the team members were on board, we lifted quickly out of the LZ and headed back to Camp Eagle. After an extraction, especially a hot one, we normally shut down after landing, checked out the aircraft, then joined the team members for a cold beer. That time we looked the aircraft over while it was still running. Amazingly, we found no damage, and soon departed to resume our original log mission.

Having a team in the field with no one on standby was one of the things we always tried to avoid, because if a team was already in contact when we were first notified of an extraction, there was a good chance we wouldn't arrive in time. The LRP company needed the same kind of support that the FOB missions demanded, dedicated air support. For the job they were doing, they deserved nothing less. Jim Riden, Dave Poley, and I wanted to make sure they got that support.

On the afternoon of June 21 we flew a VR for a first-light insertion the next morning. The area the team was going into was about five kilometers west of where Fosdick Five had been lost. Several small valleys there ran north to south. The team leader picked out a primary LZ on the floor of one of the valleys and an alternate in one of the adjoining valleys. After we returned from the VR, we stayed with the LRP company and worked on training. They'd gotten in four more replacements—John Mezaros, Jim Bacon, John Looney, and Gary Linderer—right out of SERTS. They looked so young and out of place. All of them were PFCs with an awful lot to learn, but it would not be long before those kids would be going out to play hardball with the bad guys, just like the team I was going to put on the ground in the morning.

An hour before sunrise we were back at the LRP pad. There were two slicks with a light fire team standing by at the Castle. The Castle was what we Kingsmen called our company area. I was flying as the C&C, with the LRP mission commander on board. Jim Riden was doing the insertion, and Dave Poley was flying the chase ship, with Grant as his copilot.

I left fifteen minutes before the other two aircraft, to reach the recon zone and ensure that we were able to get into the LZ. It looked to be an easy insertion. The LZ was on the floor of a valley covered with tall elephant grass and dotted here and there with trees. The two slicks and the two gunships would fly in a trail formation. There would be just enough distance between them to allow the insert ship to get in and out of the LZ between the chase and the lead gun after making the insertion. That way, unless someone was standing in the LZ, it would sound like nothing more than a flight of helicopters going down the valley.

Riden, Kingsman 18, checked in just as he was passing FSB Vehgel. I watched as the flight descended toward the treetops. They were right on the course that had been briefed, and their spacing looked to be all right.

It felt funny to be up at altitude playing C&C. I wanted to be in the lead aircraft making the insertion. I was sure Poley felt the same way. That was where the action was.

The setup looked good. All I had to do was call one left turn and call off the distance. The calls were one thousand meters, five hundred meters, and one hundred meters. At the last call I could see the nose of the insertion aircraft come up as he began to slow, with the chase ship closing the gap. Jim's aircraft settled into the LZ as Poley flew directly over him. Even before Dave had cleared the LZ, I heard, "Kingsman One-eight, coming out."

It had been a textbook insertion. Everything had gone just as planned. The flight of aircraft continued down the valley for about a mile before breaking out and climbing to three thousand feet. As briefed, they moved five miles away and went into an orbit. They would stay in the area until I heard from the team on the ground that it had not been compromised and was continuing the mission.

A short time later the team leader called and reported that one of his men had injured his leg when he'd exited the aircraft. The extent of the injury dictated that the individual be extracted immediately. After some discussion with the mission commander, it was decided that the entire team would come out, to be reinserted into the alternate LZ as a five-man patrol. Safely in, they would continue their mission. The injured man would then be returned to Camp Eagle.

Normally, the aircraft that made the insertion would make the extraction. However, things had gone so well with the first insertion that I decided to let Poley (Kingsman 19) do the second one. Besides, Grant was flying his first LRP mission, and it would allow him to see how things worked. Riden did not have a problem with that. He said he'd completed his training for the day and would be more than happy to let Dave earn his flight pay for a change.

We got Dave set up and vectored him back to the LZ. The extraction was uneventful. Once the team was on board, I began to vector Dave to get him lined up with the alternate LZ. Everything was going as it should. but just as I was about to tell him he was five hundred meters out, both sides of the valley sparkled with muzzle flashes.

As soon as I saw the flashes, I told Dave he was taking fire and ordered him to turn right, where a small saddle in the ridge line would allow him to get out of the valley more quickly. Both slicks cleared the valley, and the two gunships began firing rockets into the valley to provide as much cover as they could.

I realized then that Dave had not been fired at. The bastards were shooting at me. Even in the bright sunlight, I could see some of the tracers as they came up out of the trees. It was not the usual small-arms fire; there was .51 caliber (12.5mm), 23mm, and possibly some 37mm antiaircraft guns down there in the jungle. I instructed the Lancers to get the hell out of the area, and asked the mission commander to try to get some tac air on the scene. We were lucky. A flight of three F-4s from Da Nang was in the area, and they said they would be glad to assist.

I could not help wondering if the bad guys who'd just shot at me were the same ones who'd gotten Olsen and Link in Fosdick Five. If they were, they were sure as hell going to pay. And if not, well, then they were going to pay for shooting at me.

I had gotten a good look at where the gun positions were when I'd directed Dave and Jim out of the valley. Once the F-4s announced they had me in sight, I told them I would mark the targets for them.

I flew to the north end of the valley and dropped down to the treetops. I told Tom and the gunner that whenever they heard me say "Now," I wanted them to throw a smoke grenade out of the aircraft. I didn't care what color it was, just as long as it went out.

We were doing 120 knots as we came into the area where we'd taken fire. I was on the east side of the valley. When I reached the area where I thought a gun position was, I called for a smoke. When we came to the end of the valley, I did a 180-degree turn. There was a solid line of smoke coming out of the trees. I told them we were going to do the same thing to the west side of the valley.

After we completed the second run I climbed up to four thousand feet to watch the show. And what a show it was! Five-hundred-pound bombs and napalm are a beautiful thing to see, but I would have hated to be on the receiving end. However, I sure as hell didn't feel sorry for the bad guys.

After the air strikes were completed, we headed back to the LRP pad. I didn't know why, maybe it was the adrenaline pumping, but I was damn hungry. I knew there would still be some food left over from breakfast. It was a hell of a way to start the day.

After some cold eggs and hot coffee, I discovered that I was also slated to make the next insertion in the same general area. We flew a VR to see if we could find another LZ, and planned to make the insertion the following day. We would never attempt to go into the same area twice on the same day. After the air strikes, we knew there would be a whole lot of very pissed-off people in that particular area.

The landing zone we selected was about a thousand meters to the north of the previous insertion and closer to FSB Vehgel. It had also been defoliated, which I really did not like. There was little or no cover, and there were dead trees 150 to 200 feet high. We would have to hover straight down through them to get the team on the ground. I didn't see how we could get them in without being compromised. There was bound to be too much exposure time.

That night I sat down with Dave Poley, who would be flying the C&C aircraft the next day, and the two gunship pilots, Bill Turner and R. L. "Hootchmaid" Smith. We tried to come up with a plan for making the insertion.

It was not going to be anything like the one we'd just done. It would simply take me too long to get in and out of the LZ to do that. I wanted to keep the chase ship out of the immediate area and the two guns close by. Everyone seemed to agree that the team would not be on the ground very long.

Once again it was dark when we arrived at the LRP pad. We shut down and went to the Operations tent to check on any last-minute changes. There were none. We would just have to wait for the sun to rise.

Poley departed with the C&C party, and the team loaded on board my aircraft. Fifteen minutes later we were on our way. As we approached FSB Vehgel, I began letting down. The chase ship and the two gunships did not follow me. Dave called that he had me in sight and began to call the turns for me. When I received the two-hundred-meter call, I began to decelerate. The LZ appeared in the chin bubble and we started down through the trees.

The insertion went off without a hitch. The team was off and we climbed up out of the trees. I climbed up and joined the other four aircraft orbiting over Vehgel. After fifteen minutes the team radioed that it was moving away from the LZ. Normally, once we got word that the team was moving, everyone would be released to return to Camp Eagle, where they would go on standby. But I called the C&C aircraft and suggested we remain on station for a while just in case things turned to garbage. They agreed.

About twenty-five minutes after the men had moved off the LZ, the team called. They'd been compromised and were heading back to the LZ for immediate extraction. The bad guys were right behind them, exactly what we'd been afraid of. The fun was about to begin. I headed toward the LZ with the gunships right behind me.

As I began the descent through the trees, I saw the six members of the team setting up a 360-degree perimeter. I would try to land right in the middle of it. As soon as I was on the ground, they moved toward the aircraft and jumped on board. I pulled in power and began to climb straight up. The copilot, who was on his first LRP mission, was calling off the pounds of torque I was using. When he called out fifty pounds, I held it there and let the aircraft climb.

We'd reached about one hundred feet when I saw three NVA soldiers run directly under the helicopter. Our machine guns could not depress far enough down to fire at them. They had us cold as they began to fire into the belly of the aircraft. At this point the cool, calm, and collected aircraft commander who normally sat in the left seat seemed to have gone AWOL as I began yelling into the radio, "Goddamn it, Hootchmaid, get those assholes off me! The bastards are trying to kill me! They're shooting the shit out of us!"

The copilot was screaming at me over the intercom that I was overtorquing the aircraft. I glanced down at the torque meter and saw that it was passing sixty-two pounds. He was right. I kept right on pulling in more power, and he kept on screaming at me. I finally yelled at him, "Shut up, goddamn it! Just shut the hell up!" I didn't think he realized that our only two choices were either to overtorque the hell out of the aircraft or get blown out of the air. I, for one, did not care for the second choice.

With all of the yelling and screaming going on, I still heard Hootchmaid over the radio. "Now, damn it, Bill, just settle down, boy. I got you covered." As he said "covered," rockets began to explode under us. That took care of the bad guys, and we cleared the treetops.

I checked the instrument panel as we headed toward Camp Eagle. Everything seemed to be working properly. I was concerned because I knew we had to have taken some hits in the fuel cells. But the fuel gauges didn't show that we were losing any fuel. All I could think was, Thank God for self-sealing fuel tanks!

On the way back to Camp Eagle, I told Dave I was going to fly directly to our maintenance area. He could pick up the LRP team there and take them back to the LRP pad. It was ten minutes after eight in the morning. I'd flown one and a half hours, and I was through for the day. Now that, I had to admit, was one hell of a way to get a day off and going!

After turning the aircraft over to Maintenance, I went up the hill to Operations and filled out the afteraction report. When that was completed, the Operations officer told me to report to the Old Man.

Major Addiss asked me how the mission had gone and wanted to know why I'd come back to the company area. I explained what had happened and told him my aircraft was being worked on. After we talked for a few minutes, he handed me a stack of papers, copies of orders promoting me to the rank of captain.

That evening when I walked into the club, I threw my hat and a copy of my orders on the bar and said, "This is my promotion party. All drinks are on me for the rest of the night." Then I proceeded to see how much I could drink. It was one hell of a party, or so they told me the next morning. When the club manager presented me with the bill for $140, I had to agree. At twenty-five cents a drink, that was a hell of a lot of drinks. But it had been well worth it.

My aircraft (121) was in Maintenance for two days. We'd taken several hits but hadn't sustained any major damage. Meanwhile, W.T. was spending a lot of time in the maintenance area. When I went down to pick up the aircraft, there was a painting of Snoopy, the *Peanuts* cartoon character, on each of the front doors.

Snoopy was in a sitting position, wearing a blue World War I flight helmet with goggles down over his eyes. A long red scarf was tied around his neck, and he had a pipe clenched in his teeth. In large red letters were the words THE DOG.

The paintings were against battalion regulations, but a number of other aircraft had beautiful artwork on them. There was the "Hustler," which had crossed pool cues, a pair of dice, and a poker hand of five aces. Then there was the psychedelic painting of "Lucy in the Sky with Diamonds" (LSD). There were other aircraft, with names like "The Hell Bringer" and "Society's Child." And now we had "Wild Bill and His Dog." Damn, I liked it!

There were some fine artists in the company. W.T. and B. J. Hoyt were two of the best. Although Major Addiss knew we were breaking the regulations, he turned a blind eye. I guessed that as long as it didn't get too far out of line, he wouldn't say anything about the paintings.

On the last day of June the company was tasked with supplying ten slicks and four gunships to stage out of FSB Anzio, eight miles southeast of Camp Eagle. The mission was to move troops out of the fire base and conduct combat assaults into the low-lying hills immediately to the west.

When we arrived, we couldn't establish radio contact with the TOC on the Fox Mike (FM) radios. Both the primary and secondary radio frequencies were being jammed with conversation in Vietnamese and with Vietnamese music. After landing, I went to the TOC to talk to the Operations officer. He said the jamming had been going on all day and was driving them crazy. It seemed that every time the TOC changed frequencies, the jamming station would find them. If it continued, it would really screw up our operations.

Looking at the map of the area, I saw that the mountains began about ten miles to the southwest. FM radios worked best at line of sight, meaning there could not be any obstruction between the jamming station and the TOC. If I were a bad guy and wanted to set up a radio-jamming network, I would probably use the high ground somewhere back in those mountains. Of course, as long as the bad guys were talking and broadcasting their music, I could find them.

After laying out my plan to the Operations officer and getting his approval, I went back outside. I got together with the pilots of the two light fire teams as well as Dave Poley. I explained to them that we were going to do a little FM homing. I would have Dave and one fire team fly to the southeast until they got a ninety-degree deflection on their homing instrument, then they would turn and follow the signal. As soon as they had an indication of station passage, they would drop a smoke grenade.

I would depart FSB Anzio with the other fire team shortly after Dave left, and follow the signal directly to the target. I would try to time it so we would both reach the jamming station at about the same time. Once I received station passage, I would put out a smoke grenade too. If everything worked as it should have, the two smoke grenades should land close together and the jamming station would therefore be marked. After that, it would up to the Lancers.

As we implemented the plan, I watched Dave's aircraft come across the nose of mine about a mile in front of me. His two gunships were following a mile behind. When he was directly in front of me, two smoke grenades dropped from his aircraft. Thirty seconds later I called for Tom to drop the smoke grenade he'd been holding. When I got the aircraft turned around, I could see that all three of the smoke grenades had landed within fifty meters. I keyed the radio and said, "Okay, Lancers. Go get 'em."

"Roger that. Rolling hot."

Dave and I moved off to one side to watch the show. The first fire team lined up on the smoke and salvoed their rockets. Fifty-two 2.75-inch rockets slammed into the smoke and the surrounding area. As soon as the first fire team cleared the area, the second did a repeat performance.

I waited for the smoke to clear and then went down to take a look. The jamming had stopped but I could not see anything through the trees. I keyed the radio and said, "Good morning, Charlie. If you are still listening, that was your wake-up call, asshole." We headed back to Anzio to begin our day's work.

On the first day of July 1968 the 17th AHC ceased to exist. We officially became B Company of the 101st Aviation Battalion. I could not have been happier. Now I'd be able to wear the shoulder patch of the Screaming Eagles. I was right back where I'd started, with an Airborne unit.

Also on that day, W. T. Grant celebrated his first wedding anniversary. He came up with a case of champagne and reserved the club for that night. Unfortunately, the battalion headquarters wanted to use our club for its own party to celebrate the activation of the battalion. Grant's reservations were canceled.

At around 1830 hours Jim Thompson and I returned to the Castle after completing our mission for the day. As the two of us walked into Operations to fill out our afteraction report, I saw W.T. talking to Rick Haines. Grant was complaining about his party being canceled.

Rick looked at Grant and said, "Damn, W.T. Didn't anyone tell you? Battalion's not coming. They decided to have their party somewhere else. You can still have the club for your party."

W.T. stood there shaking his head and said, "Shit, that's no good. Everybody's gone. The company area is deserted."

When I'd finished the afteraction report, I turned to W.T. and said, "Grant, why in the hell are you complaining? You can still have your damn party."

He replied, "Didn't you hear what I said? There's nobody here."

I said, "Look at it this way. You are the assistant club officer, are you not?"

"Yes."

"And that means you have the keys to the club, does it not?"

"Yes."

"And you have Sir James, Rick, and myself. Right?" At that point Rick said he had a poker game to attend.

I said, "Okay. That means you have Sir James, a case of champagne for which you have already paid, and myself. I don't see what the problem is." That seemed to make sense to the three of us, so we headed for the club. It was four o'clock the next morning when we stumbled out to try to find our tents.

On July 7, I was flying an ash-and-trash mission out of LZ Sally when I received a call from our Operations. I was instructed to report ASAP to the FOB compound at Phu Bai. That was highly unusual. Normally, a request for air support came down the night before a planned mission.

Due to the shortage of copilots that day, I was flying with Warrant Officer Charlie Smith. We were both aircraft commanders, and had both flown FOB missions. As we landed at FOB-1, there were more aircraft than usual. Even the VNAF CH-34s that were flown by the Kingbees, the best helicopter pilots in the South Vietnamese Air Force, were there.

When we entered the briefing room, I could tell something big was going on. Everyone seemed very tense. The colonel who had given the first briefing that I'd received was on the small stage. Behind him were two map boards covered with blankets.

The colonel got right to the point. "Gentlemen, we have a major problem. As of an hour ago we had a Mike Force of one hundred sixty-four men holding a mountaintop across the border in Laos. Why they are there is none of your concern. Your only concern is getting them off that mountain and back here to safety."

He stopped for a few seconds to let that sink in. Pointing to one of the map boards, he continued, "As I said, we hold the top. The NVA holds the bottom. We knocked out a tank here, and saw two more in this area. These ridge lines are covered with antiaircraft guns. The Kingbees lost a CH-34 there this morning. It was hit by 37mm fire. It crashed and burned just down the slope from the top of the mountain. There were no survivors."

He walked over to the other map board and removed the blanket. Instead of a map, there was a board with a list of 164 names on it. Most of them were Montagnards, but also included within the list were ten Americans. The colonel said that once again he could not order us to fly the mission. He took a red grease pencil, made a large red X across the names, and said that if we did not go to pick up these men, he'd have to write them off; there was no way they could fight their way out.

After that there was really no discussion as to whether we would go, just how we'd do it. The Kingbees would lead us to where the troops were trapped on top of the mountain. Once there, their main concern would be to recover their dead from the crash site of the CH-34. It would be up to us to extract the 164 people.

The Vietnamese and the Montagnards hated each other. The Montagnards—we called them Yards—were fiercely loyal to the Americans. They would literally die for us. This was really a strange way to fight a war.

The mountain was located about three miles inside Laos at the southern end of the A Shau Valley. The only landing area was a small clearing that had been blown clear about fifty meters from the top. There was only one way in and one way out.

It would be up to the gunships to try to suppress the antiair-craft fire coming from the surrounding ridge lines. It was going to be an interesting mission.

It worked much better than I'd expected. Eight slicks were involved in the extraction. We made four trips each into the one-ship landing area. The first four aircraft were loaded with wounded when they came out. There was no panic among the Yards as they loaded onto the aircraft. They were waiting in small groups as each aircraft landed. They must have had one hell of a pathfinder with them. Probably the guy who signaled them to load in a given order.

If the Yards had been ARVN troops, we would've had to beat them off to keep them from overloading the aircraft. I had no idea how many people we were taking out on each load; when I looked back into the cargo compartment, all I could see was a mass of bodies.

The only equipment that I saw loaded onto the aircraft were their weapons, ammunition, and a few radios. This was definitely a well-planned evacuation. They were leaving their other equipment behind to cut down on the number of trips we had to make. What was left behind was either burned or booby-trapped. The NVA would not be too happy with what they found when they started going through the things left behind.

As I started my fourth approach onto the mountaintop, I was told there were only ten people left to pick up—seven Montagnards, a medic, the RTO, and the detachment com-mander, a second lieutenant. After the pickup, we headed back to the FOB compound at Phu Bai to drop off the last of the Mike Force personnel. It had turned out to be a damn good mission. As far as I knew, no one received any hits, and we were released to go back to our original assignments. It was just another day at the office.

I found out eighteen years later that the mission of the Mike Force had been to provide security for 2d Lt. Mike Clark, the detachment commander. Lieutenant Clark's as-signment had been to eliminate an NVA general staying at a rubber plantation across the border in Laos. Once they had reached the area, it took Clark two days to move into position for a clean shot. At around 0730 hours on July 5, using a sniper's rifle with a telescopic sight, Lieutenant Clark put a 7.62 NATO round between the general's eyes from a distance of five hundred meters. As soon as he'd pulled the trigger, the chase was on. For that one shot, Lieutenant Clark received the Distinguished Service Cross, the second-highest award that can be earned by an American serviceman.

On July 10, I got to fly for the LRPs again. It was a very uneventful day. I had W.T. flying as my copilot. We inserted one team, then extracted another that had been in the bush for five days. Their recon zone had come up cold. Still, they were glad to be back in the company area.

W.T. had been flying as many LRP missions as he could talk himself onto, going with Poley and Riden as well as me. Although he did not get to fly the actual insertions or extractions, he was constantly watching, listening, and learning. We, the ACs, all thought that when the time came he would make a good LRP pilot, but none of us would tell him that. We didn't want it to go to his head.

On July 16 we were given a warning order that on the following day we would be putting most of the LRP company in the field. The division was going to put a full battalion into an area where they suspected a large concentration of enemy forces. The battalion was to sweep the area using the LRPs as a blocking force. We would be using seven aircraft to put in four heavy teams of eighteen men each. After we inserted the four heavy teams, I was to put a six-man team into another area. We spent most of the day flying VRs. We located and plotted the landing zones. How we were going to get that many men on the ground without their being compromised was beyond me. The LZ for the six-man team really had me worried. The next day looked like it was going to be a busy one.

July 17 dawned crisp and clear. We began inserting the heavy teams just after daylight and had them all in before 0900 hours. We were to remain on standby for the rest of the day, but first I had to make one last insertion.

Sgt. Richard "Burnie" Burnell would be going in about eight miles west of LZ Sally along the Song Bo. The LZ was to be a sandbar right up against the south wall where the mountainside met the river. The mountainsides there were very steep, and the tops were close to two thousand feet high. A narrow gorge had formed where the two mountains came together at the water's edge. The river itself was as crooked as a snake and less than a hundred feet across. The only way to insert the team was to fly low-level down the valley for two miles, twisting and turning with the river all the way, then put the team in on the sandbar. With four aircraft in that gorge, it was going to get awfully damn crowded, with absolutely no room for evasive maneuvers. We would have to come in from the west and depart to the east.

Before the team loaded on board the aircraft, Lieutenant Owen D. Williams, who was going along as the belly man, and myself, walked over to talk to Captain Fitts. I told him that due to the narrowness of the gorge, I did not want the other three aircraft following me down the river. The only thing I would need was for the C&C to tell me when I was coming to the last turn in the river before I reached the sandbar. The chase ship and the two guns could stay with the C&C aircraft. If the world turned to shit and I needed them, he would be the first to know.

Sergeant Burnell and his people were already loaded when we returned. The C&C took off and we followed ten minutes later. The chase ship and the guns were to stay with me until I started down the river, then were to climb out and join up with the C&C.

We entered the canyon and, the mountains towering above us, started our low-level run down the river. It was like riding a goddamn roller coaster sideways. The river twisted so much, and the turns were so sharp, that it was impossible to maintain a constant airspeed. We went from a hundred knots down to twenty.

It seemed to take forever before the C&C told me the sandbar was coming up just around the next bend in the river. I was sure glad we hadn't allowed the other three aircraft to follow us into the canyon. It would have made things far too complicated. As we came around the last bend, I could see the sandbar along the south wall. I began the deceleration and had almost set down when Tom yelled over the intercom that everybody was out. It was time to get out of the area! We continued down the river for about a half a mile before climbing out of the canyon.

That was the second time in less than a month that I'd decided to make an insertion without the other aircraft following me in a trail formation. I wondered if it would work out better than the last time. I really didn't think so. Something just didn't feel right.

With as many teams as we had in the field, and the chance of a major contact imminent, Division had requested and received an Air Force FAC. The FAC who was on station had the call sign Covey. A pair of F-4 fighter-bombers was also on standby at Da Nang. The F-4s could be at our location in less than ten minutes.

As soon as I rejoined the flight, I called the C&C and got Covey's VHF radio frequency. If we needed him, I didn't want to have to relay though the C&C ship. That would take too much time.

Burnell had been on the ground for about twenty minutes when he called and reported that he'd found a battalion-size (300 to 500 men) base camp about fifty meters up from the water's edge. The NVA had spotted him and the fight was on. He requested an immediate extraction since there was no place for him to go. The team had backed down to the shoreline and had the LZ behind them.

The C&C sent the two gunships in to try to relieve the pressure on Burnell. I called Covey and told him to launch the F-4s. I was going to need them, and the sooner the better. Covey called back in less than a minute and said they were on their way.

The gunships were working over the south wall of the canyon just above the sandbar. They were keeping the bad guys from getting to Burnie's team, but the guns reported that they were also taking some fire from the north side of the river.

While that was taking place, I'd moved back up the river. I would not go back to the same place where I'd entered the river before, but I wanted to be out of sight of the area where the sandbar was located. I wondered where in the hell the F-4s were, but I knew I could not wait any longer.

Just as I started down into the canyon, Covey said the fast movers were overhead with 250-pound bombs and napalm. I told Covey I wanted to talk to them and that I would control the air strikes. Much to his credit, he didn't argue. Some people don't like you doing their jobs for them. He said he'd have them come up on my radio frequency and that their call sign was "Gunfighter."

"Kingsman Two-five, this is Gunfighter. How do you copy?"

"Gunfighter, this is Two-five. Got you Lima Chuck. Do you have me in sight?"

"That's affirm."

"Do you see the sandbar that's around the next bend to the east?"

"That's affirm also."

"Can you time your strike so that when my skids touch that damn sandbar you can hit the south wall with napalm, about fifty meters up from the water?"

"Two-five, this is Gunfighter. Can do easy."

I called the C&C and told him to get the gunships out of the area. He said Covey had already taken care of that, and that I was coming up on the bend.

As I rounded the bend I thought, holy shit! This looks like a goddamn World War II movie. Green tracers were coming from both sides of the canyon, and they were all coming up at me. Both of my door guns were firing as fast as they could, trying to suppress some of the enemy fire. Just before I reached the sandbar I heard one of the F-4s on the VHF radio: "Lead's in."

As I pulled the aircraft into a hard flare and let it settle onto the sandbar, I heard a sudden roar. The F-4 passed over me, followed by a loud swishing sound. Looking up, I saw two silver cylinders passing above my rotor blades. The cylinders slammed into the wall of the canyon and burst into a raging fireball that climbed up the canyon's sheer cliff. It seemed to suck the air right out of my lungs. Immediately, the green tracers stopped coming from the south wall and seemed to slacken from the opposite side of the river. I knew that would not last, but it gave me a breather. As soon as the shock wore off and Chuck got his shit together again, the enemy fire would pick up once more.

Burnie's people were running toward the aircraft as I heard "Two's in" on VHF. On the Fox Mike the team's RTO was yelling that he saw eight people in the open and they were on fire. I was screaming over the radio for him to get his ass on board the aircraft. I didn't like it there, plus I knew there was another dose of napalm on the way.

Everyone was finally on board. They were firing out both sides of the aircraft. Lieutenant Williams was beating on my helmet and yelling for me to go. I'd just cleared the sandbar when the next two napalm canisters hit the canyon wall. Once again there was a blaze of glory. I hoped it would force the bad guys to keep their heads down just a little longer.

The fire from the north wall began to intensify as we stayed low over the water and picked up airspeed, the tracers criss-crossing in front of us. They were hitting the water around my side as well as to the front of the aircraft. There was only one way to go and that was downstream.

It took about a minute after we departed the sandbar before we flew around another small bend in the river and the firing died out. I asked Tom to check and see how many people had been hit. Out of the eleven people on board, no one was hit. Unbelievable, just un-goddamn-believable! With all the enemy fire the team had taken on the ground, and what we'd received on the way out, we hadn't taken one casualty.

I called the C&C to let them know we had everyone on board and that all of them were all right. Then I went to the VHF radio and called the F-4s. "Gunfighter. Kingsman Two-five."

"Two-five. This is Gunfighter Lead. Go ahead."

"This is Two-five. Thanks, partner. That was as good as it gets. I owe you. We're out, all in one piece, I think, and going home."

"Anytime, Two-five. Anytime."

I then called the FAC. "Covey, are you still with us?"

"This is Covey. Two-five, that was quite a show. Do you guys do shit like this every day?"

We had climbed out of the canyon and I could feel the tension draining from me as I answered, "No, and please don't ask for an encore. Covey, there are still a hell of a lot of bad guys down there. If the fast movers have any ordnance left, you might want to let them work over both sides of the canyon. Most of the fire seemed to be coming from about two hundred meters east and west of the sandbar."

Covey answered that the F-4s still had a full load of high explosives, 250-pound bombs, and that they would put it all into the area I'd described. I asked Covey to pass along to the Gunfighters that we could confirm eight KBAs (killed by aircraft) for their efforts with the napalm. I knew there were more, but the eight bodies were all we'd seen.

We married up with the C&C aircraft and headed back to Camp Eagle. We had to shut down and check out the aircraft. We still had the four heavy teams in, and expected that once the sweep began, there would be more contact. So far we'd flown two and a half hours. As far as I was concerned, that was enough for me.

There were no further contacts that day, but the following morning Sergeant Burford's team sprung an ambush and got six confirmed kills. We remained on standby for the next two days, then extracted all of the teams. The results of the operation were not as good as Division had expected, but all things considered, I was satisfied. I was still alive.

A few days later I was flying a log mission out of Fire Support Base Vehgel. My copilot was Rick Haines. We were taking supplies up to a new fire support base called Eagles Nest, on top of a 4,700-foot mountain that overlooked the A Shau Valley. The supplies consisted of just about anything and everything that would fit inside the aircraft. There were cases of small-arms ammunition and C rations, rolls of barbed wire, concertina wire, engineer stakes, and five-gallon bottles of water, just to name a few items. It was going to be an all-day job requiring multiple trips.

I had made the first three trips into Eagles Nest, and on the way back to Vehgel, I gave the controls to Rick and told him the next trip was all his. I was going to let him supervise the loading of the aircraft and fly the approach into Eagles Nest. I told him to be especially careful of the amount of cargo they loaded onto the aircraft; he had to keep in mind that Eagles Nest was almost three thousand feet higher than where we were loading. It would take more power to land than it would to take off. Also, landing on a pinnacle with an overloaded aircraft was not in our best interest if we were planning to grow old.

I sat and watched as the aircraft was being loaded. After a short while I asked Rick how much more cargo he was going to let them load. He replied that we could take a little more. He had it figured that we would burn off a given amount of fuel on the flight up to Eagles Nest, and that should leave us with enough power to make a safe landing.

Just looking at the load we had on board, I knew we were overloaded. There was no way we'd be able to land safely. Although it was a regular log mission, it also gave the aircraft commanders a chance to let the copilots gain some flying experience and get to know what to expect when they became ACs.

When he said we were ready to go, I told him I wanted him to do a good hover check before we departed. This would entail bringing the aircraft to a three-foot hover over the helipad and holding it there for about a minute. That would determine if there was enough power to keep the aircraft in the air. I knew there wasn't, but I wanted Rick to see for himself. It would be better than my telling him.

I told him I'd watch the instruments and call off the pounds of torque to him. I also said that I wanted him to keep his eyes outside the aircraft, and whatever he did, he was not to hover off the pad.

I was calling off the power settings, and when I called out that we had fifty pounds of torque, we were only about a foot off the ground. Evidently, Rick must have looked inside the aircraft, because I felt the aircraft start to settle and the low rotor rpm warning horn began to beep. We'd moved off the helipad and lost our cushion of air. We were going down into the trees on the mountainside below us.

Without saying anything, I grabbed the controls and pushed the nose of the aircraft down. There was no way to get back to the pad. The only way to go was down. We had to get some forward airspeed and build up the rotor rpm. If those two things were not accomplished immediately, we were going to crash into the canyon floor nine hundred feet below.

As the airspeed increased and the rpm returned to 6,400, the beeping finally stopped. We were flying again. But that brought on another problem. We were still going down, and were now going so fast there was not enough room in the canyon to make a turn without hitting the wall on the other side.

Without even thinking, I pulled in all the power that was available and initiated a cyclic climb, where you trade airspeed for altitude. The aircraft stopped its descent and began to climb up the canyon wall. We were right on top of the trees as we went up. Just before we reached the top of the ridge line the low rpm audio came back on. We were running out of power and airspeed again. There was nothing to do but hold what we had and hope for the best.

We cleared the ridge line with our skids literally dragging through the trees. Once we cleared the ridge, I headed down into the valley on the other side and turned to the east. I was shaking so badly that I couldn't talk. In fact, I didn't talk to anyone for close to an hour and a half. I couldn't remember ever being so scared.

Both Rick and I had made mistakes, big mistakes. Rick had let the aircraft be overloaded and had then moved off the helipad. But I'd made the biggest mistake. I'd allowed myself to assume that everything would go just as I had planned, and had become complacent.

Later that evening Rick and I sat down and talked about what had happened during the day's mission. We both had learned a lot. I think the most important lesson we'd gotten out of it was that complacency will get you killed. We both felt very fortunate that we were still alive and would be able to profit from our mistakes.

On July 27 the LRP company got a new commanding officer. Captain Fitts was moved up to Division staff, and a Captain Sheperd took command. It was rumored that he'd been transferred from a line company because there was a contract on his life. Evidently, he'd brought his attitude and troubles with him.

On the evening of the fourth day after assuming command, Captain Sheperd walked into his tent and stepped on a toe popper—a small antipersonnel mine—that blew part of his foot off. In the investigation that followed, no one would admit to placing the mine in his tent. The bottom line was that the damn fool should have known better than to pitch his tent in a minefield.

Chapter
Twelve

August had finally arrived. On the seventh I would be meeting my wife, Carole, in Hawaii for R&R (rest and recreation). I was definitely ready. Having been in country for nine months, I was very tired.

July had been an interesting month. I'd flown eighty-two hours; been told that I'd been put in for a Silver Star for the mission with Staff Sergeant Burnell's team; and had Rick Haines try to kill me by overloading the aircraft and hovering off the helipad at FSB Vehgel. The more I thought about it, the more I knew I was ready for a rest. However, there were still missions to fly for the next six days.

During the following four days, we averaged eight hours a day as we kept flying in supplies to the fire-support bases located to the west of Camp Eagle. The CH-47 companies, the Pachyderms and Varsity, were taking literally tons of ammunition for the artillery pieces located at FSBs Vehgel, Berchtesgaden, and Eagles Nest. Something was in the wind, but we didn't know what.

A couple of nights before, Grant and I had been sitting in the club. He commented that he and Jim Riden were in the A Shau Valley that morning. I looked at him and said, "W.T., who in the hell are you trying to bullshit? Nobody goes into the A Shau single-ship."

He responded, "No shit, Bill. If you don't believe me, just ask Jim. We took Colonel Hoefling from the 2d Brigade up at LZ Sally. He had us do a low-level recon of all three of the old abandoned airfields."

Now that was food for thought. No, not even the Army

would be that dumb. They wouldn't be thinking of going back into that damn valley. The 1st Cav had done it in May and gotten their proverbial asses shot off when they tried to land on top of an antiaircraft battalion. No, not even the Army.

Later that night, as I was sitting in the club with W.T., the thought kept going around and around in my head. I finally asked Grant what he thought.

He looked at me with that little shit-eating grin he always had when the world was getting ready to turn to garbage, and said, "We're going."

"Going where?"

"Going into the A Shau Valley."

"When?"

"Don't know. Just got that feeling. We're going into the valley."

I thought about it awhile and said, "Fine! You guys go right ahead. Day after tomorrow I'm heading for Da Nang. The following day I'll be on a 707 heading for Hawaii. I'm going to forget about this place for seven whole days, and I sure as hell ain't going into that damned valley."

About an hour later Rick Haines came into the building and announced that the club was closed; all of the pilots were to report to the mess tent for a briefing on tomorrow's mission. That was unusual. Normally, we had that kind of briefing only when we were going on a company-size operation. I didn't like the way this was shaping up.

Major Addiss opened the briefing. "Good evening, gentlemen. Tomorrow morning at 0530 we will depart the Castle for FSB Birmingham to support Operation Somerset Plain. This will be a battalion-size operation and will entail the airlifting of two battalions, the 2/502d and the 2/327th Airborne Infantry into the A Shau Valley. We will be putting up twenty UH-1s plus one C&C aircraft. Alpha Company [the Comancheros] and Charlie Company [the Black Widows] will attempt to do the same." His comment drew more than a few laughs from the pilots gathered in the tent.

"At ease, gentlemen. That will be enough. The purpose of this operation is to interdict supply lines that the enemy has established through the valley going south. The Arc Lights [B-52 strikes] are not doing the job. There will be a total of fourteen B-52 strikes. The strikes began at 0800 hours this morning. The last one will be delivered at 0850 tomorrow morning.

"Immediately following the last B-52 strike, four flights of tac air will be hitting the two landing zones with daisy cutters. As soon as the fast movers clear the area, the artillery will begin and continue until we are on final. The gunships from Delta Company will supply close air support as soon as the artillery lifts. The two landing zones will be the abandoned airstrips of Ta Bat and A Luoi. Our LZ will be Ta Bat.

"We will be using the lessons learned from the 1st Cav when they made their assault back in May. This operation will be conducted differently than you are used to. The lifts will be done in flights of five with a thirty-second separation. All operations will be flown low-level to avoid antiaircraft fire from across the border.

"Gentlemen, it's going to be crowded out there tomorrow and timing is going to be critical. You are going to have to be extremely careful. We have to accept combat losses. Losses that are due to accidents and stupidity are not acceptable.

"Before I turn the briefing over to Mr. Haines, there is one more thing that I must cover. As you know, as of last month we are part of the 101st Airborne Division, and must operate from the division SOI. We are B Company, 101st Aviation Battalion, and, according to the SOI, our call sign for tomorrow is Snaky Inkwell. I will be Snaky Inkwell Four-seven."

With that last comment, the whole tent went wild. There was laughing, yelling, stomping of feet, and whistling. Even as pissed off as I was, I was laughing too. Snaky Inkwell? What in the hell kind of call sign was that? We were Kingsmen. We'd been working the area for five months. Did anybody really think the bad guys wouldn't recognize our voices? Snaky Inkwell, my ass!

Major Addiss was trying to regain some kind of order but wasn't having much success. Finally he lost his patience and yelled, "All right, damn it. Shut the hell up." The tent was suddenly silent. "I am serious about this. I do not want to hear the word Kingsman or any other personal call sign on the radio tomorrow."

The Old Man stood there looking at us for a minute to make sure we'd gotten the message. Then he turned to Rick and said, "Mr. Haines will give his part of the briefing now."

As Rick moved to the front of the mess tent I got up and headed for the rear exit. Jim "Sir James" Thompson reached over and grabbed my arm. He looked at me and asked, "Where the hell are you going?"

"I'm getting the hell out of here."

"What about the briefing?"

"Fuck 'em. I'm not going."

"What do you mean, you're not going?"

"Just what I said," I replied as I walked out of the tent.

Standing outside, I looked at the club. Unfortunately, it was closed. God, I wanted—no, I needed a drink, bad. I was doing something I'd never done before and never thought I ever would do. I was going to refuse a mission. Just the thought of that made me feel a little sick to my stomach. However, my mind was made up. The more I thought about it, the more certain I was.

I was not worried about getting killed. Hell, that happens in a war. I have always been a firm believer that when your time comes there's nothing you can do about it. What bothered me more than anything else was that some damn farmer with an old muzzle-loading rifle might hear all of the helicopters flying over and just fire into the air.

As I stood there, I could just see it. Carole sitting in the hotel in Hawaii wondering where the hell I was, and me lying in some hospital with my damn foot shot off. In my mind that was enough reason for me. I walked back to my hootch. I still needed that drink.

The company area was quiet because everyone was at the briefing. I sat alone on my bunk, seeing how big a dent I could put in a bottle of rum. For some reason, I didn't feel like drinking by myself. Picking up the bottle, I walked down to the crew chiefs' area.

I remembered that Tom Turck was getting ready to leave on his R&R in the morning. We'd worked it out so that we'd take our R&R at the same time. Although neither of us had any way of knowing of the upcoming mission, I was glad to know that he wouldn't be going either.

I sat there drinking, bitching, and complaining to Tom about how fouled up the Army was. The more I drank, the more I complained. And the more I complained, the more I drank. It didn't take long before I was literally knee-walking drunk. One of the last things I remember before someone carried me back to my hootch and dumped me on my bunk was Tom asking me, "Bill, what is the first thing you do when you get up in the morning?"

I said, "Time permitting, I shower, shave, and get ready for another shitty day in paradise."

"When you shave, do you use a mirror?"

"Yes."

"Well, just remember what you'll be looking at for the rest of your life if you don't go into that goddamn valley tomorrow."

Someone was shaking the hell out of me. My eyes wouldn't open and my head hurt like hell. I could hear my name being called, but I couldn't recognize the voice. A hand grabbed me by the front of my shirt and pulled me up into a sitting position. The hand let go and I started to lie back down. The hand grabbed me again. I heard the voice again, louder this time, "Goddamn it, Bill. Wake up."

I shook my head. Oh, shit, *that* was a mistake. I felt as if my head were going to explode, and my mouth tasted like I'd been chewing on a dirty sock.

As I slowly opened one eye, I could make out a blurred shape in front of me. The other eye began to open, and as it did, the shape began to come into focus. God, what an awful sight. Jim Thompson was holding me upright with his right hand and holding a cup of coffee in the other. I sat there looking at him. What the hell did he want? I couldn't seem to get my brain working. I was in a complete state of confusion.

Jim reached down, took my hand, wrapped it around the coffee cup, and said, "Here, drink this."

I looked at the cup, then back at him. "What do you want?" I mumbled.

"Drink your coffee and get down to the aircraft," was his only response.

I still couldn't comprehend what he was saying. "Why?"

"We've got a mission." Jim let go of the front of my shirt, but I was still sitting upright. At least it was a step in the right direction.

I still wasn't making any sense out of what he was saying. "What?"

Jim was shaking his head as he began picking up my flight gear, helmet, chicken plate, and weapon. "We gotta go fly, damn it. Now get your ass in gear and get out to the aircraft. We have to take off in thirty minutes."

The lights were on by then. Other people were up, moving around and getting dressed. Sitting on my bunk, I noticed for the first time that I was still dressed, boots and all. Whoever had brought me back to my hootch and poured me into my bunk had just dumped me there to sleep it off. Oh, well, what the hell! At least I wouldn't have to waste time getting dressed.

Looking at my watch, I saw that it was only 0430 hours. Christ, 0430! My head still hurt, but not as much. I guess the coffee was doing its job. I stood up very slowly. My head didn't fall off, and I was able to stand without holding on to anything. Shit, I might live after all! I walked outside the hootch and took a deep breath of fresh air. Damn, that felt good.

After lighting a cigarette, I started down into the gully toward the revetment area. I really didn't know why I was going to the aircraft. My decision had already been made. I wasn't going to fly. Maybe I was just going to bring back the flight gear that Jim had taken there for me.

As I reached the bottom of the gully and started up the other side, I saw the silhouette of 121. The blades were untied and pulled around ninety degrees to the nose of the aircraft. The pilot's door was open. My helmet was hanging from the hook that Tom had installed in the overhead just behind the back of the armored seat. The cargo door had been pulled open and pinned. The M-60 machine gun was mounted on the gun mount and pointed down toward the ground. I had seen that picture over a hundred times before, and yet I never failed to get "that feeling." Jim was sitting in the cargo compartment watching me as I walked up the side of the hill.

W. T. Grant described the "feeling" best: "It happened often when you were in flight school. It occurred less as you gained more flight experience. It seemed to me, though, that as I became a more experienced pilot, the feeling was far more intense when it actually happened. It was mostly a sense of awe and wonder. You look outside of the aircraft and realize it's flying. Then you look down at your hands on the controls and realize that it's you making it fly. There's something in man that has caused him to try to fly since before he learned to draw on the walls of caves. For those of us who have had the opportunity to conquer the skies, that 'something' comes out on occasion and causes that feeling. It makes you warm inside and gives you a great sense of power. It amazes and mystifies, yet there is still something in the feeling that makes you feel small and insignificant. Even after thousands of hours in the air, it still returns and reminds you of the joy of flying."

For being such a dumb-ass most of time, Grant sure had a way with words.

Jim sat watching me until I reached the rear of the aircraft. Then he stood up and walked over to where I'd stopped. As he glanced at his watch, he said, "Ten minutes. We're preflighted and ready to go."

"Okay, Jim, what have we got?"

"We've got to do a weather check of the valley."

Well, that wouldn't be too bad. We would do a quick flight over the valley at altitude to see if it was clear, then return to Camp Eagle. It would be a ninety-minute flight at most. Yeah, I could at least do that.

Without saying anything, I got into the aircraft, strapped

in, put on my helmet, and began the starting procedure. Normally I would have used the checklist. But that morning I couldn't even see the pages, much less make out the writing on them. Also, there was the fact that I knew Jim would be watching to make sure I didn't miss anything.

I confirmed that all of the switches were in the proper positions and all of the radios turned off. Before pulling the trigger to energize the starter, I called out, "Coming hot."

This got an immediate response from the gunner, who called back, "Clear right." However, there was no answer from the crew chief.

Without even trying to hide the irritation I was feeling, I said, "Goddamn it, crew chief. I said I was coming hot." The voice that answered was not the one that I'd expected to hear. Turning around, I saw Tom Turck sitting in the left-hand gunner's well, looking back at me.

Keying the intercom, I said, "Goddamn it, Tom. What in the hell are you doing here? You're supposed to be on your way to Da Nang."

He sat there looking at me and finally said, "Well, you're going, my helicopter is going, and goddamn it, I'm going too." I couldn't think of any way to argue with that. I knew it would be a waste of time even to try.

I lifted the aircraft out of the revetment at exactly 0500 and called Operations on Fox Mike. "Kingsman Operations, Kingsman Two-five off at this time." Switching to the UHF radio, I contacted the tower and said, "Eagle Tower, Kingsman Two-five off the Castle, departing to the west."

"Kingsman Two-five, this is Eagle Tower. You are cleared for departure to the west. Negative reported traffic."

After clearing the bunker line on the perimeter, we entered a gradual climb. The sky was starting to lighten in the east as we continued to gain altitude. If our timing was right, it would be light enough to see the valley floor once we arrived over the A Shau.

As we passed two thousand feet, I gave the controls to Jim, lit a cigarette, sat back, and watched the country pass below. It was such a beautiful sight. Light fog was forming in some of the small valleys. The valleys led into the foothills, which continued on into the surrounding mountains. Looking at the fog, I had to wonder how many NVA cook fires were adding their smoke to the fog.

If it hadn't been for all of the bomb craters that pockmarked the jungle, I couldn't have believed there was a war going on and that people were dying under that jungle canopy.

The silence on the radio was deafening. Normally at that time of morning we would hear other aircraft checking in with ground units for their missions, making commo checks, getting artillery clearances, and greeting the new day with "Good morning, Vietnam." That morning there was nothing. The only radio traffic had been our transmissions to Operations and to Eagle Tower.

We continued climbing until we leveled off at five thousand feet just a little east of FSB Bastogne. In the darkness below I could hardly make out Bastogne. The fire base was 1,042 feet above sea level. In the distance the sun could be seen hitting the tops of the mountains that formed the east wall of the A Shau Valley. We were still at least thirty minutes from our destination.

Fire Support Base Vehgel passed under us as Jim turned to a northwesterly heading. I wanted to pass to the north of Eagles Nest, then turn south and fly down the east side of the valley. At that altitude, and staying to the east, I figured I would be clear of antiaircraft fire from across the border.

Eagles Nest was a fire support base located on a ridge line 4,461 feet above sea level, overlooking the A Shau Valley. As we got closer, I saw that overcast seemed to cover the valley. Far to the south the cloud cover didn't seem as thick as in the northern end. Some areas looked as though there might be holes over them. With the overcast, maybe the day's mission would be canceled. Then maybe I could go back to Camp Eagle and go back to bed. Someone else could worry about the mission tomorrow. Just maybe!

We passed to the north of Eagles Nest at about four hundred feet. A lot of troops were moving around, getting ready for another day. Large amounts of ammunition were stacked by the gun tubes. All of the artillery pieces were pointed to the west and southwest. From the looks of it, those troops were likely to have a very busy day.

When Eagles Nest was behind us and we were over the A Shau Valley, I took the controls from Jim. The top of the cloud layer was about a thousand feet below us. The sun was reflecting off the cloud bank. Far to the south there appeared to be large breaks in the overcast. I had flown farther to the west than I really wanted to; I was out over the center of the valley. Directly below the aircraft was a sucker hole—a hole in the clouds that said, "Hello there. Come on down. You can make it all the way through." And then once you entered the clouds it would close up and say, "Got ya, sucker!"

I entered a left-hand 360-degree turn above the hole. Looking down, I could make out the ground, yet I was pretty sure the layer didn't extend all the way down. Now what in the hell was I going to do? I really needed to know where the base of the clouds was. If the layer was breaking up to the south, could the flights still get in? If so, was the base high enough for the gunships to give effective support? There was only one way to find out.

Without looking at Jim, I keyed the intercom and said, "Okay, guys. Hang on. We're going down to take a look." With that, I headed toward the sucker hole. As the break in the overcast appeared in the chin bubble, I slowed the aircraft to about five knots forward airspeed and applied pressure to the left pedal. The nose of the aircraft rolled down and to the left. The maneuver was the same one you'd use to put a fixed-wing airplane into a spin. You aren't supposed to spin a helicopter, but it had worked many times before without seeming to do any damage to the aircraft. It also cut your exposure time to a bare minimum.

As we entered the hole in the overcast, I kept the aircraft in trim while maintaining eighty knots forward airspeed. We were coming out of the sky like a homesick brick. The VSI was pegged at four-thousand-feet-a-minute descent. In less than one minute we passed the bottom of the cloud layer about a thousand feet above the valley floor.

Once we passed the bottom of the layer, I started pulling in power, bringing the aircraft out of its descent about fifty feet above the ground. We were heading south and were right over the dirt road that ran the length of the valley.

It was dark and was misting rain. Far to the south I could make out some lighter areas that had to be the breaks in the overcast that I'd seen before we entered the clouds. That was where I wanted to be just as fast as I was able to get there. Staying over the road, I pulled in all the power I could. The aircraft accelerated to its maximum allowable airspeed of 120 knots.

Hopefully, being as early as it was, and as dark and misty as it was, nobody would see us until we were already gone. Besides, the bad guys were probably thinking that nobody in his right mind would ever do anything as stupid as this. I almost started laughing when I thought that Grant had done the same thing just a few days before. Well, hell, maybe we would both be lucky.

Just as I'd planned, we entered the valley above A Luoi airstrip, and were just passing Ta Bat when I heard Tom say, "Holy shit, look at that!" Out of habit, as soon as I heard the phrase, I went into a hard left-hand 360-degree turn, losing airspeed as the aircraft came around.

When I completed the turn, I was right over the road. Looking down through the chin bubble, I could not believe what I was seeing. Right there in front of me were tread marks. It had rained during the night, so the tracks had to be fresh. Those tracks could have been made only by a tank, armored personnel carrier, or a self-propelled gun. Any of them would have at least one .51 caliber machine gun that could blow our helicopter out of the air with no trouble at all. I could actually feel the NVA watching us. It was time to get the hell out of there, and I wasted no time doing just that.

I'd seen enough. The tread marks told me all I needed to know. As we picked up forward airspeed, I turned to a south-easterly heading, away from the road, toward a hole in the overcast near the ridge line that would take us out of the valley. We stayed low over the jungle and continued to climb toward the clouds. Once we cleared the top of the ridge and passed through the hole in the overcast, I gave Jim the controls and told him to take us back to Birmingham.

Sitting back and lighting up a cigarette, I tried my best to relax. My hands weren't shaking and my head didn't hurt anymore. I guess the adrenaline had been the magic cure. To the best of my knowledge, no one had shot at us. I couldn't believe our luck. We'd gone down the length of the valley and gotten away with it. Maybe things would work out after all.

We had climbed back up to five thousand feet and were passing over FSB Bastogne. Off in the distance I could see Birmingham. I had never before seen so many helicopters with their rotor blades turning at the same time. There were forty UH-1Hs (slicks), twenty-five UH-1Cs (gunships), more than a dozen CH-47s (cargo), and a handful of OH-6s (scouts). It was the largest single operation I'd ever been involved in. There may be safety in numbers, yet I couldn't help but wonder if that was really true.

We landed at the refueling point, topped off, then repositioned to join up with the rest of the company. After shutting the aircraft down, I went and gave my report to the Old Man. He didn't say anything about my walking out of the briefing the night before, and neither did I. Looking around as I walked back to my aircraft, I could see that the whole company—no, not just the company—the whole damn battalion was there. How in the holy hell could I walk away from that? The bottom line was, I couldn't. The valley would get one more shot at me. How I hated that goddamn valley.

The troops we would be putting into the valley were sitting in groups of eight—what we called an ACL, aircraft load—a couple hundred feet from the aircraft. They were waiting patiently for the word to load. Once we departed with the first lift, another group of eight would move up to take their place and wait for our return. The UH-1Hs were to make five trips each. The slicks would be putting in close to sixteen hundred troops before we were done. The CH-47s would take in the heavy equipment and about four hundred additional troops. A hell of a lot of people would be inserted into the area by the time we were finished. They would be staying on the ground for seven to ten days, and I didn't envy them at all.

At 0830 hours the aircraft began taking off on a heading due west. At first there were just a few UH-1s. These were the C&C aircraft with the division commander and the battalion commanders on board. Next to leave were the gunships, four light fire teams of two aircraft each.

At 0845 hours we got the order to crank the aircraft and load the troops. The waiting was over. I had all four of my radios turned on and set to the appropriate frequencies. The VHF was on the C&C frequency, the UHF was on the gunships, FM-1 was on the company, and FM-2 was on the platoon frequency. For having been so quiet when we'd done the recon of the valley that morning, things had now done a complete 180-degree turnaround. The radios were going crazy. Over time, you learn to hear what's meant for you, and to disregard the rest. Even so, with four radios going continuously, it can, and does, get very confusing.

I heard Major Addiss call, "Birmingham Control, Snaky Inkwell Four-seven departing with a flight of five." I couldn't help but smile as I watched the first flight leave the ground. They stayed low over the trees as they gained airspeed. By the time they reached FSB Vehgel, they were doing 110 knots. Thirty seconds behind was the next section of five, then the third section, and so on.

The gun company had evidently said to hell with using the signal operating instructions, since I could hear Killer Three-six and Killer Three-five on the radio. "Killer Three-five, this is Killer Three-six on UHF. Are you with the flight?"

"Roger."

"Killer Three-six, this is Stinky . . . uh . . . uh . . . oh, to hell with this. Killer Three-six, this is Kingsman Six. Inbound with the first flight."

"Roger, Six. I have you coming across the ridge line."

"The flight's inbound."

Then on FM: "Cease-fire the artillery. Cease-fire the artillery."

On VHF: "Okay, those lifts will be coming from the river."

"Never mind the rockets. Never mind the rockets. Cease-fire the artillery."

"There's the flight."

"Man, there's artillery all over the place."

You could tell even before we crossed the ridge line that the approach was going to be a real zoo. So far no one had taken fire, but they couldn't seem to get the artillery shut off. Or was it artillery? We crossed the ridge and started a shallow right-hand turn toward the LZ. There were helicopters all over the place. The C&C aircraft were higher than I would have guessed, but they were still favoring the east side of the valley. Some of the guns were low but others were flying high, just below the C&C.

The radio traffic had picked up after we cleared the ridge.

On VHF: "Killer One-seven. Breaking right."

"I see where they are going in down there."

"Two-one, are you with us?"

"Roger."

"We're going to climb out of here and set up an orbit. Watch out."

I heard the radio call, "Kingsman Six lifting," and saw the first flight of five clearing the LZ, just as the second flight was touching down. That day timing was the name of the game.

We were on short final and the third flight was just lifting off. Everything was going according to plan. No sooner had our skids touched the ground than the troops were gone. I was just pulling in power to take off when Jim, Tom, and the gunner all started yelling at the same time for me not to take off. Looking up, I saw the skids of the lead aircraft of the following flight come right across my rotor blades. He couldn't have been ten feet above me. If I'd taken off as I had started to, we would have more than likely had sixteen dead men lying on the LZ. You don't have many survivors from a midair collision. Luckily, everyone on our aircraft was doing his job. Well, so much for plans and timing.

Coming out of the LZ, I had to go like hell to catch up with the rest of my flight. I sure as hell didn't want to get separated and be flying around all by myself. Just as I was pulling

UH-1H en route to insert a LRP team, April 1968. One of the author's first LRP missions.

A LRP team waiting to load for an insertion.

W. T. Grant, Kingsman 18, in formation after a LRP extraction and going back to the barn.

Albert D. Contreros. KIA, November 20, 1968.

Memorial service for Al Contreros, Mike Reiff, Art Heringhausen, and Terry Clifton. KIA, November 20, 1968.

Home sweet home. Company area at Camp Eagle, 1968.

(above) H-34 flown by the Kingbees in support of FOB, July 1, 1968. *(below)* UH-1C gunship flown by WO R. L. "Hootchmaid" Smith, May 1968.

AH-1G Cobra helicopter. The 2/17 Cav. gunships did one hell of a job in support of the LRPs in 1968.

OH-6 helicopter belonging to the 2/17 Cav. Captain Eklund used these for his C&C aircraft.

WO Rod Heim waiting to "go to work."

WO Rod Heim after a "bad day at the office."

UH-1H flown by Lt. Dave Greenlee and WO Jim Thompson, shot down in July 1968.

Kingsman aircraft on standby at FSB Anzio the day we took out the NVA radio-jamming station.

The company area as seen from the revetment area.

A LRP team coming home after a "walk in the woods."

Training was the name of the game. The helicopter shown here is working with the LRPs on insertion and extraction procedures.

Ladder training with the metal ladder we recovered from the downed CH-47.

Copilot Rod Heim and crew chief Tom Turck, the best crew chief who ever pinned on a damn set of wings.

Left to right, standing: Ken Roach and B. J. Hoyt. Kneeling: Ricky DeSimone (friend of the author) and author at the 1997 VHPA reunion in Orlando, Florida, twenty-nine years after the fact.

into my position in the formation, the radios went completely batshit.

"Killer Six, Killer Three-five. We are receiving fire from southeast of the LZ."

"Where is it?"

"Heading of two-one-zero, one klick from the LZ."

"Gunships, this is Killer Three-six. We took fire on a heading of two-one-zero out of the Lima Zulu, about a thousand meters."

On Uniform: "Kingsman One-two, this is One-six. Over."

"What was that?"

"Ah . . . someone put a rocket in there."

"Ah . . . those aren't rockets. Those are mortars."

"Killer Six, this is Killer One-two. Over."

"There are mortars on the west side of the LZ. Three-five, this is Three-six. I just went by you."

On Fox Mike: "Soapy Zebra One-two, this is Kingsman Eight. The Lima Zulu is cold." Soapy Zebra was one of the C&C aircraft.

As we were climbing out of the valley, things were heating up behind us. We landed back at FSB Birmingham to pick up our second load. While the troops were loading on board the aircraft, another flight landed to pick up their next lift. It was the same flight that had flown over us on the LZ.

I'd taken my helmet off and was undoing my seat belt when Jim jumped out his side of the aircraft and went at a dead run for the lead helicopter. I just sat there and watched. Although I couldn't hear what was being said, I knew it would be a one-sided conversation. Jim returned shortly, got back into his seat, and said, "Dumb son of a bitch. Said he didn't see us. Do you believe that shit?"

We headed back toward the valley with our second load. The radio traffic had gotten worse. The guns were doing most of the talking. Luckily, they were on the UHF band, and if things got too confused we could turn it off. However, I didn't think that was very smart. I wanted to know where the fire was coming from and what was going on.

"Zebra One-two, this is Killer Six. We are receiving fire from the ridge line just to the west of the LZ."

"Is that the big terrain feature to the immediate west?"

"That's affirmative."

"Roger."

"What range from the LZ are you receiving fire? Do you know, Killer Six?"

"A thousand meters."

"Ah . . . Killer Six, this is Soapy Zebra One-two. They're putting tac air in there. Tac air, remain clear . . ."

"We've got a gunship down at nine o'clock."

"Roger."

"My miniguns are jammed. I'm going to back off and orbit over here."

"Roger, the F.O.—ah—correction, the FAC is calling down tac air now."

"One-two, this is Three-six. Appears that we've got a gunship down. Do you have any knowledge?"

"Roger. I've got the gunship in sight."

"Roger. We have one down in the LZ. Should be no problem. Ground elements should be able to get to him right away. Over."

"Ah . . . roger."

"See if you can contact my One-six element and see if he is in the area now. Over."

"Black Widow Six, this is Soapy Zebra One-two. Over."

"This is One . . . uh, this is Six. I think we're out of order on the Black Bandit element. Over."

"Black Bandit Recovery One, Bandit Yellow. Can you make the recovery? Over."

"Soapy Zebra One-two, Bandit One . . . uh . . . Negative at this time."

"Killer Three-six, this is Killer Three-five."

"Bandit, what is your location?"

"I'm approaching the hillside to the northwest."

"Go ahead, Three-five."

"We've been circling to the west of the LZ. Our miniguns are jammed and we have one gunship down."

"Say again, please."

"He wants you to cap the west side of the LZ and his mini-guns are out and they have one gunship down."

"Black Widow, what is your location?"

"My white element is inbound."

"Roger. We'll pick up the west side on our next pass."

While all of that was going on, we had inserted our load of troops into the LZ and departed for Birmingham. After the first lift, the separation between flights increased. The Black Widows were taking their second load of troops in. No one was waiting for his turn to talk on the radio. They were just jumping in whenever they could. There were aircraft every-where. The only thing that kept us from colliding was that most of us did it daily and we knew what we were doing. Well, maybe not that asshole who tried to land on top of us, but most of us.

"Killer Three-five, this is Three-six. Did you monitor the west side?"

There was a long pause with no response. Then, "Killer Three-five, Three-six is moving to the west side."

"Ah . . . roger that."

"Killer One-seven, this is Six. Are you in orbit on the west side?"

"This is Killer One-six. Roger. Over."

"Roger. Which ship is down, Killer Two-one?"

"Ah . . . this is Killer One-seven. I'm not sure. He got shot down a while ago . . . before I got here."

"Roger, Killer Two-one. Are you receiving, Killer Six?"

"Black Widow Six, this is Two-one. We're inbound to get the downed bird."

"Roger. You can go ahead and recover. We have security around the downed aircraft."

"Okay. This is Killer Six. I think everything is pretty quiet right now. I'm gonna head back because my miniguns are out. Three-six, you assume control. I'm going back for fuel."

"Killer One-six, was that a second platoon aircraft?"

"Roger that."

It was hard to believe, but the C&C was staying off the

radio and letting the pilots do what they got paid to do. Killer Six was doing one hell of a job. With all of the gunships in the area, and the amount of fire they were taking, things could have gone to hell in a second if anyone had tried to micro-manage the operation. Now that Killer Six had departed for fuel, it would be interesting to see how the guns continued to operate without his presence.

"Killer One-six, Three-six on Victor."

"Receiving fire from the hills west!"

"Three-six, Three-five."

"One-six, Three-six. Our VHF is out. You're receiving fire from the hills to the west. Back off a minute . . . mm . . . see if you can locate it. We have no minigun. Over."

"Uh . . . I see it. Thanks. Roger."

Then very calmly came, "Three-six, this is Three-five."

"Three-six. Go."

"Uh . . . this is Three-five. I had to adjust my fire. I took a round in the right pod and it caught fire. I had to jettison it. Over."

He sounded pretty cool for someone who had just had a pod of high-explosive rockets catch fire on the side of his aircraft.

"Where's that fire coming from?"

"The southwest side of the runway."

"Gunships, this is Killer Three-six. Let's set up one chain, right-hand orbits about one-five-zero off the LZ. Anyone who has the target, go ahead and hit it."

"This is One-seven. Understand you want a right-hand orbit."

"Roger. Let's get 'em all over that one side. Any gunship that knows where that fire is coming from, break off a fire team and go get it."

"This is One-seven. I'm breaking off over the LZ now."

"Roger. Three-six is behind One-seven."

"Three-Six, Three-five. It's on the southwest side of the runway. I dropped the pods right near it."

Nothing was left of the old runway but the short stretch of

the original dirt strip that was still barely visible among the bomb craters.

"One-six, I see Widow Mender is with the downed ship. He just landed." Widow Mender was the call sign for C Company's maintenance platoon.

"It's okay. We've got a lot of ships with us now."

"Okay. I have the smoke off Three-five's pods where they hit."

"Okay."

"Pods mark the spot?"

"Uh, yeah, he had to drop 'em."

"One-seven, this is Three-six. Off the end of the runway the two pods are smoking. As you come around, let's dump a little on it this time."

"Understand. To the right of the runway."

"Uh . . . roger."

"Okay. I'll slap a little on 'em."

I couldn't help but be impressed. Killer Three-six, one of the gun company's platoon leaders, had taken charge of the mess that was developing. He had directed the fire teams just like he knew what he was doing.

"Yeah. Put forty mike mike down in there."

"Three-zero, Three-three. You got me now?"

"Three-zero, Three-three is with the flight that has just crossed the ridge line."

"Three-zero, Three-six is with the flight that just passed LZ Zon."

"Killer Six, this is Soapy Zebra One-two. Have you got a hot LZ?"

The C&C was sticking to the tactical call sign, most likely because he had the brigade commander on board.

"Uh . . . this is Killer Six. Keep on coming in. Negative fire."

"Zebra One-two. Eagle lead is off and it is pretty cold down here."

It was true, the LZs were all cold. Only the guns were taking fire.

The C&C aircraft had started out at about two thousand

feet. About the time our flight was crossing the ridge line into the valley, an air burst had been aimed at the C&C bird. He soon gave up and started to perform his job, yet he was careful to keep a ridge line between himself and the dreaded A Shau Valley.

"Killer Six, this is Kingsman Six. Inbound at the ridge."

"Roger, Kingsman. Keep to the low-lying terrain. We got a thirty-seven millimeter we believe is firing from your nine o'clock position. We had an air burst up here a short time ago."

Killer Six was back in the area and had taken over control of the gun support.

"Killer Six, this is Killer Three-six. Over."

"This is Killer Six, say again on UHF. Negative VHF. Over."

"Killer One-five's got a light fire team on the right side of the LZ. We are in good shape at this time."

"Roger. You still have ordnance? Over."

"Roger that."

"Roger. Any other Killer element in the area? Over."

"This is Killer Three-six. I have two lights just north of the Lima Zulu, coming in on the west side. Over."

"Roger. Well, come on down south of the Lima Zulu. You might get something. It's all quiet up there."

"Roger."

"I don't have any guns left. I'm down here to the south of the area. If I can get somebody to come down here, we'll see what's down by this road where we had the fire before. Over."

"Roger. I'll bring my light straight across the LZ."

Then came a call of, "Receiving fire. Three-eight is receiving fire."

Again still fairly calm, "Receiving fire. Three-eight is receiving fire."

"Who is receiving fire?" Killer Six was asking.

Then came the most terrifying radio transmission you'd ever want to hear. One of the most dreaded situations any pilot could imagine was to be in an aircraft when it was on fire. Most of our aircraft were not equipped with the self-sealing fuel tanks, so when we took off we were sitting on 208 gallons of highly flammable liquid. It was a fact we lived with every day. The voice came back several octaves higher. "I'm on fire! I'm on fire! God!"

Killer Six, unable to hear the transmission on VHF, was talking about his guns being jammed. A calmer voice came on the radio.

"Killer Three-eight. I'm on fire. I'm going down."

"You're on fire. Put it down."

Then an apparently inadvertent transmission: "We're on fire! Shit!"

"Killer One-five is going to cover the downed ship."

"To the west of the LZ. He's going down."

Then Killer Six's voice sounded with the obvious: "Put it on the ground. Put it on the ground."

We had just crossed the ridge line with our fourth load of troops when Killer Three-eight reported that he was receiving fire. I was trying to look for him and hold my place in the formation at the same time. When I finally did spot him, he was coming down from my left front and a little below our flight of five.

All I could clearly see were the rotor head and the cockpit area of the helicopter; the aft section and tail boom of the aircraft were engulfed in flames. Luckily, they had been working at a fairly low altitude when they were hit. If they'd been any higher when they caught fire, they would never have made it to the ground before the aircraft exploded or disintegrated in the air.

To escape the intense heat and flames, the crew chief and gunner had stepped out of the aircraft and were hanging onto the skids. The gunship seemed to be under control as it descended in a level attitude. Just before the helicopter hit the ground, both men turned loose of the skids and dropped to the ground.

It looked as though the pilot tried to flare the aircraft just before impact, but the forward airspeed must have been in excess of eighty knots when it hit the ground. On the initial impact, the main rotor snapped off and the aircraft ricocheted back into the air. It looked like a flat stone skipping across a pond.

Then I saw one of the most horrifying sights that I'd ever seen. The gunner, in his haste to get away from the fire, had forgotten to unhook his monkey (safety) strap. When the aircraft bounced back into the air, the gunner was yanked off the ground, trailing behind the burning helicopter. The pilot, for some reason, had unhooked his seat belt when the aircraft hit the ground the first time. When it hit the second time, he was ejected up and out through the greenhouse. Unhooking his seat belt had been the wrong thing to do, but it more than likely saved his life.

The copilot never remembered getting out of the aircraft. All he could recall was looking back and seeing that the windshield was missing. The aircraft was lying on its side. The crew chief escaped with some very bad burns and bruises. There was no doubt among anyone who witnessed the crash that those were three very lucky men.

However, the gunner was not so fortunate. His body was found later, pinned under the burning helicopter. All that was visible were his boots. I hoped that he was already dead when the aircraft came to rest. There is no good way to die, but I can think of a hell of a lot of ways I would rather go than by burning to death.

The crash had transpired in seconds, but it seemed to take forever. The guns were doing a good job keeping the NVA gunners off our backs but they were paying a heavy price.

We landed, off-loaded our troops, and headed back for the last lift. The fifth and final lift went off without a hitch. We returned to Birmingham, refueled, and shut down. It was time to stand by and see how things developed out in the valley.

The gunships continued coming in to refuel and rearm, then climbed back out to head back to the valley. Just because the slicks were no longer going into the LZs didn't mean the bad guys had stopped fighting.

We were standing around talking about the morning's events when somebody yelled, "Hey, Killer Six is inbound and he's been shot up."

Off in the distance I could just make out a Charlie model gunship coming toward us. He was low over the road and looked as though he was going to make a straight-in approach to the maintenance area. At the last second he made a hard left-hand turn and landed at the rearm point.

When he made his turn, I could see that the aircraft was full of holes. Both windshields had bullet holes in them. There were a number of large-caliber bullet holes in the doors and down the tail boom. I could tell by their size that they'd been made by at least a .51 caliber heavy machine gun. With the amount of hits it had taken, I couldn't believe the aircraft managed to make it all the way back.

A light fire team that had just rearmed was getting ready to depart as Killer Six's aircraft landed. Killer Six, LTC Ron Perry, the commanding officer of the gun company, jumped out of his helicopter. He'd been hit in the face and was bleeding profusely. I watched in amazement as he ran to the lead gunship, yanked the door open, and pulled the aircraft commander out.

Perry shouted at the young warrant officer, "That son of a bitch shot me and I know where he is." With that said, he jumped in the aircraft and took off, leaving the bewildered young pilot standing there watching his helicopter fly away. I guess there were times when it just didn't pay to argue with your boss.

We spent the remainder of the morning on standby. Around noon some of the aircraft were released back to their company areas. From there they were assigned to various ash-and-trash missions. I was released for the day too, along with the rest of my crew. All I wanted to do was go back to bed, but first there were a few things I had to do.

As always, the afteraction report had to be filled out and turned in. That consisted of a brief description of what had transpired from the time we took off until we landed. In those seven and a half hours a hell of lot had happened. Of course, it didn't look like much after it had been reduced to a few lines on the first page of the report. Oh well, as the saying went, the job's not finished until the paperwork's done.

Next on the agenda I had to arrange transportation to Da Nang for the first thing the following morning. Checking the status board in Operations, I saw that the first platoon had a pilot returning from R&R on August 7, the same day I was leaving. Somehow that individual had to get back to Camp Eagle. It might just work out well for everybody concerned. After talking to the Operations officer, it was agreed that he would schedule a first platoon aircraft to fly to Da Nang the following day. I would fly down with one of the first platoon's pilots, he would RON (remain over night) and then fly back with the returning pilot the next day.

Once that was taken care of, I walked out into the sunlight. Standing there, I tried to decide what to do next. Should I take a shower—God only knew I needed one—or should I go to the mess hall and get something to eat? Damn, how I hated to make decisions. Ah, to hell with it, I thought as I headed toward my hootch. I'll go to bed and worry about the other two later.

Chapter
Thirteen

The next morning, feeling a hell of a lot better after a good night's sleep, I was back in the Operations tent to check on my flight to Da Nang. Once again, looking at the status board, I saw that W. T. Grant was not flying. I asked the Operations officer if he would assign Mr. Grant to fly with me. Although Bill was not an AC, I was, and so was the pilot returning from R&R. This way, the first platoon would not have to pull one of its aircraft commanders off a mission. That seemed to be the deciding factor. No one in the Operations tent could understand why I was being so considerate. I don't think they realized that I had an ulterior motive in asking for Grant.

W.T. had been assigned to the 282d Assault Helicopter Company before being transferred to the Kingsmen. It made perfectly good sense to me to take him along. He would know the people down there. We would need a place to stay, a set of wheels, and someone to keep us out of trouble. Besides, Grant had been flying his ass off and needed a break.

He was sitting on his bunk when I walked into his tent. Trying to keep a serious look on my face I said, "W.T., I got good news and I got bad news."

He said, "Go away. I don't want to hear any of it."

"Well, you're going to hear it anyway. The good news is that you have to fly down to Da Nang with me."

He sat there looking at me with an "I don't believe this shit" look on his face.

"The bad news is that you will have to RON."

It took W.T. two or three seconds to weigh the pros and cons of the message, then he jumped up and began throwing things in an AWOL bag. With me still standing there watching, he headed for the door. When he reached it, he stopped, looked at me, and said, "Ain't we left yet?" and then he was gone. Obviously, he didn't mind flying ash and trash on one of his few days off, after all!

We departed Camp Eagle with W.T. at the controls. I just sat back and enjoyed the ride. We climbed up to 3,500 feet and headed south about a half mile out off the beach. We were far enough offshore that nobody could shoot at us, yet we were close enough that if we had an engine failure we could still put it down on the beach. Rule of thumb says that for every thousand feet you climb, you cool down two degrees in temperature. We had cooled seven or eight degrees since departing and were flying along at a hundred knots. That made for one of the most comfortable and enjoyable flights I'd experienced since arriving in country.

As we came abeam of the Hai Van Pass, Grant started letting down to below a hundred feet for the high-speed run down the beach under the approach path at Da Nang Main Air Force Base. He then climbed back up to a hundred feet as the runway at Marble Mountain came into view.

W.T. hovered into the transient parking area and proceeded to shut the aircraft down. That was it for us. The crew chief and gunner were already doing the paperwork in the logbook. Once they finished their postflight, they would be free until the return flight the next day. It was party time.

Grant took the lead as we headed for the company orderly room. They had four or five two-man rooms set aside for transient air crews. When you live in the lap of luxury, you have to expect a lot of uninvited guests!

We were assigned a room next door to the latrine. After dropping our gear, I went over to check it out. I couldn't believe it. There was hot and cold running water, as much as you wanted, both at the same time. And flush toilets, the kind where, at the push of a little handle, everything in the bottom of the bowl disappears. It was amazing. I just stood there pushing that little handle for the longest time. It was almost as if I'd been living in the Stone Age for nine months.

Grant had told me that the Officers' Club was air-conditioned. That was something I just had to experience. As we reached the front door of the club, W.T. warned me about the Black Cat emblem on the floor just inside the front door: visitors who stepped on it had to buy a round for the bar. I figured that since it was just coming up on 1300 hours, there probably wouldn't be many people there anyway. Since I knew I'd have to buy Grant a whole bunch of drinks just to shut him up about having to give up his day off to fly down with me, I walked in first and stomped all over that stupid cat. I was right. We were the only ones in the bar, so I paid for the first drinks—both of them.

We sat there nursing our drinks and enjoying the wonderful coolness of the air-conditioning. A short time later Warrant Officer "Sleepy Bear" McClure came in and joined us. The Bear and W.T. had flown together before W.T. had been transferred. They spent the next hour catching up on the last couple of months. Around 1430 hours three guys wearing 1st Cav patches walked in. Well, at least we wouldn't have a monopoly on uniforms that stank of rice, starch, and sweat. As it turned out, they were going on R&R the next day, the same as I was. They didn't seem to know anyone in the place so we asked them to join us.

The 1st of the 9th Air Cav was one of the most—if not the most—decorated units serving in Vietnam. It was rumored that when new pilots reported to the unit, they were handed a Distinguished Flying Cross and a Purple Heart and told that the paperwork wouldn't be very far behind. Looking at these kids, I had to wonder if they were really playing with a full deck.

The Bear announced that pretzels and beer would not provide an adequate transition from C rations to Stateside chow. Since four of us were going to Hawaii the next day, we would need a proper meal. He said he'd be back shortly. He was going to sign out a three-quarter-ton truck and show us some Da Nang hospitality. He said he was going to take us "main side," to the Navy Officers' Club, the Stone Elephant. Every piece of material for its construction was supposed to have been shipped over from the States.

Getting anywhere on the ground in RVN was a major production problem. First, there was the problem of getting a vehicle. Then, since Marble Mountain was on a peninsula between Da Nang and the ocean, we had to leave the Marine compound, cross a very long bridge, and drive through the suburbs of Da Nang. That was SOP for the Black Cats, so the Bear, who was driving, seemed unconcerned. The rest of us were, to say the least, a little uneasy about driving through the countryside with nothing more than four .38 caliber pistols and Grant's K-Bar knife.

When we arrived at the Stone Elephant, I saw right away that the place was every bit as nice as any Stateside O-Club I'd ever been in. The stone and mortar construction was a far cry from the plywood hut we called a club. As we walked in the front door, we were greeted by the maître d' with his bow tie and little waist-jacket tux. Grant and the Bear were in the lead, but as we neared the door they both stopped. When I got next to them, W.T. looked at me, grinning, and said, "You have the controls, Meacham." Shaking my head, I led the way into the dining room.

The floor was shiny black and was, at the very least, imitation black marble. In the distance I could see starched white tablecloths that were beautifully set with crystal and silverware. The Navy officers dining there were dressed in their whites and low quarters. All I could hear was the sound of six pairs of boots screaming, "Kiwi, Kiwi, Kiwi." There was no way this guy was going to allow our crew into his club. We would've had a better chance wearing black pajamas, carrying AK-47s, and asking if he had a reservation for a Mr. Charles.

Grant was standing in the entryway, looking around with his mouth hanging open. I walked over and said, "Damn it, Grant. Can't I take you anywhere? Are you going to eat dinner or stand there gawking like a goddamn tourist all night?"

The headwaiter looked as though he'd just allowed six

winos into the Waldorf Astoria. Either that, or judging by the look on his face when he seated us, he'd recently bitten into a grapefruit and washed it down with a lemon.

Dinner was terrific. The Bear had some type of fish plate, but for the rest of us it was steaks all around with baked potatoes. Real potatoes, not any of that powdered crap they fed us up north. We were all a little awed by the atmosphere in the place. No one threw any food, farted, burped, yelled obscenities, or did anything else of that nature. We even managed to abstain from emptying half the bar stock while eating our dinner.

That was why we were so surprised when the waiter came over and announced it would probably be best if we paid our check and left. We were astonished! The only thing that could have possibly offended anyone there was when one of the Cav guys told the waiter when we were ordering that if anything ended up on our table that even remotely reminded him of lima beans, he would cut off the waiter's head. So after taking our sweet time finishing our drinks, we finally paid for our dinner and rose to leave. Then, much to my surprise, some smart-ass young WO1 sneered at the headwaiter and said, "If you think you're hurting anybody's feelings, forget it. We've been thrown out of better places than this!" I was glad I didn't know anyone so tactless as to say something like that.

Once we were outside the club, we had a quick conference to decide what to do with the rest of our evening, since it was only about 1800 hours. I think it was one of the Cav guys who suggested rolling some Navy whites through a mud puddle. Well, since there was no mud around, and we were already getting thirsty again, we quickly discarded that idea.

After giving some long, hard thought to our situation, I suggested that since we'd just been thrown out of the Navy O-Club, we might as well get thrown out of every O-Club in Da Nang. After a quick consultation with the Bear, it was decided that the Air Force would be our next victim. So it was into the truck and off to Da Nang Air Force Base.

The trip to Da Nang Main involved a ride downtown and through parts of the city itself. The scenery was much the same as any other populated area I had seen since arriving in country. The buildings, some of them very nice, were of stucco and concrete construction. In between were shanties and shop stalls made of used lumber with roofs pieced together from flattened Coke and beer cans. The Vietnamese never threw anything away: something could always be made from it. Everywhere I looked, the castoffs of our military machine were being utilized in some form or another. The better-looking buildings gave the impression of being old but well kept. I wondered if anyone had built anything designed for permanence after the French left Vietnam. Da Nang Main had fences topped with barbed wire and large hangarlike buildings everywhere.

Sleepy drove since he signed for the truck; I rode shotgun since I was the ranking man; W.T. got to sit up against the cab in the back since he knew both guys in charge. It was the best seat in the back because the cab kept most of the wind out of his face, and he could hear what was going on up front as well as in the back.

When we pulled up to the gate at the Air Force base, we were immediately stopped by the AP (Air Police) and asked if we were either attached to or worked for the Air Force. When Sleepy answered, "No!" the airman told us we could not enter Da Nang Main.

I tried to tell the AP that we just wanted to go to the O-Club for a while. The airman said, "I'm sorry, sir, but the policy is that no one is admitted after sundown unless he is Air Force, attached to the Air Force, or working for the Air Force." Not wanting to be thrown out before we even got into the club, I then asked if there was another gate. The airman smiled and said, "Yes, sir. If you will just follow the fence to the left all the way to the end and then turn right, there is another gate about a quarter of a mile down the road."

I replied with a grin, "Thank you, Airman. You're doing an excellent job."

The airman saluted and said, "Thank you, sir. Have a good evening."

Sleepy Bear followed the directions given by the airman.

Just as he'd said, there was another gate. As we came to a stop, another gate guard approached us. "Sir, are you attached to or working for the Air Force?"

I answered, "We are attached to fly recovery missions for downed fighter pilots." We were promptly admitted to the base. Well, that meant that at least the Navy had not called around to warn the Air Force that Army derelicts were on the loose.

The Air Force O-Club was called the Gunfighter Club. It belonged to the fighter pilots who flew the F-4s that escorted our bombers north of the DMZ and provided air-strike support for the 101st and other units in I Corps. The building was not nearly as ornate as the Stone Elephant, but then, it was also not the plywood hut that served as the Kingsmen Club either. Where the Elephant was marble and crystal, the AF club was Formica and paneling. But the important thing was that the bourbon tasted the same in all three.

As ludicrous as the Navy's white uniforms seemed to us, we were in for a real treat in the Gunfighter Club. The fighter pilots in residence were wearing tailored powder blue flight suits with white silk ascots bearing the Gunfighter patch. It was obvious that the flight suits were not actually for flying but for wearing to the club.

A short time later I sat down at a table with some Air Force lieutenant colonel while the rest of the guys stayed at the bar talking to fighter pilots. Grant later told me of a conversation he had that would prove invaluable in the future. The captain he spoke with told him that once they took off in their fighters with a full load of armament and fuel, they had to expend either the ordnance or the fuel to land again. As Grant put it, "This guy must have been all right. He was wearing a working flight suit."

While the F-4 had the thrust to hurl it into the air with all that weight, to stop when the aircraft was fully loaded it needed more runway than Da Nang Main had to offer. That meant that most of the time there were aircraft circling Da Nang, burning off fuel so they could land again. The captain said that as rapidly as the F-4 sucked down jet fuel, the pilot could dump ordnance much faster. Besides, blowing things up was much more fun than boring holes in the sky.

W.T. got the Gunfighter's internal frequency. All we had to do was find a target, get clearance to fire it up, and then call. If our new friends were circling and still had the fuel to get to our target area, they would be more than glad to swing by and shoot up something for us. Since our AO was only minutes away for the jet jockeys, they didn't need a whole lot of fuel. Those guys were always looking for target-rich opportunities, and we had plenty of 'em. Most of the time it took us an hour or more to get air support if it wasn't already on standby for us. Particularly when we were working with the LRPs, that kind of time just wasn't available. When we needed fire support, we needed it right then! A chance contact had just reduced the old procedure of calling in air strikes from an hour's wait to a thirty-second radio call. I couldn't help but wonder how many bad guys had gotten away in the past or how many GIs had been killed because of the lack of coordination. A short time later the captain W.T. had been talking with left the club.

About then, one of the jet jockeys yelled, "Army pilots are just a bunch of bush pilots."

One of the 1/9th guys responded with, "Pilots with balls fly down in the trees without autopilots to keep them from crashing."

Being a little more direct, another Cav pilot said something about only faggots wear powder blue flight suits.

Grant came over and said, "Watch this," then started to sing. Well, I guess you would call it singing. It actually sounded more like feeding a live cat into an electric meat grinder tail first. However, it was not how well he sang, but what he sang that was important. "Off we go, into the wild blue yonder . . ."

It didn't take long for one of the Air Force pilots to inquire as to why he was singing their song. I smiled and said, "It is not your fucking song, it is the Army Air Corps song."

I realized that things could really get out of hand in a hurry. After about fifteen minutes I went over to W.T. and told him that the club manager said he thought it would be best if we left.

W.T. asked, "Why? Is he afraid we'll kick all their candy asses?"

My quick response to W.T. was simply, "That's it." And so we headed for the door, another successful operation completed.

It was time for yet another mission-planning session in the parking lot. Sleepy felt we'd better head back to Marble Mountain. Curfew was at 2200 hours and the ride back would take about thirty-five minutes. I looked at my Seiko and saw it was already 2150 hours. Oh well, close enough! Besides, there was still the Black Cat Club within crawling distance of our bunks.

The return trip was going very well until we got to the approach end of the bridge that would take us back to the Marble Mountain peninsula. Suddenly, there was a "queer cop" in the road. The Vietnamese MPs had QC in large letters on their helmets instead of MP, like our guys, and we were in general agreement that it stood for "queer cop." Anyway, I looked at my watch and saw that it was 2210 hours.

"Oh, shit! We've been bagged by the queer cops for curfew violation." It was bad enough to be grabbed by our own MPs, but it was even worse to deal with the South Vietnamese military police.

The queer cop came over to the truck and said, "No go bridge, GI, firefight, beaucoup VC!" We looked ahead and, sure enough, we could see red and green tracers being exchanged across the road at the foot of the bridge. Red from the left and green from the right.

Sleepy Bear told us that the only other way around was to drive to the south side of the city and cross over where the peninsula connected. That meant we would have to drive most of the night through all the little villages that were definitely in known Indian country.

I thought about that for a minute and said, "Screw this shit. Blow the horn, flash the lights, and floor it." Before anyone could protest, the Bear complied and we were on our way.

The headlight flashing continued as we approached the fire-fight. I leaned over to work the horn for Sleepy. Suddenly, the shooting stopped, and we drove through unmolested. I looked back at where we'd been just as the shooting started up again. The only thing I could imagine was that the bad guys concluded that some of their own had swiped a truck, and the ARVNs simultaneously decided not to shoot at an American vehicle for a change. Boy, those kinds of close calls made me thirsty again!

Finally, at 2215 hours, we came to a stop at the main gate to Marble Mountain. The Marine guard stationed there stopped the vehicle and said he was sorry but he couldn't let us in since it was after the curfew. That seemed almost funny at the time. The young sergeant was only doing his job, but it didn't make a whole lot of sense to us.

"Sergeant, let me see if I understand this. You are telling us that we cannot get in the gate because it's after curfew?"

He responded, "Yes, sir."

"Then because it's after curfew we have to stay out here?"

"Yes, sir."

"So, that means you are causing us to further violate the curfew by forcing us to stay outside the military compound."

The guard got a confused look on his face. For all the things Marines are famous for, telling an officer that he is full of crap is not one of them. He let us in.

Since it was a slow night, the Black Cat Club was closing up early, so we didn't have much trouble getting thrown out. Of course, it wouldn't have been such a slow night if we'd been allowed to stay there.

The only option left for us was the Marine Officers' Club on the other side of the airfield. Sleepy Bear wanted to go to bed, but we convinced him to drive us over anyway. Once we were there, it wasn't hard to talk him into a nightcap. Besides, it was a long walk back.

Marines are supposed to be pretty tough, so we figured we might have some trouble getting thrown out of their club. Just inside the door was the usual hatcheck room. But in Vietnam that was where you checked your weapons, not your hat and coat. The sergeant at the counter checked us over pretty well. He watched carefully as each of us opened the cylinders on our pistols, dumped out the rounds and put them in our pockets. We then reholstered our weapons. He didn't look happy about it, but he understood that we were people who didn't surrender our weapons to anyone.

I had come to realize that in most clubs, if you wore a 1st Cav or Screaming Eagle insignia, they would not even ask you to give up your weapon. I guess they'd already decided that it would be better to let us keep the weapons than try to take them away from us. And they were probably right.

It was not unusual for military personnel in Da Nang to arrive at the club without weapons, so he didn't question the Bear or Grant. Therefore he didn't notice the K-Bar tucked neatly under W.T.'s jungle shirt. Since no one ever noticed, Grant never offered to give it up. The only evidence that it was there was that the very tip of the sheath and the leather thong at its end always hung out from under his shirt.

Once we were seated, the ammo went right back into the weapons. The whole procedure was something we always found hard to understand. While we knew the reason was to prevent people getting blitzed and shooting up the club, they should have realized that we were not REMFs. No matter how drunk we got, we took our fighting ability seriously enough to avoid wasting ammo by merely shooting up some Officers' Club.

The place was big. It had obviously been designed and constructed with drinking in mind; it was not set up for dining. The bar was at least seventy-five feet long, and four or five bartenders were working, feverishly serving drinks. It was constructed of stone and mortar, with a black Formica top and a black vinyl pad along the front edge. The club was crowded with at least a hundred Marine officers. It was also apparent that most of them had been there awhile. Few of them looked as if they were feeling any pain.

When we stepped into the large room, a shroud of dead silence started at our side of the room and followed us as we walked across the floor. We, of course, headed directly for the bar to take care of business. We still hadn't quenched the thirst we'd developed driving through the firefight.

The bar was situated along the back wall of the room. Above it, windows looked out on the South China Sea. The tables were basic chrome and Formica. The chairs were made of box steel tubing with angled legs that allowed them to be stacked. The same chairs could be found in every military club in the galaxy. It was easy to imagine the first astronaut to arrive on some inhabited planet: he makes his landing amid great fanfare from the population, and then, after the appropriate introductions and ceremonies, some military dude invites him to the club for dinner. He walks in the door and there are all these little green officers sitting around on those damn universal stack-chairs.

About the time we reached the bar on the other side of the room, someone bellowed, "Uh-oh, here comes the Army." The volume dropped the rest of the way to total silence. Static electricity was coursing through the air. There were some empty tables diagonally across the room, on the far side, near the back door. We had to walk the entire length of the bar to get to them, but they were strategically placed for rapid exit should the need arise. The location would at least provide us with a defensive perimeter, walls on two sides and the crowd to our front. The back door was in the corner behind us, providing an escape route to the rear. I was thinking more like an LRP every day!

I ordered our drinks. That was not too complicated since everyone was drinking bourbon and Coke or rum and Coke and no one was too fussy about which one they got. When we got our drinks, we made our way back to our seats. Other than the music from the jukebox, not a sound was being made.

I could tell right off the bat that the Marines were jealous of us. I mean, after all, they were Marines, and here we were in their club with dirty clothes and scuffed and dusty boots. Even when our clothes came back from the PX laundry, the closest the Eagle on our insignia ever got to white was light brown or beige. Those Marine pilots all wore crisply starched fatigues and spit-shined boots. It was easy to see that their hootchmaids were giving them their money's worth.

After we took our seats, murmurs started all around the room, but the sound never quite reached its previous level. Several minutes passed while we slowly sipped our drinks. Then a Marine lieutenant sauntered up to the bar. He picked up the public-address mike and said, "The Army sucks swamp water through its ass."

I was not sure exactly how bad an insult that was supposed to be, but it did get my attention. I muttered to no one in particular, "That's it!" I pulled out my wallet and slapped a five-dollar bill on the table. I knew it would be automatically matched. After the other five had been anted up, I said to Grant, "Cover my back, Junior."

W.T. didn't know for sure what I was going to do. I didn't either. Grant and I stood up and walked directly to the bar, going around the edge of the room, not through the crowd of Marines.

I started to get a real bad feeling about all those Marines surrounding us. The other four guys still had the quick escape route available near the back door. Things had gotten quiet once again as we reached the bar. Everyone was waiting to see what we were up to.

I slapped thirty bucks down on the counter. At a quarter a drink, thirty dollars buys a hell of a lot of drinks. Picking up the mike, I said, "The Army may suck swamp water, but we're not cheap. Buy these jarheads a drink."

I thought Grant was going to die of heart failure. He said, "Oh, shit, Bill! You called them jarheads. I know we're going to die now. You could have called them dirtbags or something else, but not jarheads. They're going to kill us now." None of the Marines got up. They all remained seated and just stared at us. We got our drinks and went back to the table. Still no one moved or said anything. Things remained pretty quiet for at least two or three minutes. At last, one Marine lieutenant got up and went to the bar for his free drink. After he returned to his table, another man went, then another. Pretty soon it was as though the dike had broken. The noise level reached its previous volume. I don't know why they let us get away with it, but it was all right by me.

Suddenly, I looked up and there he stood at parade rest, a well-chewed cigar sticking out the corner of his mouth. The silver bar on his collar had three red squares on it. A CW4! (Chief warrant officer, paygrade W-4.) I was beginning to believe that none really existed. In my six years of military experience, I had never had any dealings with a CW4.* But there one stood in all his formal glory, almost as though he'd materialized out of the floor. We hadn't seen him coming. He was just *there!* right between our carefully selected defensive position and the door that was to serve as our escape route.

He looked us over carefully and said, "Who in the hell do you think you are?" Before any of us could whip out a smart-ass answer, he continued, "Well, I don't give a damn! Ya got balls, so you're all right by me." As he threw down a box of cigars on the table, he said, "I run the avionics shop here at Marble. If you ever have a radio problem you can't fix, you just come and see me. I'll get it taken care of even if you are Army."

This statement took us all by surprise, but Sleepy Bear looked up and said, "Have a seat, Gunner."

The Bear was probably the only one at the table who had been around Marines enough to know that Marine warrant officers are addressed as "Gunner." That form of address originally referred only to Ordnance warrants, but it was widely used to address the few warrants the Corps had.

As he took a seat at our table, he motioned with his hand above his head. A bartender soon approached with a round of drinks.

The CW4 grinned and said, "I figured I'd better come over here before you had a chance to bust up any of them college boys over there."

We didn't pay for any more drinks the remainder of the night. After a while the Marine said his good-nights and left,

---

*Several years ago the Army created the CW5! W. T. Grant was one of the first to receive the new rank.

but the free drinks kept coming. Now we were faced with a real dilemma. It was beginning to look like we might spoil our record for the evening and not get thrown out of the club. Sleepy announced that he was, in fact, getting sleepy and wanted to leave. He asked if we wanted a ride back to the other side of the base. A quick conference concluded that we needed more time to contemplate the "thrown out" thing. With the Bear gone, we would have to walk back to the other side. Just then the PA system announced "last call." If we hung around long enough, we knew they would have no choice but to throw us out. I realized that was kind of cheating, but at least it would keep our record intact. Each of us ordered two more drinks for our last call. Then all we had to do was wait.

After a short time the carrier landings started, a procedure that required at least two tables to be pulled together. Then someone would run toward the tables, leap into the air in the swan dive configuration, and "land," sliding chest-first across the table. That was supposed to represent an airplane landing on an aircraft carrier. I noticed right away that the Marine pilots were performing the ritual differently than I'd seen it done in the past. They seemed to prefer landing on tables that hadn't been cleared off, then sliding into the broken glass on the floor instead of stopping on the table.

We just sat there, two full drinks and part of another in front of each of us. We were waiting for someone to tell us that we had to leave when something caught my eye. I looked to the left just in time to see a Marine lieutenant, right at the peak of his swan dive, headed for our table. I yelled, "Heads up!" and ten hands grabbed the two full drinks in front of them just before the Marine crashed through the remaining five glasses, sweeping them to the floor along with himself.

As he got up off the floor, Grant leaped to his feet and began to chew the Marine's ass. "Lieutenant, do you realize that you have just wasted our last call?"

"I'm sorry, sir!"

"Well, you should be . . . you dumb-ass."

"I'll be glad to replace them, sir."

"You can't replace them, Lieutenant. Last call means that they will not sell me any more."

"I'm really sorry, sir!"

I was amazed that this guy was standing at attention getting his butt chewed by a WO1. Could he really be that dumb, or were my railroad tracks affecting his judgment? I felt the game had gone on long enough. I leaned over and said to Grant, "Let's get out of here before this shithead realizes who's chewing him out."

The staff was starting to kick everybody out anyway. So we soon found ourselves gathered in another parking lot anticipating the long stagger back to our rooms.

Two Marines came running to where we were standing. I wondered aloud, "Now what? Do they want to fight now that they're outnumbered?" As it turned out, they were fighter pilots who wanted us to go to their hootch to party with them. The Cav guys decided that they'd had enough of Marines for one night. They said good night and staggered off into the darkness.

Grant and I decided we could stand another drink. Besides, those guys had a vehicle. Maybe we could end up by talking them into giving us a ride back to our quarters. W.T. and I and a few additional Marines who showed up hopped in the back of their truck. After several minutes it became obvious that the truck was not moving. I peeked through the canvas and then turned back to address the Marines. "Which one of you geniuses is supposed to be driving?"

Blank stares all around, then a big argument over who was supposed to drive. When the word came down that the hootch we were going to was just one row over and six hootches down, about a hundred meters away, I suggested that we walk. The Marine lieutenants were impressed by my wisdom and started stumbling over one another to get out of the truck.

By the time we reached the hootch, only five of us were left, which turned out to be more than enough. The refreshments we were to party with consisted of a six-pack of beer and a bag of potato chips. The well had run dry; it was time to head for the barn.

W.T. and I each took a beer, thanked the guys for their generosity, and departed. Once we were outside, we debated the possibility of stealing the truck still parked by the club. Although at first we considered it to be a good idea, we soon came to the conclusion that neither of us was in shape to drive. Another thing that was certain was that the walk back would probably do us some good.

It took us about an hour to make it to our rooms, where we immediately hit the rack.

I opened my eyes as I heard my name being called. I tried without success to ignore it. I heard W.T. say, "Damn it, Meacham, wake up."

"What in the hell do you want?"

"I just wanted to say fuck you, Bill." That said, W.T. rolled over and went back to sleep.

I sat up, lit a cigarette, and tried to get the cobwebs out of my head. After a few minutes I got out of bed, picked up my shaving gear, and headed for the shower. R&R was at hand, and I had a plane to catch.

Chapter
Fourteen

After seven days in Hawaii, a paradise, I was well rested
and relaxed. For the entire week I tried hard to forget Vietnam. The moonlight walks along the beach with Carole, dining in some of the finest restaurants in Hawaii, and getting to
know my wife again, were things I would never forget. I tried
to eat all of the fresh salad on the main island, consumed
enough fresh milk to float a battleship, and fell madly in love
with a Coke machine. But now it was time to go back to
the war.

I arrived back in country on August 14, and spent a quiet
night at the 282d AHC. Early the next morning I caught a
flight back to Camp Eagle. Although I'd tried to forget about
the place, it felt good to be home again.

Nothing had changed. The two battalions of the 101st,
plus one ARVN battalion, were still operating in the A Shau
Valley. There had been two bitter firefights, the first one
against the ARVN battalion, the second against the 2/327th.
In both cases Charlie got his ass kicked good and proper.
After that the NVA, which had still not fled the area, were
forced to de-escalate to small harassing attacks on the supporting fire bases with mortar and artillery fire.

The day Grant and I departed for Da Nang, the LRP company had gotten a new company commander. Captain Ken
Eklund volunteered to take command of the unit after the
Sheperd fiasco. I guess he was looking for a challenge. If so,
he sure as hell picked the right unit. The division staff had
wanted to disband the LRPs. However, the new division com-

mander, Maj. Gen. Melvin Zais, quickly made it known that he wanted his "eyes behind the lines" to remain intact.

I went over to the LRP company to introduce myself and learn more about Captain Eklund. Ken was on his second tour. He'd been a platoon leader during his entire first tour with the 1st Brigade of the 101st in 1965–66. Amazingly, his platoon hadn't suffered anyone killed in action during that year. To me that was an unbelievable record. Any line platoon that went for twelve months in combat without having a man killed was a true oddity.

Ken was a West Point graduate, and my first thought on learning that was, Oh, shit, a damn ring knocker! But as we talked, and he told me how he planned to handle the company, that impression began to fade. The confidence and enthusiasm that radiated from the man was nearly overpowering. I could not help but think that maybe the LRPs finally had the right man for the job.

The weather had turned to shit, and the LRPs were on a two-week stand-down, because we didn't put teams in when we knew we wouldn't be able to support them. When a six-man team was in contact and needed help, they needed it *now!* not when the weather broke.

With the weather turning bad, we also had to pull the line troops out of the A Shau Valley. On August 21 the last of the paratroopers was airlifted from the valley floor. It was a hell of lot easier getting them out than it had been putting them in.

During the seventeen-day operation, 181 NVA had been killed, four were taken prisoner, and fifty-eight weapons, individual and crew-served, had been captured. As the Airborne troops left the picturesque valley, the NVA sanctuary was in a shambles. Base camps had been destroyed, roads obliterated, and caches uncovered, removed, or destroyed. The remaining NVA had been left in a valley ringed with artillery and littered with minefields to discourage its future tactical use. Friendly casualties were described as light, whatever the hell that meant.

We spent the remainder of August flying in support of

the division. There were a few sniffer missions back in the mountains, and several starlight missions in the flats north along Highway 1 and east to the ocean.

On the night of August 28, around 2200 hours, we were flying a starlight mission in the vicinity of LZ Sally. As we headed north along Highway 1 we came to a bridge approximately one thousand meters to the northeast of Sally. The bridge spanned the Song Bo, which flowed out of the mountains into the South China Sea.

I had been briefed that a platoon of M-60 tanks was securing both approaches to the bridge, and there were two tanks, one on each side of the road, at the ends of the bridge. When we got close, I made radio contact with them to let them know who I was, what I was doing, and how long I would be in their area. I figured it never hurt to let the closest ground units know what your plans were.

After flying a grid pattern for about half an hour, we moved approximately one thousand meters to the northeast. That was when we spotted movement on the ground heading in the direction of the bridge. I called the commander of the tank platoon and told him it looked as though he had people headed his way. He acknowledged the call and said they would immediately go on a hundred percent alert.

An hour later we completed our mission and turned south over the road heading back to Camp Eagle. As we approached the bridge at fifteen hundred feet, I was getting ready to check in with the tanks to let them know I was going home. I never had a chance to make that radio call.

There was a small flash on the ground, and I watched helplessly as a B-40 rocket streaked through the night and slammed into one of the tanks. After the rocket hit, everything went dark again. As I looked into the darkness around the bridge, I began to see a dull glow and then the outline of the tank. The longer I watched, the brighter it glowed. Soon I was able to make out the hull, turret, and even the 90mm gun tube as the tank glowed cherry red.

For a short time we circled the area around the bridge, looking for the bad guys, to no avail. The glow of the tank had begun to fade. Knowing the military as I did, I knew the tank would have had a basic load of ammunition and a full fuel tank. Why it didn't blow is something I'll never understand. It would have done no good to try to land, since there would have been no survivors. Nothing could have lived through that.

Before I had joined the Army, I was given the opportunity to go out on a U.S. Navy destroyer escort, the USS *Wilkerson*. I'd looked all over that damn boat and couldn't find a place to dig a foxhole anywhere. As far as I was concerned, that was reason enough not to join the Navy. After what I'd just witnessed, there was no doubt in my mind that I would never get in a tank.

August had passed. Although I'd taken time off to go on R&R, I had flown nearly 106 hours, and the lowest daily flight time that month had been two hours, on the night of the twenty-eighth. The longest, on the nineteenth, had been almost ten hours.

Captain Dave Greenlee, the other section leader in my platoon, had taken a flight of five helicopters down to III Corps to support the 3d Brigade of the 101st Airborne Division. The helicopters were staging out of Phuoc Vinh. The 3d Brigade was working out of Cu Chi, a thirty-minute flight to the south. Why they hadn't stationed the aircraft at Cu Chi, I never did find out; some military genius must have worked overtime to screw that one up.

On September 3, I was notified that I would be going down to relieve Dave. He'd come over with the unit from the States and was due to go home. With so many people rotating back to the States, I was getting to be one of the old-timers.

I was supposed to depart for Cu Chi the fifth, but a typhoon rolled in from the South China Sea and dumped a large amount of rain on us. As luck would have it, W. T. Grant was assigned to fly down with me. It would take the better part of a day to reach Phuoc Vinh. Once we arrived, we'd help load Greenlee's gear on board and head back to Camp Eagle the next day. That seemed simple enough.

The four of us, W.T., Tom, the gunner, and myself, had already loaded our gear in the helicopter. We decided to spend the night there, figuring we'd be at least as dry in the aircraft as in our tents. As the sun came up the next morning, we could see we'd been right. The company area was a mess.

We departed that morning and arrived at Phuoc Vinh late that same afternoon. Dave met us as we were shutting down the aircraft. After some small talk, he told me he wasn't due to DEROS until the twentieth and had no intention of going back to Camp Eagle and flying his last two weeks in the mountains. He was going back with just enough time to sign out and catch his plane home. Damn, Dave was not nearly as dumb as I'd thought!

We talked a little about what my responsibilities would be, and Dave said he'd take me around to get me broken in for the job. Then he looked at W.T. and said, "Mr. Grant, if Bill has no objections, I want you to get lost for two weeks."

Grant stood there looking at us as if he couldn't believe what he was hearing: two captains were giving him a two-week vacation. Grant was grinning from ear to ear as he replied, "Where's the club?"

If we'd still been up north and the LRPs had been operating, I would have gotten an argument from W.T. However, there were just ash-and-trash missions to fly, so he was content to stay on the ground. At least for the time being.

The next day Dave and I made the rounds as he showed me the operation he'd set up at Phuoc Vinh. I was impressed. He had an Operations section to handle the missions, a Commo section for flight following, and radio and land line communications with the brigade (TOC) at Cu Chi. The Maintenance section had its own hangar and didn't seem to have any problem keeping our aircraft flying. It seemed most of my work had already been done for me.

That afternoon we flew to Cu Chi. Dave told me he was required to spend most of his time at the TOC acting as the S-3 Air. I did not like the sound of that, but I'd have to wait and see how things went.

As we entered the TOC, I was introduced to the S-3, Major Sharp. For some reason, when we looked at each other there was an instant mutual dislike. He said he wanted me to carry on the same as Greenlee had. I was to report to him at 0700 hours each morning and stay in the TOC until at least 1800 hours in the evening. Then I could return to Phuoc Vinh or stay at Cu Chi. He really didn't care, as long as I was at his beck and call.

For the next three days I arrived at the TOC at 0700. When I entered, Major Sharp would ask how many aircraft we had flyable. I would tell him we had four flyable and that they were committed to various units. My aircraft, which was not counted as part of the detachment, was sitting outside. My crew was standing around with their thumbs up their asses while I was sitting in a corner waiting for someone to ask me a question about aviation. This shit was not going to work. I'd already had enough of it.

After I left the TOC at 1800 hours on the third day, I headed to the brigade headquarters. I had no idea who I was going to see, but there had to be someone there who had some common sense. Fortunately, the gods were with me once again.

Lt. Col. Julius Becton was still in his office. I'd worked with him when he was still up north with the 2/17th Cav. Lieutenant Colonel Becton was an excellent officer who appreciated and knew how to use Army Aviation. He listened intently as I described my situation and told him what a waste of manpower I thought it was. The job Major Sharp had me doing was ridiculous. The information he needed could be obtained by a simple radio call, or by telephone via land line. That would then allow me the flexibility to run my detachment. It would also give me a chance to fly a few missions and give some of my pilots a day off now and then.

I must have been convincing. After I finished, Becton thought it over for a few minutes and told me I didn't have to be present in the TOC. I was to call in a status report each morning prior to 0715 hours, and let someone in my Operations section know where I was at all times in case I was needed. I hoped that I'd never see Major Sharp again. As far as I was concerned, he was a flaming asshole on a one-sided power trip.

I was back in the saddle again. Things were working the way they were supposed to work. A couple of days later I had to fly to Cu Chi and check on one of our aircraft that had taken some hits from ground fire. The damage had been more than our maintenance could handle, so the aircraft was sent to the 725th Maintenance Battalion for repair.

As we departed Cu Chi and headed for Phuoc Vinh, a line of thunderstorms was in front of us. It began raining, and I thought, No problem. A little circumnavigation and we'll soon be sitting in the club with a cold beer.

We had entered the rain at fifteen hundred feet for the thirty-minute flight to Phuoc Vinh. Forty-five minutes into the flight we were forced down to treetop level. It was pouring like a son of a bitch. I could just make out the trees by looking through the chin bubble. To make matters worse, I didn't have the faintest idea where I was. The one thing I did know was that anything outside the wire was Indian country, and we were definitely outside the wire.

Maintaining visual contact with the trees below, I called, "Phuoc Vinh Tower, this is Kingsman Two-five on uniform. Over."

"Kingsman Two-five, this is Phuoc Vinh Tower. Go ahead."

"Yeah, Tower. This is Two-five. I'm a little bit lost out here. Could you give me a radar vector?"

"Love to, Two-five. Be advised, the radar's broken."

Well, shit, that wasn't going to work. Okay, we'd have to go to Plan B.

"Tower, Two-five. Talk to me on Fox Mike. I'll use the FM radio and home in on your location."

A few seconds later: "Two-five, Tower on Fox Mike. How do you copy?"

"Okay, Tower. I got good copy. Just keep talking and I'll get this thing pointed in the right direction and be there shortly."

"Kingsman Two-five, is being a little bit lost the same as being a little bit pregnant?"

"Smart-ass!"

It was still raining in torrents, but by following the radio signal, I had the aircraft heading toward Phuoc Vinh. We were low over the trees and could not see very much through the windshield. The guys in the tower were great. The one on the radio was telling me about his wife, his wife's boyfriend, his cat, and his dog. Then he remembered that he didn't have a dog, so it must have been somebody else's dog. Even as worried as we were, he had everyone on board laughing.

Then over the radio I heard a startled scream: "Goddamn!" I looked out the front windshield and saw the control tower, barely visible through the rain. Just before we flew over the top of it, I saw the two controllers jump from the tower. Luckily for them, the structure was only about twenty feet high and the ground was muddy from all of the rain.

We landed in the refueling area. While we topped off the aircraft, I looked back. Both controllers were climbing back up into the tower. They did not look any the worse for wear; just wet, muddy, and most likely more than a little pissed off. I watched until they were back inside and then called on the radio.

"Tower, this is Two-five."

"Go ahead, Two-five." He did not sound very happy.

"What time do you guys get off?"

After a few seconds: "In about half an hour."

"How about meeting us at the club? We owe you." This time there was no hesitation. "Yes, sir, yes, sir, three bags full. Now that is an order I can understand." So much for being pissed off.

W.T. and I were sharing a room for the two weeks he was there. After the first five days of his vacation, he was climbing the walls. He was not part of the detachment, so I couldn't use him on any of the assigned missions. He did talk himself into a little flight time with the Maintenance section, but not enough to keep him happy.

I told him a couple of times to shut up about it. Hell, he was getting as much flight time as, or more than, *I* was. His response was that it wasn't his fault that I was an RLO (real live officer). With all the big bucks I was making, I wasn't supposed to fly, I was supposed to supervise.

On September 13, Dave told Grant to be ready to leave early the next morning. Dave adhered to the principles of the "Seven P's" to the letter: "Proper Prior Planning Prevents Piss-Poor Performance." He was going to get back to Camp Eagle with just enough time to turn in his gear, sign out, and get the hell out of Dodge. Proper prior planning could not get much better than that.

I was able to fly support missions for the next two days. Nothing exciting, but it sure beat the hell out of staying on the ground. September 19, I spent the day at Phuoc Vinh doing whatever was required to keep the detachment running smoothly. I had one aircraft in maintenance and four assigned for missions on the following day. That schedule would allow one of the air crews the day off.

I arrived at the club around 1900 hours. The beer was cold and the food was better than whatever they were serving in the mess hall. Around 2200 hours a runner came from Operations and told me I had to get in touch with the TOC at Cu Chi "right now." He said it looked like there might be a mission coming up. Looking around the room, I spotted Charlie Smith. He wasn't scheduled to fly in the morning and seemed to be fairly sober. I went over and told him to get his gear, round up Tom Turck and a gunner. The latter two were to get 121 ready to go, and Charlie was to meet me in Operations.

I called the TOC on the land line. They said that one of their fire support bases was getting hit with mortar and ground attacks. They needed an aircraft to fly resupply and general support, and I was to report to the logistic pad at Cu Chi for a more detailed briefing.

We arrived at the log pad at 2315 hours. They told me they were sending a PFC with us to help with the cargo, and began loading the aircraft with cases of M-16 and M-60 ammunition, hand grenades, and LAWs (Light Antitank Weapons—one-shot disposable armor-piercing rockets in cardboard tubes). While that took place, I went over and got briefed on the mission.

The fire support base under attack was called Pope, about a twenty-minute flight west of Cu Chi. They estimated that two battalions of VC were hitting the base, one from the south and the other from the north, and a reinforced rifle company was defending it.

The company had sent out two twenty-man ambush patrols, one north and one south. Both had moved out about five hundred meters before setting up for the night. About two hours later the patrol to the south called in that they had a lot of movement that appeared to be heading toward FSB Pope. A short time later they called back and reported that column after column of VC were passing on both sides of them. Luckily, they hadn't blown their ambush and the VC hadn't stumbled over them in the dark.

The patrol set up north of the base (Charlie Two-six) was not quite so lucky. They too reported movement and let the main body of VC pass them in the dark. Just when it looked as though Charlie Two-six's patrol might get away undiscovered, one of the rear elements of the VC battalion walked into the ambush site. The fight was on. Charlie Two-six's action had disrupted the coordinated attack on Fire Support Base Pope, but Charlie Two-six was fighting for its life.

I had the radio frequencies and call signs. We climbed to three thousand feet as we headed west. The night was clear but, with a new moon, it was very dark. After fifteen minutes, from our altitude I could see the flashes from impacting mortar rounds. Green tracers were going into the fire base and red ones were coming out. One hell of a fight was still going on.

A little to the north, another firefight was taking place. That had to be Charlie Two-six. The radio was alive with traffic from the gunships, artillery, the battalion commander (Sidewinder Six), and an Air Force forward air controller. I knew that the gunships would be working low. Where in the hell was that FAC?

I was waiting for a break in the radio traffic when Charlie Two-six came up on Fox Mike. "Sidewinder Six, this is Charlie Two-six."

"This is Sidewinder Six. Go ahead."

"Six, the bad guys have got us surrounded and we're just about out of ammo. Can you get any help to us?"

"Negative, Two-six. Can you blow a hole through them and make a run for the wire?"

"This is Two-six. That's a negative. I've got eight wounded, two critical. I can't move them and I won't leave them."

For someone who was up to his ass in alligators, that guy was pretty damn calm. Maybe he was resigned to the fact that he was going to die, and could see no real point in getting excited.

At that point, I contacted Sidewinder Six and told him I was a UH-1 with five SOBs (souls on board) and a full load of small arms ammo. "If you want, I can try to resupply Charlie Two-six and evacuate his wounded."

He came back at me: "Two-five, this is Six. You understand that Two-six is surrounded and in heavy contact?"

"Roger that. Even if we can get in but can't get out, it will still give him five more people, two more machine guns, and a shit pot full of ammo."

After several moments Sidewinder Six replied: "Kingsman Two-five, use your own judgment. If you think you can do it, give it a shot."

"Six, this is Two-five. Roger. Break. Charlie Two-six, you copy?"

"This is Charlie Two-six. Good copy."

"Two-six, this is Kingsman Two-five. It's going to take us about five minutes to get to you. We'll be making our approach from the west. You hang in there, partner. We're inbound." Two clicks on the handset were the only response I received. Nothing else needed to be said.

I'd been looking out of the left window toward the area where Charlie Two-six was located. Now that I'd committed us to try to resupply him, I had to figure out the best way to get in and, more important, how to get out.

I had flown the area before, and knew there were no tall trees down there. Most of the vegetation was three to five feet high. We had almost a full tank of fuel and a heavy load of

ammunition. I would have to make a fairly shallow approach.
I could not afford to put in a big flare at the bottom and take
the chance of putting my tail rotor in one of those bushes. I
looked back inside the aircraft to check the instruments one
last time before turning the instrument panel lights off. We
would have to go in completely blacked out.

I'd been in a shallow left-hand turn, bringing the aircraft
into position to start my approach. When I looked back outside, I saw the silhouette of a fixed-wing aircraft. It was an
O-1 Bird Dog, the FAC I'd been wondering about. He was
about five hundred feet directly in front of me. If we had continued on the same course, we would have collided. I sharpened my turn and passed behind the O-1. Everyone else was
watching the firefight below. I did not say anything but wondered if the Bird Dog pilot, or anyone on board my aircraft,
had any idea how close they'd just come to dying.

After we started our approach I called, "Charlie Two-
six, this is Two-five. Can you give me a strobe to mark your
position?"

"Two-five, Charlie Two-six. Can you see where the green
tracers are making a cross?"

"That's affirm."

"Well, I'm right under them."

We continued the approach and I thought, Holy shit! What
in the hell have I gotten us into this time? Well, it was too late
to worry about it now.

"Okay, Two-six, I've got your position spotted. We'll be
coming in blacked out. You won't see us until we're almost on
the ground. I'll still need that strobe on short final. Have it
ready when I call for it." Hopefully, the VC would not be able
to see us either.

That's one time I was thankful for the darkness. I told the
crew chief and gunner they were not to fire unless I told them
to, or unless they had a hard target, that is, if they could see
the VC and the VC were shooting at us.

We continued to descend into the darkness. The only thing
I could see in front of us was the glow of the tracers as the
firefight raged on. As we neared the landing area, about half a

mile out, I called for the strobe light. It came on immediately. Being blacked out and having the gunners not return the enemy's fire seemed to be working fairly well. The VC fire continued, but they did not bring concentrated fire to bear on us.

As the aircraft touched down I spotted movement about five feet from my left skid. A man stood up. I had damn near landed on top of him. He moved to the aircraft and began helping to off-load the ammo. As soon as that was completed the wounded began to arrive. A few were able to manage on their own, but the rest were either helped or carried onto the helicopter. I knew from the radio transmissions that at least two of them were critical.

Charlie and I sat there with our hands on the controls and wondered when the bad guys would get our number and come to call. We knew it could not take the VC long to zero in on the noise of our aircraft.

Not a word had been said. Even though it seemed as if we'd been on the ground for an hour, I knew it was only a few minutes. Time flew when you were having fun. We obviously were not having very much fun.

In the cargo compartment, all I could see was bodies lying all over each other. With thirteen people on board, we had a much heavier load to take out than we'd landed with, but I could not bring myself to tell any of them that they'd have to get off. I just hoped we'd have enough power to get off the ground.

I called Charlie Two-six and let him know we were loaded and would be departing to the east. He replied that he would give us some covering fire. Now that he had more ammunition than he'd be able to use, Charlie Two-six opened up with a vengeance.

It took everything that 121 had to pull itself into the air. As soon as we lifted off, tracers converged on us. The VC could not see us so they were shooting at the noise. We stayed about ten feet off the ground as we built up airspeed and cleared the area.

After five minutes we started to climb. As we passed

through one thousand feet I made contact with the 12th Evac Hospital at Cu Chi and told them I was inbound with eight wounded. They asked what type of wounds, and I replied, "Hell, I don't know. Two were able to walk, two of them were critical, and the rest were shot full of holes." When we landed at the medevac pad fifteen minutes later, medics were waiting for us.

After the wounded were unloaded, we repositioned to the log pad and took on another load of ammunition for the fire base. With the aircraft still running, we used flashlights to check it over. With all the rounds that had been fired at us, we hadn't taken a single hit!

We spent the rest of the night, as well as most of the following day, flying in support of the fire base. We caught a little sleep whenever there was a lull in the flying requirements. At one point an NCO from the battalion rear came over and asked us for the name, rank, and serial numbers of the entire crew. We were finally released at 1700 hours. It had been a sixteen-hour mission. W.T. would have loved it.

The following morning I was instructed to report to Lieutenant Colonel Becton at brigade headquarters. I was to bring the crew that had flown with me the day before. When we reported, Becton informed me that the PFC from his unit who had accompanied us as the belly man (cargo handler) had already been awarded an Air Medal for Valor as an impact award for his part in the night's action. He said that my crew and I would be put in for other awards by his unit. (The awards would never be received.)

Lieutenant Colonel Becton further stated that in gratitude for our service to his unit, he was offering us all an additional R&R from his unit's allocation. Now *that* was too good to be true. Two R&Rs on one tour were unheard of. I let the other three guys take their pick of where they wanted to go. No one asked for Hawaii, so I did. They had one coming up in about two weeks. I told them I wanted it.

I still could not believe it: I was on a plane heading for Hawaii. Only now when we landed, there was no one to meet me. I sat through the briefing at the R&R center at Fort De Russey. Afterward I went into the men's room and changed out of my uniform, then caught a cab to the Honolulu International Airport. There, I bought a round-trip ticket to Los Angeles. That was strictly against Army regulations, but what the hell! What were they going to do to me if they caught me? Send me to Vietnam?

We were ordered to return to Camp Eagle on September 30, which gave us four days to close down the operation and pack our gear. By then we were all ready to get back up north. At least I knew damn well that I was.

I had to fly to Cu Chi each day for the next three days to coordinate our movement. On one of those visits I was informed that the 3d Brigade would be relocating to Camp Eagle and I was being requested to assist their Aviation section in getting set up. On the morning of the thirtieth we departed Phuoc Vinh and headed north as a flight of five.

After my second R&R in less than sixty days, I returned to Camp Eagle and worked again with the 3d Brigade. I really didn't have very much to do. Mostly I was giving orientation rides and helping get the brigade pilots familiar with the lay of the land. I was bored stiff.

Whenever I had any free time, which was a lot, I went over to the LRP company. They had been running a few missions and were getting a pretty good body count, even though they didn't remain on the ground very long. Most of their contacts were on or very close to their LZs. About the only thing that was learned from those missions was that there were a hell of a lot of NVA out there.

On October 29, Captain Eklund told me that the division was concerned about the 122mm rockets being launched at Camp Eagle and Hue/Phu Bai from the area around Nui Ke Mountain. The area had become known as the "rocket belt." On November 2 the LRPs would start putting teams in to locate the people firing those rockets. He also informed me that he'd requested that W.T. and I be assigned to the LRPs for the upcoming missions. The assignment would more than likely last for most of the month.

Other than my going on R&R, that was the best news I'd heard in many moons. I had been away from flying LRPs for quite a while, but I was going to be back in my element.

Chapter
Fifteen

"Kingsman Operations, Kingsman Two-five with a flight of two for departure."

"Roger, Two-five. Flight of two cleared for departure."

"One-eight . . . Two-five. You copy?"

"Two-five . . . One-eight. Copy."

We lifted off from our company area for the two-minute flight to the LRP Acid Pad.

It was 0550 hours, November 1, 1968, and boy did I feel good! Sixty days left in country. I was what they called "short." Things were starting to look up. We landed at the Acid Pad and shut down the aircraft.

I keyed the radio. "One-eight . . . Two-five."

"This is One-eight. Go."

"Short."

"Two-five . . . One-eight. Say again."

"Short."

There was no reply.

W.T. and I started walking up the hill toward the LRP Operations tent. He looked at me and said, "What's this short shit?"

"That's right, partner. Sixty days and I'm going home."

W.T. looked at me with disbelief and said, "Asshole."

I laughed and asked, "What's the matter, W.T.? Jealous?"

"Fuck you, Meacham, you ain't ever going home. You like it here."

I laughed. "That's right, I like it here. You know, this Army is all right."

Lieutenant Williams was in the Operations tent when we

arrived. He started to say something but Grant cut him off. "Don't say anything, LT. I already told this dumb son of a bitch that he ain't never going home." Everybody in Operations started laughing.

Captain Eklund was waiting for us at the mess tent. Over breakfast he gave us a very brief overview of what we'd be doing. A more detailed briefing would come later. W.T. and I had been requested to work for the LRP company for an indefinite period of time. The C&C and the gunships would be supplied by the 2d of the 17th Cav. It appeared that Division wanted to try to disrupt the rocket attacks on Camp Eagle, which were coming from the area we referred to as the rocket belt. The plan was to try to have teams in close, so when the NVA fired the rockets, the nearest team could either take the bad guys out themselves or call in gunships or artillery. We had entered the rainy season, and the weather prevented us from inserting teams deep into the mountains.

We would spend the day doing the VRs for the areas we'd be working in. Eklund knew the general area where we'd be inserting the teams, but not the exact location. With the team leaders on board, we flew over the AO about fifteen hundred feet above ground level (AGL) so the TLs could select their insertion and extraction points. We would be looking at two areas: Leech Island and Nui Ke Mountain. Both were known to be bad news.

Leech Island was located where one fork of the Perfume River flowed to the north and the other to the south. The island was about three and a half miles long, and a half mile across at its widest point. An abandoned fire support base was on the northern end. The ridge line that ran the length of the island rose to about one hundred feet in the center and tapered down on both sides to the north and south. The only part not covered with vegetation was where the old fire support base was located.

There was also a small area on the southern end of the island where a helicopter could land. Several large bomb craters were also suitable for inserting a team and one of them was selected as the LZ. It was approximately five hundred meters from the clearing on the southern end of the island. The clearing was the team's designated primary extraction point. I didn't like it, not even a little bit.

Nui Ke Mountain was a lone peak at the eastern edge of the mountains west of Camp Eagle, at a spot where the mountainous jungle met the rolling foothills of the coastal piedmont. It was the ideal spot from which Chuck could, and did, launch 122mm rockets to fly eight to nine miles and blow the shit out of Camp Eagle. Chuck really had the advantage there. Most of his rocket launches were at night. If there wasn't a gun team on station to see the rockets lift off when they were fired, there was no chance of catching the men who'd fired them. One thing we had learned: Chuck was not dumb. Anyone who underestimated him would pay the price.

The rolling hills of the piedmont extended about eight miles to the west of Camp Eagle and then began a gradual climb to the mountains. The top of the nearest mountain peaks was about 2,300 feet. Five fingers extended from about one-third of the way from the top of Nui Ke toward the piedmont below. One of them pointed to the north into the South Huu Valley. The next one ran to the northeast to where the South Huu and Song Ta valleys intersected. The other three fingers, or ridge lines, extended off the mountain to the east into the Song Ta Valley, which bordered the Perfume River.

We'd flown over the area for seven months. I knew before we even arrived in the AO that there would be very few places suitable for LZs or PZs. The area was definitely "number fucking ten."

There were a few bomb craters on two of the fingers that one could get an aircraft into, but it would be tight, and they would have to be used as extraction points because they were too far down the mountainside to qualify as LZs. The only area where we might have been able to insert the team without it being compromised was the old fire support base on top of the mountain. And I did not like that idea at all. With just a few places to land, you could bet your sweet ass that Chuck would have them all under observation. There was no use trying to discuss my concerns during the VR, when the TLs had their hands full trying to figure out their best course of action. There would be time to talk about them after we landed.

Back at the Acid Pad, I listened to the CO and the TLs go over the information they'd gathered on the VR. Captain Eklund told Sgt. John Burford to be prepared for a 1700 hours briefing for a morning insertion the next day. I still said nothing about my concerns. The time didn't seem right. Let them work out a plan for the upcoming mission, I thought, and once I knew where we were going to insert, I could make my recommendations. I'd already decided to discuss the situation with Captain Eklund before the mission briefing with the entire team.

We met in Eklund's tent. I requested that all four pilots be present at the meeting. First Lieutenant Owen Williams, the LRP company's XO, was also there. The other three pilots were all WO1s. There was W. T. Grant and his copilot, Ken "the Teenybopper" Roach, and my copilot, Jim Cline. All of us were considered certifiably insane by our peers.

I think my outburst was directed at Ken Eklund, but it may have been at everyone in the tent. "What in the fuck is Division trying to do? We know, and they know, that there are 25,000 NVA troops in those goddamn mountains. We've been playing tag with Colonel Mot for the last seven months. That son of a bitch ain't dumb. He knows goddamn well that with this weather we can't insert deep into the mountains. He also knows we can only put people into a clearing large enough to get a helicopter into, or we have to insert by rappelling. With the people he has, you can bet your sweet ass he'll have every single LZ under observation or booby-trapped."

I had to stop to catch my breath. Without giving anyone a chance to say anything, I started again. "We're going to get our shit shot away. You know that, don't you? Does Division want us to get a bunch of people killed just so they can confirm something that they, and we, already know? For Christ sake, we already know Chuck's there. He's on Leech Island, and he's all over Nui Ke Mountain. Who was the dumb bastard who came up with this asinine, stupid goddamn idea?"

When I finally ran down, absolute quiet reigned in the tent.

Ken Eklund and Owen Williams were looking at each other in disbelief. The two copilots were looking at anything in the tent except me.

The only person who didn't seem surprised was Grant. W.T. was smiling and shaking his head. "Okay, Captain Asshole. Do you feel better now?"

I had already begun to simmer down a little. "Yeah, I guess so, but damn it, W.T., I'm getting tired of this shit. We keep going out there day after day, and sooner or later it's going to catch up with us."

I looked at Eklund and said, "Okay, Ken. Let's get down to the mission-planning part of this brilliantly conceived operation that's been sent down from the powers that be. You know, the ones who think they're God."

The 1700 briefing was completed in about forty-five minutes. We were going to insert Honest John Burford's team into a bomb crater on Leech Island. The LZ would also serve as an extraction point if the team was compromised within the first twenty minutes and could make it back to that point. Once the team moved off the LZ to set up the recon base, the extraction point would become a small clearing five hundred meters to the southwest. Luckily, the clearing was downhill from the LZ. Nobody thought the team had much of a chance of staying on the ground very long. However, "Ours is not to reason why, ours is just to do or . . ."

After Sergeant Burford completed his briefing and Captain Eklund cleared up a few points, I asked everyone to remain in the Operations tent so I could cover one more item. "Okay, guys, we haven't worked together very much since some damn fool pitched his tent in a minefield, so I want to go over a few things you may have forgotten." Looking around, I could see faint smiles on the faces of all the team members.

I let that sink in, then went on. "I want to go over the responsibility and chain of command while we're involved in this mission. It goes without saying that while you're in or around the aircraft, I'm the boss. If anything happens to me, and the aircraft is still flyable, then Mr. Cline will take over and the mission will be aborted. If we go down and have to leave the aircraft, time permitting, I want everything of value destroyed. Once on the ground, the ranking team member, regardless of rank, will take charge. I want to make it clear to all air-crew members that your best chance for survival is to listen to the guys who know what the hell they're doing on the ground." It wasn't the first time I'd made the speech, and it probably wouldn't be the last, but it was a necessary bit of understanding I wasn't willing to leave to chance. For a day when I had begun to feel things were looking up, it had sure done a quick turnaround.

We arrived at the Acid Pad at 0600, and the insertion was scheduled for 0730 hours. W.T. and I always showed up early for a mission, in case there were last-minute changes. Besides, the LRPs had better chow than we did.

The team soon filed down the hill to the helicopter pad. Damn, they looked out of place. They were dressed in tiger-stripe fatigues with camouflage paint covering their hands and faces. Their rucksacks weighed close to a hundred pounds each, and they were loaded for bear. Sgt. John Burford, the team leader, led the way followed by Sp4. Jim "Boom Boom" Evans; Sp4. Kenn Miller—the ATL; Sp4. John Looney—the senior RTO radio; Sgt. Don Harris at point; and Sp4. Ken Munoz—the junior RTO.

Grant was already in his aircraft, waiting for the blades of 121 to start to turn. We'd been through the routine so many times that it was automatic.

The 2/17th Cav helicopter pads were just across a small ravine from the LRP Acid Pad. I saw the blades of the C&C ship start to turn. A little farther down the Cav ramp, two AH-1G Cobra gunships were starting to crank. I reached up and turned the battery switch on. As soon as I did, Jim reached over and turned on the VHF radio. A few seconds later the radio came alive.

"Kingsman Two-five, this is Windy Guard Six."

"Windy Guard Six, this is Kingsman Two-five. Go ahead."

"Two-five, this is Six. You ready?"

"Six . . . Two-five. Affirm."

"This is Windy Guard Six, follow me out in zero five."

"Six . . . Two-five. Copy."

The aircraft was set in what we called the "shotgun load." The starter generator was set in the start position, fuel on, throttle set, just below the flight-idle detent, and the battery switch was in the off position. The only thing required to start the aircraft was to turn on the battery and pull the trigger.

I looked at Jim and nodded. He turned the radio off as I engaged the starter trigger. The sound of 121 coming to life was something that never ceased to amaze me. I could hear the ticking of the igniters, hear the sound of the raw fuel as it erupted into a flaming fireball within the engine. I could smell the exhaust fumes as the main rotor blades began to turn between eight and ten percent N1 speed. The sound and smells were only the beginning of what she was trying to tell me. The instruments inside the aircraft informed me that she was really alive and well. At forty percent N1, I released the starter, throttle set to flight idle, inverters on, then attitude indicator caged. The oil pressure, engine exhaust temperature, engine oil temperature, transmission oil pressure, and temperature were all in the green. The AC and DC voltage were good. But most of all, as the rpm passed through 6,400 going to 6,600, I could almost feel her through the controls telling me, "Okay, Captain Bill, let's do it." God, how I loved that feeling!

"Kingsman One-eight, this is Two-five. You up?" I heard the squelch break twice, as W.T. keyed his radio transmit switch in acknowledgment. As 121 became light on the skids, I made a final, quick scan of the instrument panel to confirm that everything was where it was supposed to be.

"Okay, One-eight. Let's go to work."

All the fear, doubt, and apprehension were suddenly gone. Now, the completion of the mission was the only thing that mattered, and that would definitely be accomplished.

"Eagle Tower, Kingsman Two-five, Acid Pad. Flight of two for departure to the west."

"Kingsman Two-five, this is Eagle Tower. Flight of two cleared from present position for departure to the west."

Coming off the Acid Pad, in my mind's eye I could see 348 coming off the ground behind me as if attached by a long rope.

"Windy Guard Six, this is Kingsman Two-five. Off at this time en route your location with a flight of two."

"Roger, Two-five. This is Windy Guard Six. Continue."

At one hundred knots it would be only a ten-minute flight to the LZ. We stayed low at about five hundred feet AGL, with W.T. dropping back into trail position with a quarter-mile separation. Once I started my approach, he would adjust his airspeed so he'd overfly the LZ just as I was coming out. If all went as planned, and the NVA were not watching the LZ, we'd be able to insert the team and get the hell out of Dodge without the enemy ever knowing we'd been in. "Windy Guard Six, Kingsman Two-five. One mile."

"Roger, Two-five. I have you in sight. Setup looks good. Your gun lead is Saber Two-three."

"Two-five, roger. Break. Saber Two-three, how do you copy?"

"Saber Two-three. Lima Chuck." (Loud and clear.)

From that point on there would be very little radio traffic. Eklund would call when I was five hundred meters from the LZ, and again at one hundred meters. I would be at five hundred feet and one hundred knots forward airspeed.

"Kingsman Two-five. Five hundred meters." I keyed the radio transmit switch twice.

The wide part of the island was to my left. I saw the abandoned fire support base out of my window. The LZ was three hundred feet above my line of flight and about five hundred meters to my front.

"Kingsman Two-five. One hundred meters."

There was no need to respond. I lowered the collective and put a little back pressure on the cyclic. I had to gain three hundred feet of altitude and lose one hundred knots of forward airspeed. All of that would transpire within those one hundred meters. The nose of the aircraft came up, the airspeed began to bleed off, the attitude indicator started to show a positive climb. The trees were getting bigger and bigger in the chin bubble.

As the airspeed indicator wound down to zero, the opening of the bomb crater appeared under my feet. The timing had been perfect. The helicopter started to settle into the opening created by the bomb blast. The trees were higher than we'd anticipated. Instead of being one hundred feet tall, they were at least 150 to 200 feet. As we settled into the trees I thought, Oh, God, don't let this be the extraction point! If we have to come back in here, those assholes are going to eat us alive.

The opening that was our LZ was a lot smaller than I'd anticipated, and it was a *long* way down. As planned, the team took five seconds to unass the aircraft. We'd come down on the right-hand side of the crater. As I pulled in power to stop the descent, I felt the aircraft wobble from side to side as the team dropped from the skids before we contacted the ground.

With the departure of the team, I lost fifteen hundred pounds of weight, and the aircraft started to rise with little or no adjustment in power. It felt good to know that the team was on the ground and we hadn't taken any fire. Maybe, just maybe . . . Oh, shit. For a second I'd seen a flash of light brown in the trees on the left side of the LZ.

"Kingsman Two-five. Coming out."

I looked up through the greenhouse and saw One-eight come across the top of the LZ. Knowing that I was clear, as I came to the top of the trees I keyed the radio. "Windy Guard Six, Two-five. Dinks in the LZ."

"Two-five, this is Six. Say again."

"Six, Two-five. There are dinks on the east side of the LZ."

"Two-five, Six. Are you sure?"

"Goddamn it, Six, if I wasn't sure, I wouldn't have said so. Advise Windy Guard Two-eight to head south if possible. I don't think we can get them out where they are."

The team moved just off the LZ to the south, where they'd planned to lay dog for fifteen to twenty minutes. However, when they were notified that they were spotted coming in, they continued moving south. I was monitoring their company radio and heard Six talking to the team on the ground. I could only be thankful that the extraction point was downhill.

"Windy Guard Six, this is Kingsman Two-five. Get me some guns in here now. I'll talk to Windy Guard Two-eight."

"Two-five, Six. Roger."

When I came out of the LZ, I made a right turn to the northwest and was climbing. I was completely out of position and had to do a 180-degree turn to get back into the AO. I wanted to overfly the extraction point once before making an approach into it; the approach was going to be a real bitch. The PZ was about six hundred feet lower than the LZ. There were two-hundred-foot-high trees on the west side of the ridge line. I would have to come in from west to east. That would give me a better route, and a lower barrier for departure.

"Windy Guard Two-eight, this is Kingsman Two-five."

"Kingsman Two-five, Windy Guard Two-eight. Go ahead."

I could tell by the heavy breathing that they were on the move. "Windy Guard Two-eight. Sitrep."

"This is Windy Guard Two-eight. We're moving to the PZ. We got dinks right on our ass."

"Windy Guard Two-eight, how far are you from the PZ?"

"Two-five, Two-eight. About two hundred meters."

Shit, it would take them at least another ten minutes, if they didn't have to stop and fight.

"Windy Guard Two-eight, let me know when you're within seventy-five to fifty meters out."

"This is Windy Guard Two-eight. Roger."

"Windy Guard Six, this is Kingsman Two-five. You copy?"

"Two-five, Six. Go ahead."

"Six, Two-five. Did you monitor the traffic with Two-eight?"

"Two-five, Six. That's affirm."

"Okay, Six. As soon as I get their call, I'll start my approach. I'll be coming over the top of the ridge on the west side of the island. I don't know how this is going to work, so just stay out of my way. It's going to be one hell of a steep approach."

"Two-five, Six. Roger. I'll keep everybody to the north of the PZ."

"Six, Two-five. Keep those guns close by. I've got a feeling I'm going to need them."

"Two-five, Six. As soon as you get to three hundred feet below the ridge line, I'll bring the guns into position to the west of the PZ."

"Roger, Six. Break. Kingsman One-eight, where are you?"

"Two-five, One-eight. Behind you in a loose trail."

"Okay, One-eight. Stay high and keep an eye on me. Sure as hell hope I don't need your help down here. And, no, you can't have my watch."

As far as I could figure, we were as ready as we could get. It was up to the men who were running for their lives down there in the jungle. Damn, how I hated the waiting! I'd flown down the river to the south, and then turned back to the north at about one hundred feet. The main purpose of that maneuver was to avoid letting the NVA know the location of the PZ. Of course, with only one other place to land, I was pretty sure I was spinning my wheels; they had to know where we were going to try for the pickup.

"Kingsman Two-five, Windy Guard Two-eight. We're seventy-five meters out and the bad guys are still with us. We can hear them behind us. It sounds like they're paralleling us on both sides. If they get ahead of us, we're going to be in deep doo-doo."

"Roger, Two-eight. Two-five's inbound."

Then the fun began. The die had been cast. We would get the team out or die trying; nobody would be left behind. As I moved into a hard descending right-hand turn, I looked at Jim. The damn fool was smiling. I thought, He likes this shit.

I don't know why I even bothered to ask. My crew knew that when it came to decision time, there was no democratic process. I made the decisions, and if they didn't like it, they could get out and walk. Looking at Jim, I asked anyway. "Okay, guys. Are you ready?"

Tom Turck and the gunner both shouted at the same time, "What are we waiting for?"

Jim moved his hands and feet a little closer to the controls and said, "Let's do it, boss."

Shit, with a good aircraft and crew like that, what more could a person ask for?

Coming out of the turn, I was heading to the east. We were set up to clear the trees on top of the ridge line by no more than five feet. I had planned to make a steep approach, but as I cleared the trees, I could see the PZ was almost straight down. A steep approach sure as hell would not work.

The only way I might be able to make the PZ was to try a power-on autorotation. I was going to have to make the damn helicopter fall out of the sky like a homesick brick. I dropped the collective to the bottom and raised the nose of the aircraft to keep the forward airspeed from building up. The aircraft began to sink. The vertical speed indicator showed a fifteen-hundred-foot-per-minute descent. At that rate I would be on the ground in thirty seconds. Christ, thirty seconds doesn't sound very long, but sometimes, when you're living 'em, they seem like a lifetime.

"Windy Guard Two-eight, this is Kingsman Two-five. Talk to me."

"Two-five, Guard Two-eight. We're still short of the PZ and they're still with us."

"Okay, Two-eight. We're about twenty seconds out of the PZ."

"Two-five, Two-eight. We can't make it there that fast."

"That's okay, Two-eight. If you don't stop for a coffee break, we'll wait for you."

"Roger, Two-five. No coffee." Looney had to be the coolest son of a bitch on the radio that I'd ever heard.

We continued our descent toward the PZ. Christ, it was a lot rougher terrain than it had seemed from altitude. I hoped the area I'd picked out for my touchdown point was level enough to land on.

Hot extract procedure had all been covered and rehearsed before, but I wanted to go over it one more time before we got on the ground.

"Jim, stay on the controls with me. Warner, I want you to shoot the shit out of anything that moves on your side of the aircraft. There ain't no friendlies to the south. Tom, they'll be coming out of the trees on our side, so be careful. The bad guys are right on their ass." All three responded that they understood and were ready. There was a level spot right under me. Thank God! Then we were on the ground.

I couldn't understand why there were no NVA troops covering the clearing. Maybe they'd been pulled out to try to cut off the team as it moved down from the LZ. Whatever the reason, I was very thankful. There really must be a God who looks out for drunks and dumb animals. I think that I qualified on both counts.

"Windy Guard Two-eight, this is Kingsman Two-five. We're on the ground. Break. Six, you copy?"

"Six. Copy."

"Kingsman Two-five, Two-eight. We're just coming to the edge of the PZ."

Looking out of my left window, I saw the first man, followed closely by the second. The M-60 on the right side of the aircraft started to fire. I couldn't see what the target was, but I didn't have the time to ask.

I let out a yell over the intercom to Turck. "Watch it, Tom. They're coming out of the tree line at nine o'clock." Even as I watched the last of the team members clear the tree line, three NVA soldiers in khaki uniforms and carrying AK-47 assault rifles broke into the open.

Before I could say anything I heard Tom yell, "You rotten son of a bitch!"

Turning as far as I could, I saw the M-60 pointing with the muzzle down toward the ground and Tom bringing his M-16 up to his shoulder. I think the NVA were surprised to see a helicopter sitting in the clearing, because they hesitated for a moment. That was all it took. I had always insisted that the crew chief and gunner keep their M-16 magazines loaded with tracers so they could mark targets. As I watched, thirty tracer rounds tore into the bodies of the three NVA soldiers.

As they went down, I saw more figures in light brown uniforms moving in the tree line. All I could think was, Now ain't this a bitch? The team's not on board, the goddamn machine gun on the left side of the aircraft doesn't work, and a whole shit pot full of very pissed dinks with just one thing on their minds is coming after us.

"Windy Guard Six, Kingsman Two-five. The team is clear of the tree line. Get me some guns in here now. These bastards are all over the place down here. Start on the tree line and work back into the trees."

"Roger, Two-five. Break. Saber Two-three, you are cleared to fire."

Saber Two-three did not take the time to answer over the radio, but his response was something to behold. It all seemed to be happening in slow motion. The last three members of the team were almost to the aircraft. Tom was emptying magazines from his M-16 into the trees, and Warner was keeping the M-60 on the right-hand side of the aircraft on steady rock 'n' roll. I still did not know what in the hell he was shooting at. I remember Ken clearing the guns to fire, and the next thing I saw and heard was a ring of red fire and the sound of an onrushing tornado.

The ring of fire was the two miniguns firing six thousand to seven thousand rounds a minute. Every fifth round was a tracer. The tracers were coming down at a rate of twenty per second. The sound was the one hundred rounds of 7.62 ammunition striking the ground every second, and tearing the shit out of all the vegetation in sight. It was beyond my comprehension how these rounds could be coming straight down in such a steady stream.

Looking up through the greenhouse, I was treated to the sight of an AH-1G Cobra doing pedal turns while the copilot worked the turret. His wingman was making rocket runs starting about fifty meters north of the edge of the PZ. It was fascinating. But now I had another problem. The Cobra that had been my savior was hovering right above me, preventing me from getting out of the PZ.

Jim had been watching the team when the gunships started firing. He keyed the intercom and said, "We got 'em all. Let's get the hell out of here." That seemed reasonable to me.

"Windy Guard Six, Kingsman Two-five. Coming out."

"Two-five, Six. Roger."

Saber Two-three had also heard my transmission and replied, "Going cold. Breaking to the south."

I began applying power, and the aircraft started to rise. Jim was staying close to the controls and monitoring the instruments. That was the worst time when extracting a team. The aircraft was climbing straight up very slowly. We knew the bad guys were down there, although we also knew that the gunships had taken the fight out of them. But you couldn't help but think, What if one of those silly little bastards didn't get the word?

I was keeping my eyes focused outside the cockpit, watching the trees in front of me, as Jim called out the power setting. "Forty-five . . . forty-six . . . forty-seven . . . forty-eight. You're coming up on fifty pounds. Fifty. Hold it." Fifty pounds of torque was the maximum amount of power you were supposed to use without causing damage to the transmission and power train of the aircraft.

I couldn't apply any more power. All I could do was sit and wait as the aircraft made its ascent to the tops of the trees. Goddamn, it seemed to take forever. Still, we hadn't taken any fire from the area around the PZ. Saber Two-three had joined his wingman and was trying to sink the damn island. They were blowing the shit out of everything in sight. God love 'em! The tops of the trees began to appear in my windshield as we continued to climb. Just a little longer. Please, God, just a little longer. Then I saw the treetops in the chin bubble and the river four hundred feet below. I pushed the nose over and dove for the river, keeping in full power to gain airspeed as fast as possible.

"Windy Guard Six, Kingsman Two-five is clear."

"Kingsman Two-five, this is Windy Guard Six. Do you have any WIAs on board?"

"Six, Two-five. Negative. We got away clean."

"Roger, Two-five. This is Six. Take them home."

By the time I reached the river and made a left turn, I finally had my emotions somewhat under control. I was also hauling ass.

"Kingsman One-eight, this is Kingsman Two-five. Where are you?"

"Two-five, One-eight. Two thousand feet above and about three-quarters of a mile behind you."

"Okay, One-eight. Join up and let's head back to the Acid Pad."

"Two-five, One-eight. I'd be more than glad to join up if you'd slow that son of a bitch down a little so I can catch you." I looked at the airspeed indicator and saw that I had it pegged at 120 knots.

Looking over at Jim, I saw the sweat rolling out from under his helmet and down his face. Hell, it was just a little after nine o'clock in the morning, and the outside air temperature was only eighty-five degrees. What the hell was he sweating for?

"Jim, you have the controls. Go ahead and climb to two thousand feet. Let One-eight catch up to us, and take us back to the Acid Pad." With a nod, Jim took the controls.

As we began to climb I leaned back in my seat and tried to relax. Reaching for my cigarettes and lighter, which were on the radio console, I noticed that my gloves were dark with sweat. As I tried to take off the gloves, I discovered they were soaked. Shit, so was I.

After Jim took over the flying and I lit up a cigarette, I looked into the back of the aircraft and couldn't help but laugh. There were six of the biggest grins I'd ever seen. If those grins had gotten any bigger, the faces behind them would have cracked. If I'd thought I was soaked with sweat, then these guys must have been swimming in it. There was not a dry spot on any of them.

"Kingsman One-eight, this is Two-five."

"Two-five, One-eight. Go."

"One eight, Two-five. Get us cleared to the Acid Pad with Eagle Tower. I'll be talking to Windy Guard Six on Victor."

"Two-five . . . One-eight. Roger."

After changing the radio selector switch to the VHF radio, I keyed the transmit switch. "Windy Guard Six, this is Kingsman Two-five. Say location."

"Two-five, Six. We're still over the PZ. I'm going to work the Cobras until they have expended all of their ordnance."

"Six, Two-five. We are five minutes out of the Acid Pad. Do we have any more work for today?"

"Two-five . . . Six. No more work for today. Shut down and stand by."

"Six, Two-five. Good copy."

Going back to the FM radio, I called W.T. "One-eight, Two-five. You copy?"

"Two-five, One-eight. Copy. We're cleared to land."

"Thank you, One-eight. What time do you have?"

"This is One-eight. It has to be twelve o'clock somewhere in the world." With that thought in mind, we proceeded to the Acid Pad and shut the aircraft down.

By the time Eklund arrived back in the company area, the two air crews, the six team members, and I were on our third or fourth beer apiece. The adrenaline rush was over. Everybody was beginning to realize what had just happened. Although it was only ten o'clock, we all agreed we were fourteen very tired people. When Ken arrived, we decided to make it fifteen.

The debriefing went pretty fast. There was not an awful lot to cover. The dinks had been in the landing zone and had followed Honest John and his team as they left the LZ. The team never made actual contact with the NVA, but they heard the enemy soldiers moving through the jungle as the NVA tried to cut them off from the PZ. Tom Turck had killed three of the NVA soldiers with his M-16 rifle when his M-60 failed to operate. After we landed, Tom broke the machine gun down and found that the firing pin had broken after firing only two rounds. It was nothing he could have foreseen, but it sure as shit could have spoiled our entire morning.

Ken had told the gunship pilots he would call over to their unit and let them know what kind of a body count they would get for the morning's action. Then he asked me what we thought we could claim for total enemy KIAs. When I said three, he looked at me like I was crazy.

I told him, "Ken, you know that I don't play the goddamn

numbers game. I saw three people hit and three people go down. I know that the Cobras killed a bunch of bad guys around the PZ, but I didn't see the bodies. Nobody else, including Sergeant Burford's team, saw anything they could call a confirmed kill. I sure hope I don't piss off the gun pilots too bad, but three is all I can and will claim. You can claim whatever the hell you want to."

The briefing terminated shortly afterward. The team was told to recheck its gear and stand by. W.T. and I were ordered to remain in the company area while Ken went to Division to see what was in store for tomorrow.

Eklund returned two hours later. He told us we would be going back to Leech Island at first light. Division wanted to find out what was going on there. I didn't see any use complaining about it. That was the mission we'd been given, and that was the mission we would attempt to carry out, like it or not.

Once again Sergeant Burford's team would be going in, and I would be flying the insert ship. There was no need to do a VR. We already knew all of the areas that could be used as LZs and PZs. Next time the landing zone would be the abandoned fire support base, on the northern part of the island, where a large pentaprime area had been set up as a helipad. That would be the touchdown point. The PZ would be a large bomb crater down the eastern slope of the ridge toward the river, or back at the LZ if things went down quickly. Again, nobody thought the team would be on the ground very long.

Chapter Sixteen

It was 0545 hours on November 3, 1968. Everything was set. Captain Eklund had already departed in the C&C aircraft. The two Cobras were cranked and ready to go. I sure hoped they were not still pissed off about my lack of confirmation about the body count from the day before.

Honest John and his team were loaded on board my aircraft. W.T. was ready to depart behind me. I called Eklund and let him know we were ready whenever he was. His reply was, "Let's do it."

There were no shadows. The sun had not yet come up over the eastern horizon. There was only the first faint gray light before the dawn. We were just a few feet above the river when I saw the island ahead of me. W.T. was behind me about half a mile, and the two Cobras were following him. If all went according to plan, I would land, W.T. would overfly me, and I would come out between him and the lead Cobra. It was all set up very nicely.

"Kingsman Two-five. Five hundred meters."

I keyed my transmit switch twice in acknowledgment. Eklund in the C&C was calling the distances to the LZ. There was no point in my tying up the radio with transmissions, as I knew what the next call would be. I gave the instruments a last quick look. From then until I came out of the LZ, my attention would be outside the aircraft. Jim would be close to the controls and monitoring the instruments.

"Kingsman Two-five, Windy Guard Six. Two hundred meters."

Two hundred meters out from the LZ, one hundred knots of

airspeed, and a little over five hundred feet of altitude to gain. Here we go again. With a little back pressure on the cyclic, the nose of the aircraft came up and we started to climb, trading airspeed for altitude. The LZ got larger as the airspeed continued to bleed off. The airspeed indicator settled on zero and the aircraft began to settle. Piece of cake. Everything was looking good, just like we knew what we were doing.

Tom's voice came in over the intercom: "Oh, my God. They're in the trees."

Tom was already firing by the time I keyed the mike and said, "If they're in the trees, then kill the silly sons of bitches." Looking out of the left window, I saw three figures in light brown uniforms falling to the ground from about thirty feet up.

The next thing I heard over the radio was Saber Two-three saying, "Roger. Kill the sons of bitches."

Rockets were exploding on both sides of us. I couldn't help but think how much damage we'd have because of those damn rockets, if we got out of there. That was a stupid thought. If it wasn't for those "damn rockets," I wouldn't be getting out of there at all.

I stopped the helicopter's descent ten feet off the ground. Now the trick was getting it to fly again. I pulled in power until I had fifty pounds of torque and we started to climb. "Kingsman Two-five. Coming out."

The Cobras were still putting rockets into the trees around the LZ and under the aircraft. Eklund told me I was clear. One-eight had overflown the LZ and was swinging back around so he could come in behind me as I got clear of the LZ. The treetops disappeared below the chin bubble. I did a repeat performance of yesterday's departure, as W.T. and I headed north up the river at low level.

"Windy Guard Six, this is Kingsman Two-five. We're clear to the north. Going home." It was a hell of a way to start the day. We'd already been shot out of an LZ, and it was only eight o'clock in the morning. Well, at least we'd be back home in time for breakfast. I didn't know if it was getting shot at that caused it, but I was damn hungry.

A while later Eklund came into the mess tent grinning from ear to ear. It had been a pretty good morning for him, all things considered. He had remained on station with the Cobras after W.T. and I departed the area. While the gunships were expending their ordnance on the island, Ken called for tac air and got a pair of Fox-4s (F-4s) to add to the firepower demonstration being provided firsthand for members of the 5th NVA Regiment. He also made arrangements to have artillery hit the island off and on for the rest of the day and throughout the night. If nothing else, it would sure as hell screw up their sleep.

Ken kept looking at us in a way that made me feel uneasy. The thought of what a virgin bride must feel like came to mind: I had something coming, but I didn't know what. What did the silly bastard have up his sleeve?

"Okay, guys," Eklund said, still smiling. "I've got good news and I've got bad news. Which do you want first?"

What the hell was he talking about? W.T. and I looked at each other and said at the same time, "Let's have the good news."

Ken continued, serious now. "The good news is, Bill, you don't have to go back to Leech Island. Instead you'll be putting a team onto Nui Ke in the morning. The bad news is that W.T. will be inserting a team back on the island at first light."

Those people at Division had to be out of their minds. I'd been shot out of two LZs on that damn island in twenty-four hours, and they wanted Grant to go back and try his luck!

I sat there thinking of all the negative aspects of what Ken had just said when Grant brought me back to reality. His comment was, "All right, it's about time you let a real helicopter pilot do the job right. So far the only thing you've done is let Captain Asshole here have all the fun. Now I get to show you how a real live warrant officer can get the job accomplished."

That statement really woke me up. It was as if a glass of

cold water had been thrown in my face. The bottom line was mission accomplishment. Our job was to insert the team and bring them home. Trying to second-guess the powers that be was not in our job description. I felt like a complete goddamn fool. It's not a very good feeling. I was there to do a job, not to let my fears, doubts, and frustrations get the best of me. I was flying in Vietnam because I wanted to, not because I'd been ordered to. In my own mind, I was better at doing that type of work than anyone else. So it was time to get off my dead ass and do the job I'd chosen to do.

Eklund then explained the reasoning behind the decision to go back to Leech Island. The NVA had lost a lot of people there yesterday and even more today. The hope was that if we kept hitting the island with artillery throughout the day, and again at night, they might just pull back across the river and up into the mountains to lick their wounds. If they did, we might be able to get a team inserted. We knew something was going on in there, and Division wanted to find out what it was. The plan was to get the team inserted undetected, then have them set up a patrol base from which they could observe the movement of the NVA when they returned.

W.T. was going to insert Sgt. "Snuffy" Smith's team on the island first, and then I would put Sgt. Ray "Zo" Zoschak's team on the mountain.

As far as I was concerned, there was only one place to insert Zo's team on Nui Ke: the old fire support base on the crest. However, both teams wanted to do another VR so they could get an overview of their AO. That suited me. Anything was better than sitting on the ground doing nothing and not being able to drink. W.T. took Snuffy and his ATL out to take a quick look at Leech Island. Zo and his ATL, Sp4. Gary Linderer, went with me to see if Nui Ke Mountain was still there.

The Fox-4s had blown a new bomb crater while they were working on the island the day before. W.T. and Snuffy selected that crater as the LZ. They hoped the NVA hadn't had time to put people there to observe the insertion in the morning. The PZ would be another bomb crater about three hundred meters to the south.

Well, the mountain was still there. For some reason, I'd hoped that it had disappeared. After taking a good, hard look, Zo decided that the fire base would definitely have to serve as the LZ. A large bomb crater down the third finger to the east would be the PZ. If the team was compromised and couldn't reach the PZ, then the men were to try to get back to the old fire support base.

Grant had returned to the Acid Pad before I completed my VR. When I landed, he was waiting with a six-pack of cold beer in his hand for my crew and myself. All the time I'd spent training that dumb-ass had not gone completely to waste. Our flying day was over. It was up to the team leaders to prepare and give their final briefings to the CO and their team members.

At zero dark thirty the next day, W.T. had his aircraft cranked up to operating rpm. Sgt. Snuffy Smith's team was loaded on board and ready to go. Jim and I were parked behind him going through our run-up procedures.

"Kingsman Two-five, One-eight. You up?"

"One-eight, Two-five. Roger that."

We went through the commo checks on all four of our radios. Everything was working as advertised. It was time to go.

"Two-five, One-eight. Going victor."

I keyed my mike twice in acknowledgment and switched to my VHF radio.

"Windy Guard Six, Kingsman One-eight. Flight of two. We're up."

"Kingsman One-eight, Windy Guard Six. Come on out to the playground. I'll pick you up en route."

I watched as Grant's aircraft got light on the skids.

"Two-five, One-eight. On the go."

When he broke ground, I was right with him. "One-eight, Two-five. You're up with a flight of two."

I could almost feel the tension in the cockpit of W.T.'s aircraft. All of the "what ifs." It was comforting to know that I was not going back onto that damned island.

"Kingsman One-eight, Windy Guard Six. I have you in sight."

Two clicks on the radio. W.T. started descending to five hundred feet as I dropped back to a trail position about a half mile back. I could see the two Cobras swinging into position behind me. The C&C was about fifteen hundred feet above us. There was no bullshit on the radio. Eklund had learned his lesson well. The island was right in front of us.

I heard Eklund on the radio. "One thousand meters." Two clicks on the radio from Grant. "Five hundred meters." Two more clicks. "Two hundred meters."

I saw 384 starting to flare and lose airspeed. He began to settle into the trees. Then he was out of my sight. I adjusted my airspeed to ninety knots. The trick was for me to come across the LZ just as Grant was coming out of the trees. If all went as it was supposed to, he would come back up between the lead gunship and me.

As I approached the LZ, I heard, "One-eight coming out." The LZ was starting to appear in my chin bubble. I saw Grant's aircraft coming up through the trees. The team was nowhere in sight. After passing over the LZ, W.T. came up on the radio. "One-eight's clear."

We continued up the river for about ten miles and waited to see if the team had been compromised on the insertion. After thirty minutes they reported they were moving off the LZ to the area where they'd set up their patrol base. I couldn't believe that shit. Grant had gotten them in on his first try. Jesus H. Christ! That silly son of a bitch would never let me live it down.

After we were assured that Smith's team hadn't been compromised, I headed back to the Acid Pad to pick up the team going into Nui Ke. They were waiting on the pad. It was a very experienced group of people. The team leader was Sgt. Ray Zoschak. Gary Linderer was the assistant team leader and pointman. Terry Clifton was his slack. Zo would fill the third slot in the patrol formation, then Billy B. "Indian" Walkabout, the senior radio operator, Dave Biedron with the artillery radio, and finally Jim "Stinky" Schwartz at rear security. With the exception of Clifton, everyone had at least ten missions under his belt. Even Clifton was a very experienced soldier. He had extended for six months to become an LRP after having completed a one-year tour with a Screaming Eagle line unit.

The team was on board. "Windy Guard Six, Kingsman Two-five."

"Two-five, this is Windy Guard Six. Go ahead."

"Six, Two-five. Can I come out and play?"

"Roger, Two-five. Come on out to the playground. We'll meet you there."

Now it was my turn. The insertion should be a piece of cake. Coming at Nui Ke from the northeast, I decided to use a flat approach. The old fire support base was as good an LZ as anyone could ask for. There were no obstacles anywhere near the PSP helicopter-landing pad that was to be my touchdown point. The Army combat engineers had previously cleared the vegetation back away from the fire base for a distance of two hundred meters. The only disadvantage I could think of was that if we could see everything so well, so could the NVA.

I had an unrestricted view of the LZ and didn't need any assistance from the C&C. At two hundred meters out I started deceleration. As the nose of the aircraft came up, the airspeed began to bleed off. The team was already standing out on the skids, ready to drop off when I came three to five feet off the ground. I continued holding the nose up as the airspeed indicator showed zero, and as we started to settle I got a good look at the PSP chopper pad through the chin bubble. We were still about fifteen feet off the ground, but something didn't look right. I noticed that a piece of the PSP near the center of the pad wasn't lying flat like the rest. Why in the center? Why not one of the pieces around the outer edge?

I yelled over the intercom to the crew chief and gunner not to let the team leave the aircraft. The vacant sandbagged command bunker was only about twenty meters to my right front. That was the only other place I could put them down other than the helipad. The bunker had been erected next to a large vine-covered boulder as big as a house, making it a close fit to get the team in on top of the bunker.

As we hovered just above the bunker, facing the boulder head-on, I could see how close the rotor blades were to it. When the tips of the blades began to cut the vines hanging over the face of the boulder, I told the crew chief to get the team off the aircraft. I felt them dropping from the skids. It was time to get the hell out of there. We'd already spent too much time on top of the damn mountain.

Coming off the bunker, I moved back over the PSP helipad and took a final good look at it as we made our departure. Something was definitely under the pad. The planned departure route was to the north. I stayed low over the trees and dove toward the valley floor two thousand feet below to keep our exposure time to a minimum. Besides, the valley floor provided a large forced-landing area in case we encountered any problems coming out.

"Windy Guard Six, Kingsman Two-five. We're clear to the north low level. Be advised there is something under the PSP pad. Have Windy Guard Two-two check it out."

"Two-five, Six. Roger."

After inserting the team, we moved across to the other side of the valley, about five miles away over the mountains. We were far enough from the LZ not to draw attention to it, but close enough to give support if the team was compromised. We'd been orbiting for about fifteen minutes when Eklund came on the radio.

"Kingsman Two-five, Windy Guard Six on victor."

"Six, this is Two-five. Go ahead."

"Two-five, Six. Why did you overfly the PSP?"

"Six, Two-five. It just didn't feel right."

"Two-five, Six. Man, don't ever distrust your feelings. There is a BFB"—big fucking bomb—"under the center section of the PSP. It wasn't wired, so it couldn't be command detonated, but if you'd set down, there wouldn't have been anything left."

"Roger, Six. How big is the bomb?"

"Zo doesn't know. He said it's either a two-fifty or a five hundred pounder."

Jim and I looked at each other and grinned: cheated death once again! It was getting to be a habit. I wondered how much longer I would have Jim as a copilot. He had to be getting tired of my trying to get him killed.

W.T. married up with me over the mountains after the insertion. Eklund and the two guns were about a mile to our south, also in an orbit. So far, so good. We'd inserted two teams and neither had made contact. But we were well aware of Murphy's law.

"Kingsman One-eight, Two-five. How are you doing on fuel?"

We'd been flying for about an hour and ten minutes. That left me with forty minutes of usable fuel on board.

"Two-five, One-eight. I've got forty minutes left on station."

"One-eight, Two-five. Stand by."

"Windy Guard Six, Kingsman Two-five."

"Two-five, Six. Go ahead."

"Six, Two-five. One-eight and Two-five are going to break for fuel. Suggest you and the two Saber aircraft remain on station until we return."

"Two-five, Six. Good copy. Don't be gone too long."

"Six, Two-five. Roger."

"Kingsman One-eight, Two-five. You copy?"

"Roger, Wild Bill. Lead the way."

I detected a sound of relief in his voice. It was that ever-present "what if" again. What if Meacham had landed on that PSP pad? What if it had been a command-detonated booby trap? What if the bunker had been mined or booby-trapped? There were more "what ifs" than I could count as I led the way back to Camp Eagle and the refueling point.

We spent the rest of the morning and the early part of the afternoon on standby. W.T. and Ken Roach were asleep on the ground by their aircraft, and I occupied most of my time in the TOC. Zo's team had worked its way off the top of the mountain to the east and covered about two hundred meters down the middle finger. All was still quiet. I didn't know how they could have gotten off the LZ without being seen. It seemed too good to be true.

At around 1200 hours the world turned to shit for the team on Nui Ke.

"Windy Guard One-zero, this is Windy Guard Two-two. We're being mortared. I'm calling in artillery, but we sure could use some guns." One-zero was the call sign for Operations.

"Windy Guard Two-two, this is One-zero. Contact Windy Guard Six on this frequency. He is up with the C&C."

"Roger, One-zero. Break. Windy Guard Six, this is Two-two. Did you copy?"

"Two-two, Six. Give me a sitrep."

"Six, Two-two. We are receiving mortar fire from the north. They're close enough that we can hear the rounds leaving the tubes. Sounds like they are firing from down in the valley to the north of us."

"Okay, Two-two. I've got four gunships coming out of Eagle, and I'm working on getting a pair of fast movers on station. The guns should be with you in less than ten minutes."

As soon as I heard enough to get a basic idea of what was going on, I headed for the helipad at a full run. Jim, who had been in Operations with me, had left when the first radio transmission came in. Tom had the blades untied and Jim was starting the engine. By the time I got strapped in, the aircraft was running and ready to go. It sure takes a load off your mind when you have a well-coordinated crew you can count on. Eklund had not called for me to take off, but I wanted to be as close as possible in case I was needed to make the extraction. If he didn't like it, then to hell with him.

W.T. and his crew had been sacked out in and around his aircraft. Jim had yelled at them on his way from Operations. They didn't know what was going on, but the crew chief was already untying the blades. W.T. was looking at me as if I were some kind of a fool. I yelled at him as I ran by, "Zo's hot. Brief on victor." He sprang into action.

We were en route to Nui Ke when Eklund called. "Kingsman One-eight, Windy Guard Six. Your team has been compromised. They are requesting immediate extraction."

"Windy Guard Six, Kingsman One-eight. Good copy. We're on our way."

"Two-five, One-eight. You copy?"

"Yeah, Bill. You take the lead."

It looked as though Murphy had struck again. Snuffy Smith's team had come across a trail watcher and killed him. There were no other NVA in their immediate area, but the sound of their gunfire would be sure to alert them of the team's presence. With the island as small as it was, there was little chance the team would remain undetected for long. Snuffy's decision to call for extraction was the only choice he had. We all headed back to the Acid Pad. I hadn't counted on going back to Leech Island for some time to come yet. Shit, Division should have been able to see it was just not going to work.

After extracting Snuffy's team, we still had to get Zo's team out. I contacted Kingsman Operations on the UHF radio to let them know what area I'd be working. When I informed them that I'd be operating in the Nui Ke area, they responded, "Kingsman Two-five, this is Kingsman Operations. Be advised Kingsman One-two received fire from a .51 caliber in the vicinity of YD 850032 about an hour ago."

"Kingsman Two-five. Good copy. Thank you."

Jim was plotting the map coordinates as we left the pad en route to Nui Ke. I heard him groan, "Oh, shit." He handed me the map, and I couldn't have agreed with him more. The coordinates of the suspected gun emplacement were on the fourth finger coming off the mountain. The PZ was on the third finger. They were only about four hundred meters apart and at the same elevation. At four hundred meters, a .51 cal will tear a helicopter into very tiny pieces. Not a very nice way to end your day.

"Windy Guard Six, Kingsman Two-five on victor."

"Two-five, Six. Go ahead."

"Six, Two-five. I've received a report that there is a possible .51 cal on the east side of the mountain. I'm going to take a look. If it's there, I think we're going to have a problem."

"Kingsman Two-five, this is Windy Guard Six. I want you to RTB [return to base] and stand by with Kingsman One-eight."

"Six, Two-five. Negative. If that son of a bitch has that damn gun dug in where I think he does, it may be a setup. Your people and us will be suckered into the biggest fucking ambush you have ever seen. I'm going down to have a look."

As the old saying went, "The silence was deafening." It seemed a long time before Eklund came back on the radio.

"Two-Five, Six. Be advised, I don't have any gun support for you at this time."

"Roger, Six. Understand. No gun cover. I know you're kind of busy right now, but if time permits, try to keep an eye on this side of the mountain. If you see a very large cloud of smoke coming out of the trees, you'll know that I won't be able to make the extraction."

"Two-five, Six. Okay, wise-ass. Try to be careful."

We knew that he was there. Now all we had to do was get him to give us his home address. If we could do that, we'd be able to deliver his package airmail. I figured the only way to get him to reveal his location was to get so close that he would have to fire at us.

With the gunships working on the northeast flank of the mountain, I had to be careful not to fly into their impact area. My plan was to come off the top and make a high-speed run down the finger where the enemy gun emplacement had been plotted. I stayed as low as possible over the trees as we came down the finger. The airspeed had built up to one hundred knots as we approached the suspected location.

I saw out of my left window the bomb crater on the other finger that was to be used as the PZ. Using this as a reference point, I was able to determine when I would be directly over the gun position. If I was correct, when the PZ was at my nine o'clock position, I would be directly over the gun. I'd explained all of this to the crew before commencing my run. If we didn't have any luck on the first try, I planned to do a 180-degree turn at the bottom of the finger and come back uphill at a slower speed.

Jim, Tom Turck, Warner, and I were looking as we passed over the point we'd plotted on the map. All we saw were trees. At the bottom of the mountain, we were heading due east. I continued out over the valley before turning back to the west. I wanted to be at an airspeed of 120 knots before we started our climb back up the mountain. I hoped my calculations had been right. If they were, we should have airspeed of between fifty and sixty knots when we passed over the plotted position.

Everything was looking good as we reached the base of the mountain. Airspeed was 120 knots. Then we started our run back up the way we'd just come down. I saw that the four gunships had pulled off the target area, and Eklund had two F-4s hitting the area on the south side of the mountain. The gunships were holding off to the northwest at about five thousand feet. As we came abreast of the PZ, we were paying so much attention to the ground, trying to spot that damn gun, that I hadn't noticed our airspeed. When I finally looked back inside the aircraft, it scared the shit out of me. We were right on the trees and the airspeed had bled down to thirty knots. That was too damn slow in anybody's book. Low and slow like we were, the bad guys could have hit us with a goddamn rock if they'd wanted to. And still all we saw were trees.

"Kingsman Two-five, this is Windy Guard Six on victor."

"Six, Two-five. Go ahead."

"Two-five, Six. How are you doing down there?"

"Six, Two-five. I've made two runs down that damn finger and back up again, but can't get them to fire at me."

"Two-five, Six. Why don't you head on back to the Acid Pad and take a break?"

"Six, Two-five. Goddamn it, Ken, he's there. I know he's there. I can feel the son of a bitch watching me. I'm going to try one more time. This time I'll come from north to south and have my door guns start firing as I cross the PZ. If we can get close enough, maybe I can make him return fire."

"Two-five, Six. Roger. I'll try to keep you in sight."

We'd been trying to get the damn fool to come out and play for the past half hour. If he didn't come out next time, I was going to take my ball and go home. We moved up about five miles to the north. Turning back to the south, I set up to cross the PZ at five hundred feet above the trees. As soon as we were over it, the door gunners began firing as far forward as possible. I'd told them I wanted them to hit the top of the finger where we thought the gun emplacement was located.

I watched the red tracers going into the trees ahead as both door guns were firing. The sound of the two M-60s with their muzzles pointed forward was very loud. He was down there. I knew he was down there.

Green tracers leaped at us out of the trees, mixing with the red tracers from my door guns as they passed. Then I saw the camouflage being pulled away from the gun. The gun pit was a large round hole in the ground about six feet across. There was a mound of dirt in the center, upon which the gun was mounted. In this way, the gun could be fired 360 degrees. There were four men in the pit. The tracers from Tom's M-60 were hitting all around them and down in the pit.

I brought the aircraft into a hard left-hand turn right over the gun pit, and watched as the red tracers tore into the bodies of the four men moving frantically inside the hole. Well, that was one part of their plan that didn't work. Now all I had to do was figure out what to do about the gun itself. The gun crew was down, but as soon as I departed the area the enemy would simply bring in another crew.

"Windy Guard Six, this is Kingsman Two-five."

"Two-five, Six. Go."

"Six, Two-five. I found the .51 cal and have knocked out the gun crew, but I'm going to need some help in taking care of the gun itself."

"Kingsman Two-five, Six. You did what?"

"Six, Two-five. I say again, I just got the goddamn gun crew. Now I need a little help with the gun."

"Roger, Two-five. Stand by."

We continued to orbit the gun position. The one thing I

didn't want to happen was for the NVA to get another crew into that hole where the .51 cal was sitting. I couldn't see any movement under the trees, and we weren't taking any fire, but that didn't mean a whole hell of a lot. They could have the entire North Vietnamese Army under that vegetation and I still wouldn't have been able to see them.

"Kingsman Two-five, Windy Guard Six. I'm sending you Saber Three-three with a light fire team. They've only got twenty minutes left on station."

"Roger, Six. Break. Saber Three-three, Kingsman Two-five. Are you with me?"

"Two-five, Saber Three-three. Roger that. What have you got for me?"

"Three-three, Two-five. There is a .51 cal with a dead crew just below my location. I need you to beat up the gun. I'll mark the target with smoke for you."

I saw the two gunships coming in from the north at about 2,500 feet. However, they had only a short time on station, so I wanted to make sure I got a good mark on the target. So here we go, low and slow. As we came across the gun position, I came to a hover and Tom dropped the smoke grenade into the hole.

"Saber Three-three, Kingsman Two-five. Smoke's out."

"Okay, Two-five. I've got strawberry." (Red smoke.)

"Roger, Three-three. It's all yours."

We climbed up and to the left so we could watch the show. The lead Cobra started his dive and fired the first pair of rockets from about a quarter of a mile out from the target. Before the first pair had reached the target, he'd punched off three more pairs. As we watched, the first two rockets disappeared into the center of the red smoke. In the explosion that followed, I saw the machine gun fly into the air and then fall back into the pit. The next three pairs of rockets impacted in and around the place that used to be an enemy gun position. When I looked up, I saw that the wingman had just fired four more pairs of rockets into the same area. Well, one thing was for certain, they wouldn't have to worry about burying the bodies.

"Windy Guard Six, Kingsman Two-five. I'm back with you. Saber Three-three and his partner done good. We won't have to worry about our friends with the .51 anymore."

"Two-five, Six. That's good, but now we have another minor problem. Windy Guard Two-two has people after him, so we have to get them out. He's back to the top of the mountain and they've got movement below them."

"Roger, Six. Understand he is to be picked up at the same spot where I dropped him off."

So, being the wise-ass that I was, and trying to show how unconcerned and nonchalant I could be, I came back on the radio. "Six, Two-five. So what's the problem?"

"Problem is, Two-five, the Two-two element is being mortared again, and the guns have to return to base to refuel and rearm. There are no other guns available."

I didn't think Eklund was aware of all of the problems this situation brought up, the most obvious being the lack of gun support. The next was that I had only an hour of fuel on board, so the extraction would have to be made soon. The Two-two element was in contact, and they had no place to go but off that mountain. Who would get there first?

My most serious concern was the mortars. The NVA of course knew about the bomb under the fire base helipad, so they had to have zeroed the pad with their mortars. If I was anywhere over the fire base on the top of the mountain, and they dropped a mortar round on that pad, it would detonate the damn bomb. And some dumb-ass helicopter pilot and his crew would become its first and last victims. Christ, how did I ever get myself into those ungodly situations?

What was it that Walkabout had said? "We can hear the rounds when they leave the tubes. Sounds like they were firing from down in the valley just to the north of us." Okay, if that was the case, why not go have a look while we were en route to the extraction point?

"Windy Guard Six, Kingsman Two-five. What is your fuel state?"

"Two-five, Six. I have about thirty minutes before I turn into a pumpkin."

"Okay, Six. It's just you and me. Is Two-two still receiving mortar fire?"

"Two-five, Six. That's affirm."

"Six. I'm going to move down the valley to their north and see what I can find. That's where they reported the rounds were coming from."

"Two-five, Six. You understand you won't have any guns to back you up."

"Yeah, Ken, I understand."

We dropped down to the valley floor and moved to the north. The team had reached the top of the mountain, so I didn't have to worry about it for the moment. I could see the finger starting to rise toward the top of Nui Ke. It was going to be very interesting. There was only one way to make the extract work: I'd have to climb up the side of the mountain at zero forward airspeed, hanging our ass out in the worst possible way. We were going to have to climb close to two thousand feet to reach the top of the mountain. I knew somewhere in the past I'd had better days.

"Okay, guys. You all know the drill. Those of you who want to go to the party can stay on the aircraft. Those who don't want to go can get out and walk." I believe if we hadn't been fifty feet over a triple-canopy jungle, everybody would have gotten out and walked. My guys didn't think the extraction was fun anymore.

I couldn't figure out in my own mind just what I was trying to prove. I seemed to be obsessed with doing the impossible. Well, fuck it. The difficult we do immediately. The impossible will take just a little longer.

We continued our slow climb up the finger. I didn't know what I hoped to find, but something was down there. I could feel it. After climbing about two-thirds of the way up the mountain, I saw in my chin bubble something I couldn't quite bring myself to believe. There, right in front of me, were three mortar tubes and about fifteen people milling around them. They were firing rounds just as fast as they could drop them into the tubes. Tom saw them at the same time I did. There was no need for me to say anything. He was already firing before the sight in front of me had a chance to register.

I guess, in a case like that, instinct took over. I don't remember doing anything, but the next thing I knew, the aircraft was in a hard left-hand turn, almost lying on its side, and Tom was pouring M-60 machine-gun fire into the mortar position. People were running and falling, falling and running. I didn't even try to count them. It was like a beautiful dream. Then came the explosions. First, there was one, then another, and another and another, until I lost count. Ken told me later there were twenty-two secondary explosions. We must have hit a round just as it was leaving the tube.

After the fifth or sixth explosion, I pulled in all the power I could and started to climb. It just so happened that the aircraft was heading to the north. I would probably still be climbing if I hadn't heard Eklund on the radio.

"Kingsman Two-five, Windy Guard Six. Where are you going?"

That call brought me back to reality. I didn't know where I'd been, but I sure as hell knew I didn't belong there.

"Six, Two-five. I'm trying to get in a position so I can get an overall view of the LZ."

"Two-five, Six. The team is ready for extraction on the top of the hill. They still have uninvited guests below them."

"Six, Two-five. Tell them I will meet them on top of the penthouse. If they can't make that, let me know."

"Two-five, Six. The penthouse is agreeable to them."

I had to lose fifteen hundred feet in a hurry. A high overhead approach was the only thing that would work because it would provide the least amount of exposure time. So we fell out of the air at an indicated two thousand feet a minute. When we rolled out at the bottom of the approach, we were lined up with the abandoned fire support base. The command bunker was in sight, but I didn't see any of the people I was supposed to pick up.

"Windy Guard Two-two. Where the hell are you?"

"Two-five, Two-two. We're on the edge of the fire base. We have you in sight."

The team was firing down the hill as we flew over the PSP pad toward the bunker. Looking down through my chin bubble, I could see the bomb still under the PSP. As we reached the bunker, four of the team members got up and started running toward the aircraft. Clifton and Linderer remained back on the edge to provide covering fire. When the first four were on board, Clifton and Linderer came at a dead run.

At last everybody was on the aircraft, and I decided it was time to go home. I'd had enough of this shit for one day. One more takeoff, one more landing, and then I was going to get knee-walking drunk.

We'd been flying for well over an hour and had used over half of our fuel load. The aircraft was fairly light, so the departure wouldn't be a problem. I moved off the bunker and pointed the nose of the aircraft toward Camp Eagle. As we came off the top of the mountain, everyone started firing into the jungle below. They couldn't see anything, but hopefully the fire would keep the bad guys' heads down. And, who knew, maybe we would get lucky and send some of the NVA on an extended vacation to Buddha.

"Windy Guard One-zero, this is Kingsman Two-five. We're off Nui Ke with all of your people on board and en route to your location."

"Kingsman Two-five, Windy Guard One-zero. Roger."

"One-zero, Two-five. Would you call my Operations and ask them to send a fuel truck to your location? It's getting late, and I want to shut this thing down and take a good look at it before it gets too dark."

"Two-five, One-zero. Good copy."

When we were on short final to the Acid Pad, it looked like the entire LRP community had turned out to welcome the team home. I was beginning to wonder if I'd have a place to land. As soon as we were on the ground and the team had gotten off the aircraft, they were mobbed. The hugging and backslapping began in earnest. Most of the LRPs there had figured they would never see those six men again.

I was so damn tired I just sat there watching as Jim began

shutting down the aircraft and Tom and Warner checked to see if we'd taken any hits. Fortunately, we hadn't, but I sure as hell couldn't see why not.

Eklund landed behind us just as we finished refueling. Off the helipad, the celebration was still going on full tilt. I got out of my aircraft and joined in along with the rest of my crew. Eklund was walking toward us but he didn't look happy. What the hell was his problem? I thought everything had gone pretty well. We'd beaten up the bad guys and hadn't lost anybody in the process. What more could anyone ask for? Maybe he was pissed off at my playing John Wayne. If so, to hell with him.

As it turned out, Eklund was not mad at me. After I heard what he had to say, I wished he had been. "There's no easy way to tell you this," he said. "Zo, your team is going back out."

Zo looked at him like he was someone from another world. The only thing he said was, "When?"

Eklund stood there looking as though he was going to be sick. Shaking his head from side to side, he replied, "Tonight."

"Where?"

"Back to the base of Nui Ke."

Zo's face didn't show any emotion at all. "Sir, you've got to be kidding! Nobody in his right mind would send us back out there."

"Zo, we don't have any choice in the matter. Division wants to find out what you stumbled onto out there that made the NVA come out and fight."

"Okay, if that's the way you want it. But I want to replace Schwartz. He's suffering from heat prostration. I'll take Larry Saenz in his place."

"I don't have any problem with that, Zo. Get them ready."

Sgt. Ray Zoschak and the other members of his team picked up their gear and headed slowly toward the ammo bunker. The decision had been made for them. There was no time or need for further discussion. We were going back.

We hadn't had the opportunity to do a VR of the backside

of the mountain. Finding an LZ in the dark was going to be an interesting proposition. Air strikes and artillery had been hitting the area off and on all day. With some luck, we'd be able to find a suitable place to insert the team. We would have to make our approach from north to south, flying up the narrow valley. That would mean we'd be climbing as well as trying to spot a hole in the jungle in the dark. I guess it could have been worse, but I really couldn't see how.

Chapter
Seventeen

"Mr. Grant, I don't really give a good rat's ass what you want or think. This is my team. I've been working them all day and this will be my insertion."

"Goddamn it, Bill. You had your turn with the last extraction. It's my turn now."

Grant was pissed off. He wanted the mission, but there was no way in hell I was going to give it to him. I knew that he thought I'd already had enough for that day, and he may have been right. It had indeed been a very long and stressful day. But the LRPs were my people, and I was going to put them in, or no one was.

"Look, W.T., this is no longer open for discussion. I don't want to hear any more about it."

There hadn't been time for a formal briefing before the team came back down to the helipad. The aircraft were running, with the copilots sitting at the controls. W.T., Captain Eklund, and I were yelling above the sound of the running helicopters.

The plan we came up with would not have been approved by anyone who had the least bit of common sense. Since we hadn't done a visual reconnaissance, we had no idea what we'd find out there. Eklund decided he'd lead the way up the valley with his position lights on bright, and use his searchlight to light up the left (east) side of the mountain. I would follow him, blacked out. If I saw an area I thought could serve as an LZ, I'd let him know over the VHF radio. W.T., with his lights on as well, would be following me.

I hoped the NVA would be concentrating on the lead ship,

as well as the trail aircraft, and fail to notice me. Once I made my approach, W.T. would overfly me and continue up the valley behind Eklund. After I completed the insertion, I'd come out of the LZ, do a hard pedal turn, then head back down the valley the way I'd come. There was no doubt the other two aircraft would take fire. Their lights would make too tempting a target for the NVA to pass up.

We departed Camp Eagle as a flight of three, with Eklund in the C&C aircraft in the lead. I dropped back about a quarter of a mile behind the C&C, and W.T. was about the same distance behind me.

Damn, it was dark! There was no moon, and a slight over-cast. As we headed toward the mountains, the only things I could see were the lights of the C&C aircraft in front of me.

Looking in the back of the aircraft, I got the feeling that all the team members felt the way I did. We'd just been issued death warrants. How could that be? Even a condemned man is always given the opportunity for a final meal; hell, we hadn't even been offered a drink before taking off.

There was no chatter on the radio. The only sound was the thumping of the rotor blades. A single thought kept playing through my mind: What in the hell am I doing here? And the answer kept coming back the same: This is what you get paid to do. I should have asked for a raise.

"Kingsman Two-five, Windy Guard Six on victor."

"Six, Two-five. Go ahead."

"Are you ready to go to work?"

"Roger that."

"Okay, Two-five. I'm starting my turn up the valley."

"Roger, Six. I'm right behind you. Break. One-eight, you copy?" Two clicks on the radio told me that W.T. had moni-tored the exchange between Ken and myself. Strange, but W.T. was not very talkative that night. I wondered why.

I kept my distance behind the C&C as we started up the valley. With all of its lights on, I didn't have any problem keeping the C&C aircraft in sight. W.T. would not be as fortu-nate. With my aircraft blacked out, he could only guess at my location.

As soon as we entered the valley, Ken in the lead helicopter had the searchlight and landing light turned on. He was doing a hell of a job lighting up the east side of the slope. We would have to make the insertion on the first pass or not do it at all. As soon as his lights came on, my night vision went to hell. Damn, none of us had thought much about that. Well, shit! There was nothing that could be done about it now.

Ken continued moving up the valley. The lights revealed where the earlier air strikes and artillery had torn up the mountainside. They'd done one hell of a job. I would have hated to be down there during the day. But for some reason, we couldn't spot any of the bomb craters suitable for LZs that we had spotted during the overflights.

We continued moving up the valley. The searchlight was moving back and forth over the slope when it hesitated momentarily on a huge anvil-shaped boulder near the base of the ridge, about the size of a two-and-a-half-ton truck. It was about eight feet high and seemed relatively flat on top. I keyed the radio twice to let Ken know I'd spotted the boulder and believed I could use it as an LZ. I heard W.T. key his radio twice to confirm that he'd also gotten a fix on the area.

The C&C continued to move up the valley as I began the approach. I knew W.T. would be coming up to overfly the LZ but would keep his lights shining on the west slope so as not give away my position. I sure as shit hoped our system would work.

Up the valley, lines of green tracers were arcing upward toward the C&C aircraft from both sides. Well, that was his problem. I had my own problems, and they seemed to be coming in bunches.

My instrument lights were dimmed as low as possible and I could only just make out the attitude indicator. With the loss of my night vision, I was damn near blind. Spotting the boulder I had to use as the LZ, I immediately set up an angle of approach that would take me right to that point, if all went well.

It was so dark that I almost had to feel my way down the approach angle. Luckily, earlier in the day, air strikes and artillery had hit the area I was going into. The vegetation had been blown away, making the area around the boulder a little cleaner. However, I still couldn't see the boulder well enough to determine if I could land on it. W.T. passed over me from a little to the right side. Goddamn perfect! By then he was taking fire. But still none was being directed at me.

I could just barely make out the top of the boulder, and concluded there was no way I'd be able to land on top of it. It was just too small. We continued the approach to the boulder area without really knowing what else was down there. I'd managed to get a brief but good look at it in the bright light from Eklund's slick, and thought I might be able to get in close enough for the team to jump down on top of it. I could feel Jim almost touching the controls as we got closer and closer to the point of termination.

Our airspeed zeroed out as we came to a hover. To my left front, about forty meters away, was the boulder. Again I could see it was too small to land on and leave room for the team to jump out onto it. I eased the aircraft toward the top of the boulder with the idea of just getting close. In the daylight it might have been fun, but at night with no landing light and no moon to provide illumination, it was a real bitch. I could hear and feel the main rotor blade as it struck the limbs of trees overhanging the boulder.

We continued to inch toward the "LZ." I'd already made up my mind that we'd gone far enough when the left skid grazed the top edge of the boulder. The aircraft lifted slightly, then settled back down. I held it as steady as I could. It was not the ideal way to make an insertion, but it was too late to quibble over ideals. The aircraft's left skid was resting on top of the boulder, and the right skid was hanging out in thin air. The only way I could tell if I was moving forward was when the rotor blades started to hit the trees again. It might have been only seconds, but it seemed a lot longer.

I felt the weight change as the team left the aircraft. Tom yelled over the intercom that the team was out and we were clear. It was time to get the hell out of there! Knowing I could not go forward, and not knowing what was above me, I would have to back out—once again, no easy task in the dark. I couldn't allow the aircraft to lose any altitude. If I let the tail rotor hit a tree, or even a tree limb, it would be all over but the hand-clapping.

Turck and Warner were hanging out of their gunners' wells trying to see what was behind us. Jim was watching the instruments and trying to see if there was anything on the right side of the aircraft. Finally we were clear. Looking up ahead, I could see the other two aircraft climbing out of the valley with lines of green tracers following them.

It felt good to be away from the trees and the side of the mountain. It was time for a right pedal turn and to get the hell out of Dodge. Lowering the nose of the aircraft, we dove back down into the valley. Up to that point, nothing more had been said over the radio.

"Windy Guard Six, Kingsman Two-five is clear."

"Two-five, Six. Let's meet at three thousand feet."

"Six, Two-five. Roger."

Looking up, I could see the lights of the two aircraft high above me. Man, I was beat! I looked over at Jim; he was sitting back with his eyes closed. He hadn't said a word during the entire flight. I wondered if he still loved our kind of work. I decided I might as well let him earn his flight pay for a while. "Okay, Jim, take the controls and marry up with Six and One-eight."

It was my turn to try to relax. After lighting a cigarette, I let my mind replay what had just happened. We'd made the insertion without receiving any fire, but I didn't think we fooled anyone. The NVA had to know we'd just put people in, and it would not take them long to find them. We were going to have to make an extraction, probably soon. Going back to land on the boulder was out of the question. Trying to make a McGuire extraction would be next to suicidal. The only thing left was to use the ladders.

We were in a high orbit for about five minutes when we received an all clear from Windy Guard Two-two. They'd moved to the base of the boulder and were lying dog. They hadn't yet heard any movement immediately around them.

"Windy Guard Six, Kingsman Two-five on victor."

"This is Six. Go ahead."

"Six, we are going to need the ladders."

"Two-five, Six. I agree. I'll have them waiting on the pad for you."

"Six, I want ladders for both aircraft."

"Roger, Two-five. They'll be ready when you land."

Jim pointed the aircraft toward Camp Eagle and rolled the nose over to gain airspeed. We knew we had no time to spare.

"One-eight, where are you?"

"Two-five, don't slow up or I'll be kissing your ass."

Shit, I should have known. W.T. knew what I was thinking before I did. Well, the easy part was done. Then the fun began.

As promised, the ladders were waiting on the pad when we arrived. After landing, W.T. and I headed for the Operations tent. The rest of the crew checked the aircraft for battle damage and supervised the installation of the ladders.

Grant and I discussed the insertion and what we knew was soon to come. It was agreed we'd do a repeat performance on the extraction, the only difference being that we would have to use the ladders since we couldn't sit down on top of the boulder. For the extraction we would have a light fire team of Cobras on hand to give us some cover. I described what I'd seen, or better yet, what I hadn't seen, when I had put the team in. It had been so dark going in that I felt I'd been flying by Braille.

We were in the Operations tent for just a few minutes when Jim came in and told us that both aircraft were flyable and the ladders had been installed. As he left, all I could think was, Thank God for a good crew. It made our kind of life bearable.

I'd just sat down and lit up a cigarette when the radio broke squelch. It was as if everyone in the tent had been jabbed with a pin. The tension was unbearable. But not for long. Lieutenant Owens grabbed the radio handset and stood there looking at it. We knew what the next transmission would be.

"Windy Guard Six, this is Windy Guard Two-two. Over."

"Windy Guard Two-two, this is Windy Guard Five. Go ahead."

"Five, Two-two. We're in deep—"

I think his last word was "shit," but I didn't know for sure because I was already out the door at a dead run, with W.T. right on my heals. Both aircraft were already cranking as we reached the helipad. When the call came in, either Cline or Roach must have been monitoring the radio, because by the time I got strapped in, everything was up to speed. All I could think about was getting back to that damn mountain as fast as we could. I didn't even take time to call the tower. To hell with regulations. They could chew my ass later. If I still had one for them to chew. I didn't even get a commo check with W.T. If he was with me, that was fine. If he wasn't, so be it.

We departed the helipad to the north up the valley, then made a hard left-hand break over the 2/17 Cav area. Looking down as I made my break, I could see two Cobras had already cranked and were lifting off.

"Two-five, One-eight. You're up with a flight of two."

Things were starting to fall into place. W.T. was right behind me. A light fire team was on the way. The only thing I didn't know was where in the hell Eklund was. To hell with that too. I'd worry about him later.

"Windy Guard Two-two, this is Kingsman Two-five."

"Kingsman Two-five, this is Windy Guard Two-two. Go."

"Two-two, Two-five. Give me a sitrep."

"Two-five, we're right where you dropped us off. We've got dinks above us on both ridge lines. They're moving down on us."

"Two-two, are you in contact?"

"Negative contact, Two-five, but they're all around us. We can hear them talking. They're tapping sticks together and blowing whistles. Shit, Two-five, they're even blowing bugles."

"Okay, guys, hang on. We're on our way."

I didn't like the situation at all. The voices meant that they were *really* close. The tapping sticks were used to keep the enemy troops in line as they swept forward in the dark.

Whistles were nothing but a method of giving orders. One blast on the whistle might mean go forward, two could mean stop, and three could mean attack. But bugles? Christ, in the ten months I'd been flying in Vietnam, I had never heard of anyone using bugles. The last time I had heard of that was during the Korean War. Why in hell were the NVA using bugles?

"Kingsman Two-five, this is Windy Guard Six."

"Six, this is Two-five. Go ahead."

"I'm over the area now at five thousand feet. I was en route back from Division when the call from Two-two came in."

"Roger, Six. I'm about zero five out with a flight of two."

"Two-Five, Six. Where are the snakes?" The Cobras.

Before I had a chance to reply to Eklund, I heard the following: "Windy Guard Six, this is Saber Two-three with a light fire team. We're passing Two-five on his right side now. Will be with you shortly."

"Six, Two-five. Let's do this just like we did before. You lead and One-eight will bring up the rear."

"Okay, Two-five. I'm coming down. Fall in behind me and let's do it."

I watched as the C&C aircraft descended out of five thousand feet. The Cobras were swinging around so they would be behind and above us. It was very comforting. There was no doubt in anybody's mind that they would likely soon be used to their fullest capacity.

"Okay, Six. I'm at your six o'clock, quarter mile. Let's head inbound."

Ken was heading to the east. We would be required to make a right-hand turn to enter the valley low-level and start our climb to the LZ. Once again we'd be right on top of the trees. I watched as the C&C aircraft made a hard ninety-degree bank to the right. Luckily for me, he had his position lights on bright. If he hadn't, I would never have been able to see where he'd made his turn. At that point I had my lights on dim so W.T. could keep me in sight as I made the turn. Once the turn was completed, I would turn off my lights and be completely blacked out. I knew W.T. wouldn't be far behind.

I reached the point where I thought Ken had made his turn and rolled the aircraft into a sharp right-hand turn. When I brought the aircraft level, I heard Jim say over the intercom, "Aw, shit! Bill, look at your attitude indicator."

I glanced down and saw the goddamn thing rolling over and over. It was doing flip-flops and tumbling. Going into that black hole with no horizon, no attitude indicator, and no illumination was about the best way I could think of to kill not only myself and my crew, but also the LRP team I was trying to pick up.

The first thing that entered my mind was to let Jim fly the extraction from the right seat. His attitude indicator was working fine. Scratch that idea. It was not the time or place to find out what kind of a teacher I'd been.

Over the intercom I told Jim, "Hit the lights. Come up steady bright, and turn on the landing and searchlights." All of those thoughts and decisions were made in about a second and a half.

"Kingsman One-eight, this is Two-five. My attitude indicator just went tits up. I'm pulling up. You've got the extraction."

Talk about not missing a beat. With about sixty seconds from the boulder, the only thing I heard from W.T. was, "Okay, Two-five. I've got it."

By that time Eklund and the crew in the C&C had their hands full. They were taking fire from both sides of the valley. The Cobras had been cleared to fire and were shooting the shit out of the west side of the valley. They didn't know where the LZ was located on the east side, so the only fire going in there was from the door gun on the left side of the C&C aircraft.

Since we were low and on the left side of the valley, our only option was to make a climbing right-hand turn 360 degrees to bring us back in behind W.T. Jim stated that he had the controls, and rolled into the turn. I saw the lights of One-eight's aircraft as we started our turn, then they went out. As soon as we were on a heading back up the valley, I took the controls and tried to locate the LZ. It sure was dark down there. Where was One-eight?

Up toward the top of the valley I saw that the C&C was still receiving fire. The whole area seemed to be alive with muzzle flashes, and green tracers were crisscrossing all around the C&C aircraft. Funny, at the time it never occurred to me that I would be next.

I heard W.T. call for a strobe light, and seconds later saw it begin to flash. Then the position lights of his aircraft came on steady bright. He was using the reflection of his lights to judge his distance from the trees. Would I have thought of that? Well, you do whatever works!

We continued up the valley toward the LZ. I'd seen what kind of reception Eklund's aircraft had received on his pass. Now it was my turn. We stayed over the center of the valley. Just before we came abreast of where W.T. was hovering, the green tracers began to converge on us.

We knew there were four bullets between every one of those tracers, and not everyone who was shooting at us was using tracers, so a whole lot of lead was heading up at us. At least little of the fire was directed at W.T.'s hovering aircraft. He was getting some, but not very much.

As I reached the top of the valley, the C&C had already made a 180-degree turn and was headed back down the way he'd come. The enemy fire had not let up at all. I completed my turn and had just started down the valley when I heard W.T. call that he was coming out. I saw the lights of his aircraft and some of the tracers starting to reach up to grab him. Then his lights went out. Eklund had already passed the LZ when One-eight came off the boulder. I completed my run down the valley and was climbing when W.T. turned his lights back on.

"One-eight, Two-five. How are you doing?"

"Two-five, One-eight. Doing fine. I've got five on board and one riding the ladder home."

Pulling up on the left side of W.T.'s aircraft, I saw a figure hanging on the ladder about halfway up. When we got closer, I saw the guy waving at us. I should have known. It was Zoschak!

After falling into a position to the left rear of One-eight's aircraft, I followed him back to the Acid Pad. The plan was simple: We would drop off the team, take the aircraft back to the Castle, and do a good postflight. After that we'd return to the LRP company for one hell of a party.

Well, we put the aircraft to bed, but decided the party would have to wait. W.T. and I had both come to the same conclusion: Our asses were dragging. Talk about cheating death and getting away with it! I'd been shot at more that day than during any other single day in the previous ten months.

We discovered that Eklund's aircraft had taken some hits. Amazingly, W.T. still had his cherry. I will never know how, but I'd gotten away clean. No hits, and the rotor blades hadn't been damaged during the insertion, when I had the blade strikes. When the day began, I thought the mission would be a piece of cake. Little did I realize I'd soon have to eat the whole damn cake, including the plate it came on.

It had been one hell of a long day. Grant, both air crews, and I had been up since 0430 hours. We'd arrived at the Acid Pad at 0600 hours, and it was 2045 hours when we touched down. Fourteen hours and forty-five minutes of mission time, and we still had to take care of our aircraft before we could call it a night. During the last part of the day's activities, it had been exactly forty-two minutes from the time we departed the Acid Pad with Zo's team on board until we made the extraction and returned them to the LRP compound. It was not a very good return on investment in my book.

Two hours later the aircraft had been taken care of and the aftermission reports turned in. Grant and I were standing outside the Operations tent looking at the club, which was about forty feet away. W.T. looked at me and said, "Well, Wild Bill, what do you think?"

Grinning, I looked at him and replied, "Shit, Grant, just another day at the office. I'm going to bed."

Chapter Eighteen

We were back at the Acid Pad at 0800 the following morning. From the looks of the people we saw moving around the area, it was a good thing W.T. and I had decided not to return for the party the night before. We saw some very hungover, very sick people. There would not be any teams going in today. Even if a mission had been planned, I don't think they could have found enough people in any kind of shape to make up a team to go. It must have been some party! I was almost sorry I missed it. Almost.

That was to be a day of rest, a day set aside to come down from yesterday's adrenaline high. In the early afternoon I took Captain Eklund and Lieutenant Williams on an overflight of the east side of the A Shau Valley, as there was a possibility we would be putting teams into the area in the very near future.

I'd worked around there before and didn't like it at all. It was so deep in the mountains that refueling would be a real problem. It would also limit our on-station time. We'd put two infantry battalions into the valley in August, and they had to be extracted after ten days due to the deteriorating weather. Of course, that was a planned operation, and the bad weather had been forecast.

On our way back to Camp Eagle we saw the clouds building in the north. From the looks of the giant thunderheads, I didn't figure there would be any operations for the next few days. And I was right. In late afternoon the rains started. It rained steadily for six days. The tents leaked, and everything we owned was damp and soon began to mildew.

The clouds hung so low that they covered the mountains and obscured the valleys. There was no possible way to insert a team, or even to support the fire bases that were already established. If it hadn't been so damn cold, it would have been nice just to have the time off.

To combat the deplorable conditions, we kept our company Officers' Club (a GP-medium tent) open as much as possible. When we were forced to close, we would head for the Ranger Lounge at the LRP company compound. Very few pilots and crew members were welcome there. If you didn't fly for them, it was immediately made clear that you should find another place to visit for your relaxation.

The weather began to clear on the afternoon of the twelfth. The time off had done a lot for our morale, and all of us were anxious to go back to work. It had already been decided, even before the weather broke, that we would be putting four teams on the east slope of the A Shau Valley. The LRPs had not worked the A Shau since July, so they had no idea what was there. The next day would be used for conducting VRs for all four team leaders.

After the VRs were completed the following afternoon, I took the X-ray team (radio relay team) to Eagles Nest, the fire support base located on top of a 4,700-foot mountain overlooking the valley. It was a small fire base and didn't have enough room where the aircraft could stand by. Because of that, our response time would be close to thirty minutes if a team was compromised.

The insertions began at first light the following morning. All four teams were inserted without incident. All of the aircraft returned to the Acid Pad to stand by. The remainder of the day was uneventful.

Over the next two days we listened as all of the teams reported NVA units moving through their areas of operation. Late in the afternoon of the seventeenth, one of the teams was compromised. The men were able to break contact and were extracted without incident. The other three teams remained undetected, and were brought out the next morning.

After the last extraction, we were given a warning order for a mission scheduled for the afternoon of the next day. Two "heavy teams" (twelve men each) would be going into the Ruong Ruong Valley. S.Sgt. Richard Burnell would take the first team in, with the primary mission of observing enemy troop movement. His secondary mission would be to try to locate and destroy an NVA radio transmitter that was working in his area of operation.

Burnell's heavy team would consist of "Honest" John Burford as the ATL; John Looney, the senior RTO; Lieutenant Owen Williams, junior RTO; Kenn Miller, John Meszaros, Terry Clifton, Don Harris, "Snuffy" Smith, Jim Evans, Larry Chambers, and the team medic.

The second team, led by S.Sgt. Al Contreros, had a primary reconnaissance mission, and a secondary mission to intercept and ambush small NVA units that might be moving through their AO. Army Intelligence had information that the commander of the 5th NVA Regiment, Colonel Mot, was in the vicinity of the team. They also knew that Colonel Mot was wearing two 9mm pistols with pearl handles, and that he made a habit of frequently moving from one jungle outpost to another, with only a small escort for security, to make sure his soldiers stayed on their toes. Colonel Mot had been a thorn in our side for many months. To get him would be the icing on the cake of any operation conducted by the 101st Airborne Division. Strange as it may have seemed, even though he was the enemy commander, the division staff had a grudging respect for him.

Aside from Al Contreros, the second team consisted of Jim Venable, the ATL; Jim Schwartz, Riley Cox, Steve Czepurny, Art Heringhausen, Gary Linderer, Mike Reiff, Frank Souza, and John Sours. Billy B. Walkabout and Jim Bacon were the RTOs. Both teams were made up of experienced people.

After the teams were assigned their missions, Terry Clifton, who had been on Burnell's team, traded places with Jim Schwartz. Clifton, a very good friend of Gary Linderer, wanted to be with him for the mission.

The VRs were flown that afternoon. The area Burnell's team was going into had seven good LZs. There was no problem picking the insertion and extraction points. It looked like a good AO to recon.

The second area, just five klicks to the south, was not so desirable. There was only one spot that could serve as an LZ. That could be a real problem area. If Contreros and his people got into trouble and we couldn't get them out of their original LZ, we'd be forced to attempt a McGuire extraction, and a twelve-man heavy team would require the use of four slicks. If that proved unfeasible, the team would have to break contact and E&E into Burnell's area of operation. In either case, it would be extremely difficult.

Another major cause for concern was the distance to the target area. The teams would be just a little over twenty miles to the southwest of Camp Eagle. Response time could be critical. Maybe it was the memory of the mission of the fourth, but no one seemed to feel good about the one coming up, myself included.

The first team was to be inserted at 1730 hours on the afternoon of the nineteenth, with the second team going in an hour later at coordinates YC 345876. Most of that morning was spent trying to cheer each other up and take our minds off the things that were bothering us. The air crews did not seem too concerned about what was coming up, but the team members were an entirely different story. They were not in the mood for our lighthearted jokes; they were focused and deadly serious about preparations for the upcoming mission.

At one point during the day, I wandered over to the ammo bunker. These guys were crazy or they were planning to start and finish World War III, all in one day. They were loading so much ordnance into their rucksacks that it seemed impossible for them to carry everything. They were loading extra claymores, frags, bandoliers of M-16 ammo, and anything else they could think to pick up. Watching them, I wondered if I'd be able to get the aircraft off the ground if they continued to stuff all of that shit into their rucksacks.

That evening, I departed the Acid Pad with Burnell and five of his team members on board. W.T. followed with the other six. The sun was already getting low in the west. Although it would not be dark for another two hours, the shadows cast by the mountains gave the impression that nightfall was near. The insertion went off as planned. Burnell moved off the LZ, laid dog for about fifteen minutes, then reported no movement, no problems. One down and one to go.

Contreros and his team were on the pad when we returned. It took only a minute to load and we were on our way. With the two LZs so close together, we had to be careful not to draw attention to the area where we'd inserted the first team. We flew west out of Camp Eagle toward FSB Birmingham, then turned south until we came to the Ruong Ruong Valley. At that point we turned east toward the LZ.

The LZ was in sight, and so far everything was looking good. As we got closer, however, we saw that the LZ was nowhere near what we'd planned for; it was nothing more than a steep ravine covered with elephant grass that looked eight to ten feet tall. Hovering over the ravine, I called Eklund and advised him of what we were facing. Just as he told me to abort the mission, I felt the ship go light as the first of the team dropped from the aircraft! There would be no abort! Once one man has gone into the LZ, they all would go. No one on the team would ever allow one man to be left on the ground by himself.

As I pulled out of the LZ, I advised W.T. of the conditions. With half of the team on the ground, there was no doubt that the other half would follow. Going into a climbing left-hand turn, I saw that Grant was already hovering over the ravine. Watching the other half of the heavy team dropping into the LZ, I thought, These people have to be out of their rabbit-ass minds.

With the insertion completed, we pulled out of the area to wait for the all-clear call from Contreros. Ten minutes later we were advised that the elephant grass in the LZ had actually been twelve to fifteen feet high, and that Sgt. John Sours had injured both ankles when he landed on a log hidden in the grass. The team leader had tried to get Sours to go out at that time, but the courageous NCO from Kansas insisted that he'd only twisted his ankles. He wanted to stay with the team, and they would have had to drag him kicking and screaming to the LZ and physically tie him to a McGuire rig, so Contreros decided not to extract him. Also, no one was willing to risk the noise.

With both teams in safely and no contact, we returned to Camp Eagle to stand by until an hour after dark. With the exception of the one man being injured, it had been a perfect day.

We landed back at the Castle a little after 2100 hours. As we were shutting the aircraft down, I received instructions to report to Operations. I left the dirty work of postflighting the aircraft and making sure that it was flyable for the next morning's mission to Cline and the rest of the crew. After dropping off my gear at my hootch, I headed for the Operations tent.

The Operations officer didn't waste any time getting to the point. "Bill, you and Grant have been pulled off the LRP mission for tomorrow." I was not happy to hear that, and he could see I was getting ready to come unglued, so he held his hands up and said, "It won't do any good to argue with me. The orders came from the Old Man. If you think it will do you any good, you can try talking him out of it. Personally, I think you'll be wasting your time. Tomorrow every ship we have flyable will be flying CAs."

Major Addiss, the CO, was still in his office, even at that late hour. Although it was not unusual, since he made a habit of keeping long hours, he seemed to be waiting for me. As I walked in he looked up from the paperwork on his desk and said, "The order stands."

I was not expecting anything quite so abrupt, and it took me by surprise. I guess he could see I wasn't going to take this without an argument. "Look, Bill, you've been working with the LRP units," he said, "so you've got to know how much the NVA are moving. Division is going to be moving a lot of people around to try to upset their plans. In the morning, every damn helicopter that's flyable in the division will be used to move those troops."

That didn't make any sense to me, or maybe I just wasn't

ready to accept what I was hearing. "If all of the aircraft are going to be committed, who's going to cover the teams we have in?"

Major Addiss sat there staring at me, shaking his head, and said, "Nobody."

I couldn't believe it. "What the fuck do you mean, nobody? Who is the stupid son of a bitch who dreamed this up? I'm not going to leave those teams out there to die, just so we can haul a bunch of troops from one place to another." As soon as I stopped yelling, I could see from the look on the major's face that I'd gone too far.

But before he had a chance to nail my hide to the wall, I held my hands up and continued, "Sorry, sir. That was out of line. Look, boss, I've got twenty-four men in the field right now who are depending on me. Based on the amount of activity in the area, and their missions, there's no doubt that they're going to get their shit shot away. I cannot just abandon them. They go on these missions knowing they won't be left behind. I've never left anyone before. Everybody comes home. That includes the dead and the wounded."

Major Addiss said, "Captain, there's nothing I can do. The mission came down from Division. I asked them about your situation and was told that all available aircraft would be committed to the morning's operation."

"Bullshit, boss. I'm not going to write them off. There's got to be a way to cover them. If I have to, I'll go see General Zais right now, tonight, and try to get this goddamn thing straightened out. The LRP company is the division's eyes and ears. I know damn well that the general is not going to knowingly write off those assets."

I'm sure Major Addiss could see I was dead serious about it and wouldn't be put off. I was not being disrespectful, but I was simply not going to back down. "Bill," he said, "you just can't go waking up a two-star general at eleven-thirty at night just because you don't like the mission you've been assigned." Well, that was his opinion. Now it became a test of wills.

The major must have thought I was completely out of my

mind. Looking at him with absolutely no expression on my face, I asked, "How much do you want to bet? The worst thing they can do is decide I'm out of my mind and send me home early. At this point, I really don't care. If I'm not allowed to support those teams, then they'll never trust me again. As for myself, I'll never be able to look anyone from that company in the face again. Unlike a lot of people in this division, I'd like to think that my word still means something."

Major Addiss must have believed I would do exactly as I'd said. "Well, let me call Division and see what can be done." I sat there for a few minutes waiting, until the CO told me to leave and come back in fifteen or twenty minutes. I wondered what kind of conversation would take place on the phone while I was gone. It must have been very interesting, because when I returned, the CO informed me that if there was a problem with either of the teams, Grant and I would be released from the mission we were on to support the LRPs. I could buy that solution; the only other thing I was insistent about was that W.T., who was in the first platoon, should be assigned to fly with the second platoon. I did not want us to become separated at any time during the morning's mission.

After leaving the Orderly Room, I started to go to Grant's hootch to let him know what was going to happen in the morning. Then I realized it was already after midnight and he'd be asleep so there was no good reason to wake him. Besides, if I told him we'd been pulled off of the LRP mission, he would more than likely want to try to kill the person who'd come up with that dumb-ass idea. And if I hadn't been so damn tired myself, I probably would have led the charge. In about four and half hours we would be up and getting ready to start another day. I had a feeling it would be a very, very long one.

Chapter Nineteen

It couldn't have been time to get up already. I'd just closed my eyes. Yet the lights were on, and the other people in the hootch were up and moving around. I sat up and put my feet on the floor. That was the hard part; as long as I had my feet on the floor, I wouldn't fall asleep. If I let my head hit the pillow again, it would all be over. They would never be able to get me up and moving. I looked around for the cigarettes and lighter that should have been on my footlocker, but they weren't there. I realized then that I still had my uniform on. I'd taken my boots off, but that was as far as I'd gotten undressed before falling asleep.

After showering and shaving, I headed for the mess tent. Food was the last thing I wanted; just coffee, lots of hot, black coffee, to get my mind functioning.

As I approached the mess tent I saw Grant on his way back to his hootch. Damn, I had to figure out how I was going to tell him about being pulled off the LRP mission. I wasn't looking forward to that.

Leaving the mess tent, I carried all my gear to my aircraft. Jim, Tom, and Warner were already there preflighting the aircraft and loading their M-60s and ammo on board. After briefing them on the mission change, and trying to answer all of their questions—the same ones I'd asked the CO the night before—I headed for the first platoon area to find Grant.

The sun was up, and it looked like it would be good day for flying. There were no clouds in the sky, and a light breeze was blowing in from the east. On a normal day one would ordinarily think, What more could I ask for? However, we didn't think it was going to be a normal day.

W.T. was the only one in his hootch. He'd just finished shaving, and I could still see a bit of soap on his sideburns and at one corner of his mustache, where he hadn't rinsed his face yet. He was brushing his teeth as I entered. Damn, he was in a cheerful mood.

He greeted me as always, "Good morning, you old turkey. What's up?"

I couldn't bring myself to look at him. Staring out the door toward the CO's hootch, I muttered, "W.T., we've been pulled."

Still brushing his teeth, he asked, "What do you mean, pulled?"

"We've been pulled off the LRP mission."

"What the hell do you mean?" he said. Now I had his full attention. "That's got to be the dumbest damn thing they could do. We already know where the teams are. Who are they putting on to cover them?"

"Nobody. Every aircraft in the battalion is going to be used on CAs today."

His reaction was even more violent than mine had been. He reached over and grabbed his knife from his bunk. He must have slept with that damn K-Bar. I'd never seen him without it.

Luckily, I was standing between Grant and the door. I didn't know where he thought he was going, and I doubted seriously if he knew. But I had to make certain he didn't get out of there. With toothpaste running down his chin, he looked as though he had a full-blown case of rabies.

Putting both of my hands on his chest to hold him, and blocking the door with my body, I said, "Relax, partner; there's nothing you can do about it. I tried last night. The only thing we have going for us is that if the teams get into contact, the Old Man will release us from the CA."

That calmed him down a little. I was sure glad he wasn't mad at me; for a young guy, he could get as mean as a snake.

"Okay, here's the other part of what I worked out with the major. You'll be flying with the second platoon today. If we're needed, I don't want you off having fun without me. Now get your shit together, and don't cause any trouble."

W.T. stood looking at me, that little shit-eating grin flashing across his face. I knew then that he would be all right.

Looking at my watch, I saw it was a few minutes before six o'clock in the morning. "Okay, briefing at 0600, crank at 0645, and pull pitch at 0700. See you at the briefing."

As I was going out the door I heard him behind me saying, "Yes, sir, boss. I'll be a good boy." I felt a lot better.

Grant and I had made the worst mistake a combat soldier could possibly make. We'd become too close to the people we were supporting. We'd made friends with them. We knew them by their first names, knew about their families, their wives, children, mothers, fathers, and girlfriends. If something happened to any of them, it would be like losing a part of ourselves. It was too late to do anything about that now.

The 0645 hours crank was put on hold; it was stand by the aircraft and wait. The waiting was always the hardest part, especially with the situation we were in. I wanted to get the CAs over with and be released back to the LRP company. We waited ninety minutes, and still nothing happened.

At 0820 hours a runner came out of Operations. He informed me that Lieutenant Williams had called to relay the information that John Sours had just been medevacked; both his ankles had been broken on the insertion the night before. He'd thought they were only sprained, and took his boots off during the night. By morning he couldn't lace them up again. It was good news to hear that he was on his way to the hospital, but his loss would leave the team one experienced man short. However, that was better than having someone along who could not E&E if it became necessary.

I headed down the line to let W.T. and Barry Schreiber, Grant's "peter" pilot (copilot) for the day, know about Sours. I told W.T. that John had been pulled out, and he was so happy to hear that John was safe, you'd have thought that I'd given him a three-day pass.

A little after 0900 hours we were given the word to crank. Finally we were on the move. Anything was better than waiting. The sooner we started, the sooner we'd be released. Our first pickup was a unit staging out of FSB Vehgel. Using all ten aircraft, we would be able to relocate the entire company in two lifts.

Ten minutes into the flight the FM radio, on which we were monitoring the LRP frequency, came alive. Contreros's team had just sprung an ambush and killed nine NVA. They were searching the bodies. It looked like they'd caught a headquarters unit, including a staff officer and four nurses. The search of the bodies produced four .45 caliber pistols and four AK-47 rifles. More important, they recovered a large number of documents, as well as several maps, in a canvas case that the officer had been carrying.

There was still no word on our release, so we continued with our mission, moving the troops off the fire base to the field. After two hours we went back to Camp Eagle to refuel. The POL point was busier than I'd ever seen it before. It seemed every aircraft in the battalion needed to gas up at the same time. We had to sit there and wait our turn. Damn, the waiting was maddening.

W.T. and I were still monitoring the LRP frequency. A ready-reaction force was supposed to be inserted to develop the situation. The LRP team was to be extracted after the reaction force was on the ground. But something had gone wrong and this had failed to materialize. The team was still in the area of the ambush two hours after springing it. That was really asking for trouble. They should have been pulled immediately after the action, or moved the hell out of the area.

Our next mission was the same as before, with the exception that we were working out of FSB Birmingham. That was good because it put us closer to the LRP teams. We worked with that unit for the next hour, then headed back to the refueling point.

There had been no other radio traffic from the Linwood team Two-one, which had sprung the ambush. Then it dawned on me that we wouldn't hear anything unless they were relaying through the X-ray team. I suddenly got a very cold feeling. I knew something was wrong.

"Kingsman Six, this is Kingsman Two-five on victor."

"Two-five, Six. Go ahead."

"Six, Two-five. Boss, I've got a team in trouble. You've got to get me out of here now."

We'd just started refueling. I sat in the cockpit waiting for a reply. The silence on the radio was deafening. Christ, what was taking so damn long? Then came the answer to my prayer.

"Kingsman Two-five and One-eight are released for their LRP mission."

"Six, Two-five. Good copy."

Just as Tom climbed back into the aircraft, W.T. called and said he was ready to go. I called the tower and advised them I had a flight of two departing the POL point to the west. Without waiting for their reply, I pulled in maximum power—fifty pounds of torque. The aircraft leaped off the ground as if it had a mind of its own. Holding the nose down, I let the aircraft accelerate, while gaining only one hundred feet of altitude. By the time we came to the perimeter fence, we were going through one hundred knots forward airspeed.

After passing over the fence, I put the aircraft into a fifteen-hundred-foot-a-minute climb. I knew without looking that W.T. was right behind me. There was no reason to ask where he was. If he'd had a problem, he would have let me know.

We were passing through sixteen hundred feet when we started picking up radio transmissions. At first they were broken and unreadable. Then, as we continued to climb, I could make out that the team was in heavy contact. One man had been hit, but the medevac was not on station and it would be some time before it would be available. Linwood Six—Captain Eklund—was in the area in a LOH, working as the C&C.

"Linwood Six, this is Kingsman Two-five."

"Two-five, Six. Go ahead."

"This is Two-five with a flight of two, five minutes out."

"Two-five, we've got a man down."

"Can he wait for a medevac?"

"Negative, Bill. We've got to get him out as soon as possible. He's hurt bad."

In the distance I saw a faint cloud of yellow smoke drifting up through the trees. Off to the west were two Cobras and an OH-6, the Cobras making gun runs from north to south on the west side of the smoke.

There was no way we could land there or even get low enough to use a ladder, if we'd had a ladder on board, which we did not. The team had moved uphill from the LZ after the insertion, and the trees were between 100 and 150 feet high. I kept thanking my lucky stars that I'd let W.T. convince me to leave the McGuire rigs on the aircraft. I had wanted to take them off before starting on the CAs that morning, but he talked me out of it. Now it looked as though the McGuire rigs would be the only way to get the wounded man out, if we could get him out at all.

I asked Eklund for more information. The wounded man was the ATL, Jim Venable, who had been hit as he was attempting to signal the C&C aircraft with a mirror to pinpoint the team's location. He was hit at least three times, in the arm, the neck, and the chest. He needed to get out of there fast.

The team was still receiving heavy fire from the south and southeast. The NVA had gotten between them and the LZ. The only way to make the extraction would be by McGuire rig. I had a multitude of questions. Was Venable conscious? What type of chest wound did he have? Could he stand the ride at the bottom of a 120-foot rope? Would we be able to take him all the way back to Camp Eagle dangling under the aircraft, or would we have to land somewhere and pull him inside? If we had to land, where would be a safe place? There were many more questions to be answered, but the biggest was whether we'd be able to get the McGuire rig through the trees to the team below. Hell, would we even be able to find them?

"Linwood Six, Kingsman Two-five. We're going to try getting him out with the McGuire."

"Roger, Two-five. Contact Linwood Two-one on this frequency."

"Linwood Two-one, this is Kingsman Two-five. How do you copy?"

"Two-five, I've got you loud and clear. We've got big trouble down here."

"Okay, hang on. I'm going to try to get Jim out. Can he handle a McGuire?"

"He keeps drifting in and out. We can get him hooked up if you can get it to us."

"Two-one, Two-five. I'm about one minute out. Try to guide me over your position."

The jungle canopy below was almost solid. The only way we could find the team was by their vectoring us in by the sound of the aircraft. We would then try to use our rotor wash to blow some of the top layer of vegetation away so we could see the ground. Once that was accomplished, we'd try to lower the McGuire rig to them. We would have to be directly over them to make the extraction. Venable could not be moved due to the enemy fire. Learning the art of hovering in flight school had been a challenge, but once again, this was where all of the work, sweat, and frustration paid off.

Jim Bacon, the RTO, kept talking to us, moving us closer and closer to the point right above them. Finally he said we sounded like we were in the right spot. Still, I saw nothing but green canopy through my chin bubble. We were about fifty feet above the treetops. I began lowering the aircraft straight down. The lower we descended, the more effect the rotor wash had. The crew chief and gunner were lying on the floor of the aircraft trying to see through the trees. They were also watching to make sure that the tail rotor stayed out of the branches.

But it wasn't going to work. My skids were already in the trees, and I couldn't go any lower. Now what was I going to do? There must have been a God out there somewhere. I was just at the point of pulling up when Tom started yelling, "I see them, I see them!"

I still could not see anything but green. I told Tom he'd have to keep me in position while he lowered the McGuire rig. The aircraft shifted as Warner scrambled over to help Tom.

A sandbag was attached to the end of the McGuire rig rope to help drop it through the tree limbs. Tom had lowered it about halfway when Bacon told us that the sandbag was caught in the branches. It was wrapped around a forked tree limb, and Tom couldn't pull it loose. I told him to fasten the rope to one of the tie-down rings on the aircraft floor, then I raised the aircraft up just a few feet and the sandbag came free.

Hovering the way we were was not too hard. We were sitting down in the trees with just the main rotor and the tail rotor clear. It was very easy to tell if the aircraft moved. We had all of the references that were required. After the rig made it to the ground, it took the LRPs only a few minutes to get Venable strapped into the harness. Bacon radioed that Venable was conscious and able to hold on to the rope attached to the McGuire harness.

I'd made a shit pot full of McGuire extractions, but never one like that: none of the others had been with a single wounded man on the rope. They'd all been with three people. Under those circumstances, the people who weren't wounded had been able to hold on to the injured man. This situation was frightfully different.

We heard the sound of gunfire below and saw the Cobras making gun runs not more than fifty meters from where we were hovering. Because of the noise of the door guns, the only way we could tell if we were taking fire was if we took hits. So far I hadn't felt anything hit the aircraft. I had no idea what was happening on the ground except that they were still in contact. And they seemed to be holding the NVA at bay.

I had to block all of that out of my mind and try to concentrate on getting Venable up through the trees. The opening through which we had to extract him was very small. If we drifted in any direction at all, we would drag him through the trees, which might very well finish what the NVA had started. Tom was doing one hell of a job, telling me where I should move the aircraft. It got down to moving forward or back, left or right, just a matter of inches.

Once we got the aircraft out of the trees, I lost all my reference points, so Tom was the only one who could ensure that I did what was required. He did one fine job. The aircraft continued to rise until Tom told me that the McGuire rig was clear of the trees. By then I was sweating as I'd never sweated before. Now we still had to get Venable back to the 22d Surgical Hospital at Phu Bai as fast as we could.

Unfortunately, with Jim hanging under the aircraft we were unable to fly very fast. If we tried to go faster than forty knots, he would start to spin. The faster we went, the faster he spun. But at the speed we were flying, it would take us close to forty-five minutes to make it back to Phu Bai. I didn't think Venable would be able to last that long hanging on the end of the rope.

I was considering landing in order to pull him inside the aircraft when Tom told me that Jim was hanging limp and was not moving. He thought he'd passed out. We would have to get him inside.

Now the question was, where could we land? The closest place was the abandoned fire base on Leech Island. We'd been shot out of there earlier in the month, but I couldn't see that we had any other option. Jim would bleed to death or fall out of the rig if we didn't get him inside the aircraft.

Leech Island was only five minutes away, so we set up an approach for landing there.

Fortunately, we were able to land and get Jim on board without any interference from the bad guys.

Jim was a mess. The bandages on his neck and chest had worked loose, probably when we pulled him up through the trees, and the wounds were bleeding. With some effort Tom was able to get the bandages tightened and the bleeding stopped.

The red line on the airspeed indicator read 120 knots; we reached 147 knots en route to the hospital. I thought the aircraft was going to shake itself apart, but we made the trip in record time. The orderlies at the hospital were waiting on the helipad when we arrived. They had Jim off the aircraft and away to triage almost before the skids touched the ground.

After leaving the helipad, I climbed up to two thousand feet and checked in with W.T. The Cobras were still working over the area, and the NVA had backed off for the moment. I informed Grant that I was going to refuel and look over the aircraft. I hadn't felt anything hit us, but it was best to be safe.

The POL point was not nearly as crowded as before, so we didn't have to wait. In fifteen minutes we were heading back to the Ruong Ruong. Along the way, we passed the Cobras and the C&C heading back to rearm and refuel. That meant W.T. and I were the only aircraft on station above the surrounded team. I found it unbelievable that Eklund had not yet given the order to extract them.

"Linwood Six, this is Kingsman Two-five. Are we going to extract Linwood Two-one at this time?"

"Two-five, this is Six. That's a negative. We are trying to get a reaction force to insert into the area to develop the situation."

"Roger, Six. I'll join up with One-eight and stay on station until you return."

"Okay, Bill. One-eight can brief you on the arty that will be on call. I'll be back as soon as I can."

This was not the way LRPs were supposed to operate. They were not a strong enough force to stay and defend a piece of territory. They had sprung the ambush at around 0930 hours and it was 1300 hours. Shit! Three and a half hours was too damn long for ten men to stay alive out there. They should have been extracted as soon as the ambush was blown. There was no doubt about it: they were going to get their asses waxed. Even if they hadn't been two men short, they were no match for what was going to be coming at them. The NVA had taken some heavy losses at the hands of the LRP teams the past month. They were pissed. I was certain they'd be willing to pay almost any price to take out an entire team.

"Kingsman One-eight, Two-five. I've got you in sight. I'll fall in behind you and follow you for a while. Don't get us lost."

Jim Cline had been flying since we departed the POL

point, so I had a chance to sit back and relax. W.T. filled us in on what had happened while we were gone, which wasn't very much. The Cobras had worked to within thirty meters of the team's defensive position. The NVA seemed to have taken enough punishment for the time being, but with the guns and the C&C out of the area, I was sure the enemy activity would quickly increase.

Contreros had artillery on call from fire support bases Brick and Spear. Grant had plotted the GT (gun-target) line and suggested we move to the west end of the valley to keep from getting blown out of the air by friendly fire. Sounded like a reasonable request to me. Maybe he'd been paying a little attention to what Dave Poley and I had been trying to teach him for the previous four months.

I followed W.T. west about four miles before entering a left-hand orbit. A few minutes later we watched the explosions among the trees near the team. I tuned in the artillery frequency on one of my FM radios. Al Contreros was reporting movement all around his position. Jesus! Ken and the guns had better get back out there soon. All W.T. and I could do was sit and watch the show.

Contreros's requests for artillery were something to hear. Normally, when adjusting artillery, corrections are made in increments of fifty to one hundred meters, such as "drop one hundred, right two hundred." Meaning, shorten the range one hundred meters and move it two hundred meters to the right. Contreros was moving the artillery rounds ten to fifteen meters at a time. That meant the bad guys were getting in *real* close, and so was the artillery. Artillery adjustment was an art, and I was watching an artist at work.

Thirty minutes later Eklund in the C&C was back on station with four Cobras. It was about goddamn time! The NVA were getting real serious about this thing. W.T. was low on fuel, so I contacted Eklund and informed him that we were both going back to top off because it would be better if we both had full tanks of fuel. If it became necessary to make an extraction, it wouldn't do for one of us to run out of fuel in the middle of the operation.

W.T. and I departed the area of operation around 1345 hours and returned forty-five minutes later.

By then five hours had passed since the LRPs had initiated the ambush. We were very concerned about the amount of time Contreros and his team had remained in one place. Eklund had called off the artillery and put the Cobras to work. After the artillery had been stopped, we moved back to within a mile of the team and went into a new orbit. There was nothing we could do at the time to help the team, but it felt a lot better just being close.

Contreros reported the enemy was pressing closer and said he was going to tighten up the perimeter. The Cobra gunships moved in to make a much closer rocket run to keep the NVA off the team.

At 1505 hours a large part of the vegetation above the team seemed to jump straight up into the air. Then smoke came rolling out of the jungle. What the hell had happened? Eklund was on the radio immediately, trying to contact Linwood Two-one.

"Linwood Two-one, this is Linwood Six."

There was no response.

"Linwood Two-one, what the hell is going on down there?" Still no answer. That had been one hell of an explosion. The smoke was still coming up from a large hole in the middle of the jungle. Unfortunately, the hole was right where team Two-one had been.

"Linwood Two-One, this is Six. Goddamn it, talk to me."

The radio remained silent. It was maddening. Then the sound of the radio handset being keyed crackled over the air. Someone down there was still alive, or the NVA were in possession of the radio. Then came one of the most welcome sounds I have ever heard. The voice was very weak, and we could barely make out what he was saying.

"Cease fire . . . cease fire. You've hit us. Everybody's down . . . I think I'm . . . the only . . . one . . . alive."

My God, we couldn't have lost the whole damn team that fast.

The voice came back on the radio. "Indian . . . I see Indian. I'm not alone."

The voice on the radio sounded like Jim Bacon, the senior RTO, and he was in pain. I couldn't understand what he meant by, "You've hit us." Surely the Cobras hadn't caused that kind of explosion with their 2.75-inch rockets.

Up to that point, everyone was in a state of shock and disbelief. Eklund was the only one who'd been doing anything. Now he needed some help, and he needed it immediately.

"Linwood Six, Kingsman Two-five. We'll get the medevac on the way."

Without waiting for him to acknowledge, I called Grant. "One-eight, get some altitude, and get the Dustoff out here now. I'm going down to have a look."

As I hovered over the trees where the explosion occurred, I was amazed at the devastation I saw. Where earlier we'd had to work so hard to get the McGuire rig in, there now was a large opening over the team's perimeter. I could see numerous bodies of the NVA soldiers who had tried to overrun the ten men formed up in that tiny defensive position on top of a wooded knoll. I could also see the members of the LRP team lying where they'd fallen.

I remained over the team's location and reported what I could observe to Eklund in the C&C aircraft circling overhead. He wanted me to try to extract the people on the ground, but there was no way to accomplish that. I could make out two figures still moving. Only one seemed able to stand. Hovering over the ridge line, I felt totally helpless. Then Bacon's voice was back on the radio.

"Are you going to leave us?"

I could see the man with the radio looking up at me. It had to be Bacon.

"Fuck, no. We're not going to leave anybody. You know better than that. Now get your shit together and tell me how bad your people are hurt."

While I was talking on the radio I spotted more movement among the fallen figures in the tiger-striped uniforms. I wasn't trying to take over the operation from Eklund, but he was busy controlling the gunships. I hoped he was also working on getting a reaction force out there to help those people. If the reaction force was not sent out soon, there would be no need to send one at all. About that time, a new player tried to get into the game.

"This is Dragon Six. I am one mile to the south with four ARA [aerial rocket artillery] aircraft, and will be assuming command and control of this operation."

Six was the designation of a unit commander. The ARA was an aviation company and was commanded by a major. I couldn't help thinking what an asshole this guy was. He had absolutely no idea what the tactical situation was, who was involved, who the Cobras belonged to, what their call signs were, who W.T. and I were, or what the situation on the ground was. It sounded to me like the guy was looking for a fast way to get a medal.

I guess Eklund had had enough bullshit for one day. There was no hesitation in his response. "Dragon Six, this is Linwood Six. This is my operation, and those are my people down there. So get out of the area. If I need you, I'll call and let you know. Until that time, stay off of my frequency, or I'll turn the Cobras loose and let them blow your ass out of the air."

Good for you, Ken!

I had to do something, but I didn't know what. As I understood it, Bacon couldn't move, Walkabout was able to move on his feet but was unable to use his hands, and Linderer had been hit in the right leg. He couldn't walk, but he could crawl and he could still shoot and use his hands.

I watched as Walkabout and Linderer moved from person to person checking to see whether they were alive. Bacon reported that Czepurny had been hit in both feet and couldn't walk, but he could still fire his weapon. Riley Cox had been hit hard in the stomach and right arm; Bacon didn't think he would make it, although at the time Riley was trying to fire his shotgun with one hand. Out of the ten LRPs on the ridge, three were dead and seven wounded. Of the seven wounded, only three were able to fight.

I contacted Eklund to advise him that I was going to try to get the McGuire rigs down to the ground to get some of the wounded out. He said that Grant had contacted Eagle Dust-off. They were on the way, but were still fifteen minutes out. God, they had better hurry!

The NVA were shooting at the Cobras and at us. They didn't seem to realize how bad the team had been hurt. So far, they hadn't tried to follow up with a ground assault after the explosion. Clearly they did not know that they were missing a great opportunity. I ordered both of my door guns to fire as fast as they could to try to keep the bad guys' heads down. With all of the shit going on under and around me, I was not in a very good mood when the next radio call came.

"Kingsman Two-five, this is Lucky Eagle. What's your situation?"

"This is Two-five. Situation critical. Get the fuck off my radio."

I couldn't believe I'd just said that. Lucky Eagle was the call sign of Maj. Gen. Melvin Zais, commander of the 101st Airborne Division. Oh well, so much for a brief but brilliant military career! However, just then I couldn't be bothered with rank protocol; I had important things on my mind.

The general's reply came back seconds later. It was short. It also showed what kind of great leader he was.

"This is Lucky Eagle. Roger. Out."

Even with the vegetation blown away, the McGuire rigs kept getting caught up in the trees. It really didn't matter. There was nobody on the ground capable of getting anyone into the harnesses. I had never felt so helpless.

I called W.T. and told him I couldn't get the rigs through the trees and that we were still taking ground fire. He told me to get out of the way and let him try. I pulled up and W.T. took my place. After ten minutes he called and said he'd had the same results. He pulled out of the trees, and I headed back down once again. If nothing else, we could still use our door guns to keep the bad guys from focusing all of their attention on the wounded LRPs.

"This is Dustoff Two-two. I have the aircraft hovering down in the trees. Is that where the wounded are?"

"Two-two, Two-five. That's affirm. Be advised that it's hot down here."

"Two-five, Two-two. Roger that. Now how about getting the hell out of my way."

Those medevac pilots would have made great LRP pilots. They were already crazy, and there was no doubt in my mind that they had more balls than brains. They did this shit every day.

Eklund had departed for Camp Eagle for fuel before the medevac arrived. That left me the man in charge. I hoped I wouldn't hear from Dragon Six. I'd already gotten my ass in a crack with the division commander, so I didn't figure a major would be able to do much more to me.

"Kingsman Two-five, this is One-eight. What's the status of the reaction force?"

"This is Two-five. No word yet."

"Bill, this is bullshit. Let's go get the LRPs back at the Acid Pad for a reaction force."

Before I had a chance to answer, Eklund, who was still monitoring our radio frequency, came on the radio and said, "Do it."

As I headed after W.T., I informed Saber Three-seven that he had the ball until Linwood Six returned. The race was on. If we lost, we wouldn't be the losers. The seven men still alive back there in the jungle would be.

We radioed ahead to tell the LRPs to have sixteen men ready when we reached the Acid Pad. When we approached their company area, it bore no resemblance to a military compound. It looked more like a Gypsy camp. People were milling around all over the hillside between the helipad and the tents. None of them seemed to be wearing any standard uniform, if you could accuse them of being in uniform at all: some were wearing civilian shorts and tiger-striped shirts, others were not even wearing shirts. There was every conceivable combination of clothing you could imagine. It was a rainbow of color. However, they all had two things in common. One: they all had weapons. And two: they all had their load-bearing equipment harnesses.

I was on short final, just behind W.T. It looked like there were fistfights taking place to one side of the helipad. As Grant's skids hit the ground, people began piling into his aircraft. I was not yet on the ground, but I couldn't help but laugh as the first four guys who got onto his aircraft on the left side were pushed right out on the other side by the weight of those behind them. And there was no way they could fight their way back on board. There was one hell of a free-for-all going on down there.

Then we were on the ground, and it was not so funny anymore. The LRPs were swarming over my aircraft like ants. I looked in the back and saw that the cargo area was packed with bodies. I knew I was overloaded.

One of the guys sitting there, Tony Tercero, was due to leave for home the next morning. He was wearing OD boxer shorts and his web gear. On his feet was a pair of flip-flop shower shoes. This guy had to be nuts. I looked him square in the face and yelled for him to get off the aircraft. He smiled, then pointed his M-16 right between my eyes and said, "You just take off." Well, shit! His argument was much more persuasive than mine.

I asked Tom to give me a head count. He couldn't. There was a man sitting in the gunner's well with him and Tom couldn't move. There was also a LRP in the well with Warner.

"Two-five, One-eight. You ready?"

"Go."

I heard Barry, Grant's copilot, call Eagle Tower for clearance for a flight of two departing the Acid Pad. The tower told him to hold for traffic. Barry advised the tower that we had a team in contact and were on the go. Tower came back that we were cleared for departure. They must have been used to us by then.

Grant's aircraft, 348, was struggling into the air, and I could tell he was also overloaded. I held my position to make sure he'd be able to get off of the ground. Once he hit transitional lift, I began pulling in power. I still didn't know how many people I had on board. At fifty pounds of torque, the aircraft lifted to a hover. It was not the way they had taught us in flight school, but I figured if it would hover, it would fly.

As we crossed the perimeter fence W.T. was about a mile ahead of me. I wanted to take the lead, but there was no way I could catch him. It wouldn't have done me any good to tell him to slow up; he had the bit in his mouth and only one thing on his mind. It would've been embarrassing for the whole world to hear him tell me to go to hell so I just kept my mouth shut.

Cline had finally gotten a count of the number of troops we had on board. There were eleven in the cargo compartment and two in the gunner's wells. Shit, that aircraft was not supposed to fly with that much weight on board. W.T. was still holding his lead on me. I called and asked him how many people he had. He answered that he had ten on board. Twenty-three people on two aircraft! Normally four aircraft would be needed to carry that many troops.

Grant had used forty-seven pounds of torque taking off, and I had used fifty. That had been at sea level. But we were going to have to try to bring our aircraft to an out-of-ground-effect hover at 2,200 feet above sea level. That could easily put us into a very dangerous situation. If the aircraft didn't have enough power to maintain that hover, it would start to settle, and very possibly descend into the trees where the team was located. The troops we were carrying would have to exit the aircraft as fast as they could.

We could hear the Dustoff calling that he was taking intense automatic-weapons fire from the left and right front as well as the left rear. The Cobras were working in as close as they possibly could. Eklund was back on station in a UH-1 that had replaced his LOH. It was good to have him back; it was his show. He had a pair of F-4s working the outlying ridge lines in an attempt to keep NVA reinforcements from joining in the fight.

The confrontation was turning into a major battle. The NVA wanted to destroy the LRP team at any price. And they were paying a heavy toll for their effort. I still couldn't figure out why they had not already overrun the team—unless they were using them as bait in an attempt to take out a couple of helicopters or an F-4. Well, if they were using the team on the ground as bait, they were in for one hell of a surprise. The worm at the end of the hook was about to grow teeth, twenty-three sets of them.

Dustoff Two-two extracted Al Contreros while W.T. and I were picking up the reaction force. Now Dustoff Nine-four was hoisting Frank Souza up through trees on a jungle penetrator. That left five LRPs still alive on the ground, only three able to fight.

We were still five minutes out. There was a LRP voice on the radio; Bacon had started to lose focus and was unable to remain coherent. Walkabout had gotten on the radio, but was having trouble depressing the talk key on the handset. Then Linderer took over. I heard Eklund telling the team to hang on, the reaction force was on the way. Linderer's reply was that if they didn't get there in ten minutes, they wouldn't have to worry about it. There was no panic in his voice. He made his comment sound matter-of-fact. It sent a cold chill down my spine. So things were that bad down there!

I was still trailing W.T. by about a mile. As he began his approach into the original LZ, two Cobras picked him up and escorted him in, laying down covering fire below the LZ and in the area between the LZ and the team's location on the ridge line. I didn't know what W.T. had told the troops on his aircraft, but as soon as he slowed to a hover, they came spilling out like water over a waterfall.

I'd already started my approach. As Grant was pulling out of the LZ, I was coming to a hover in the spot he'd just vacated. The LZ bore no resemblance to the area we had used the day before. It had been hit by rocket and artillery fire so savagely that the ravine, once so well concealed by the elephant grass, was plainly visible.

As we came to a hover the aircraft began to settle; I didn't have enough power to keep it in the air. But as the troops dropped off the skids, the aircraft handled better. Tom finally reported that they had all exited. I took a moment to look down at the area where we'd just inserted twenty-three people who had insisted on laying their lives on the line for their comrades. God, the pride and respect I felt for those men!

As my group dropped to the ground, the group off Grant's aircraft had set up a perimeter to secure the LZ. Then they started up the hill. As the reaction force moved up, I saw the bodies of NVA soldiers lying on the hillside.

With the gunships and the F-4s still working over the area, I took the same route W.T. had taken, down the hill with a right break. I didn't know where Grant was anymore, but I thought the best plan of action was to get the hell out of everybody's way. As Jim was reminding me that we were getting low on fuel, W.T. called.

"Two-five, One-eight. What do you think about getting some gas?"

"Yeah, One-eight. I'm down to 260 pounds."

With six and one half pounds per gallon, I had forty gallons of fuel left. The UH-1 consumed eighty gallons an hour, so we had thirty minutes of flight time left. We would reach the refueling point with ten minutes of fuel left. That was cutting it kind of close.

"Kingsman Two-five, this is Linwood Six. The Cav is sending a platoon of blues as a reaction force. They are en route at this time."

"Well, la de goddamn da. What took them so fucking long?"

"Come on, Bill. At least we've got some help."

That was true. It was not the fault of the troops that were going in. But some staff officer somewhere up the line should have been taken out and shot. If given the chance, I would gladly volunteer to pull the trigger.

"Okay, Six. How many people are the Cav going to insert?"

"Twenty-five."

"Are the Cav going to reinforce and hold the position, or are they going to be extracted?"

"We're going to get our people out, and the Cav are coming out also."

There was not an LZ anywhere in the neighborhood where we would be able to land to pick up people on the ground. It would have to be a ladder extraction.

I told Eklund that after we refueled we would reposition to the Acid Pad and have the ladders installed in both aircraft. We would also pick up a belly man for each aircraft. In making a ladder extraction, it was essential to have a belly man on board to assist the soldiers climbing up the ladder.

W.T. and I met at the refueling point. He told me he couldn't believe how fast the last two and a half hours had gone. I said, "Shit, man, time flies when you're having fun." We both checked over our helicopters and repositioned to the Acid Pad.

After shutting down the aircraft, and while the ladders were being installed, we headed to the Operations tent. We wanted to get an update on what had happened out in the Ruong Ruong while we'd been out of the area. This also gave us a chance to move around outside the aircraft. We'd been flying for almost eight continuous hours, and we knew that our day was still a long way from being over.

The mood of those who remained in the company area was one I hadn't seen before. It was almost as if everyone's belief in his own immortality had suddenly been shattered. Things like that were supposed to happen to other units, to other people, not to them. Regardless of how, why, or whose fault it was, it was just not supposed to happen.

There was not much they could tell us in Operations. In the time it took us to get back to Camp Eagle, refuel, and reposition to the Acid Pad, the LRPs we'd inserted had reached the survivors on the hill. The Cav platoon had also been inserted, and was still on the LZ. Dustoff aircraft had medevacked Cox and had taken out Bacon and Czepurny. That left just two wounded still on the ground: Billy Walkabout and Gary Linderer. It also enabled us to figure out who had been killed: Mike Reiff, Art Heringhausen, and Terry Clifton.

We departed the Acid Pad as soon as the ladders were ready. It was 1720 hours. We were about five minutes out when we heard Dustoff Two-two pull out of the area with the last of the wounded. It had taken two and a half hours to get all of the wounded out. God, what those guys must have gone through waiting for the medevac and the reaction force to reach them! But the most important thing was that the living were safe and would soon get all the help they needed.

The three LRPs still on the ground were beyond anyone's help. However, they would be brought out. They would be going home. Knowledge of that was what had kept them going out time after time, knowing they would be going back to their loved ones, and not be left lying out in the jungle somewhere to rot. "Nobody gets left behind."

There was nothing for us to do but hold off to one side and watch the show. Eklund had been busy while we were gone. An endless stream of Cobras was being directed into the fight. The LRP CO had also used six pairs of F-4s to hold the NVA back.

The LRP reaction force on the ground had actually had some trouble getting up the hill due to the large number of NVA bodies strewn about. The blood had made the ground slick and difficult to climb. I'd seen quite a few bodies scattered about in the jungle, but had no idea of the number of people the NVA had committed to the action.

The medevac aircraft had done a remarkable job, having taken out all the wounded, including six members of the reaction force. Of the twenty-three troops we put in, six had been wounded. Dave Bennett, Joe Beilisch, Richard Fadley, William R. Kirby, Joe Miller, and Tim Coleman had all been hit during the rescue.

One of the Cav aircraft was to bring the three dead LRPs out, tying the three bodies together, by the feet, to a single rope, and slinging them all out at one time. Christ, I don't know if I would have been able to bring my friends out like that. But the only alternative was to leave them behind, and that was not an option.

Division was still very interested in the bag of documents and equipment that had been taken off the NVA killed in the initial ambush. Eklund wanted me to try to get a rope down

into the area to retrieve the bag and take it to the division helipad. Although the earlier attempt with the McGuire rig had
not been successful, I was determined to try again. We were
able to get the rope all the way down, and, after the bag had
been retrieved, we headed back to Camp Eagle. En route, we
were advised that the entire reaction force was to be extracted, including the people the Cav had put in. W.T. called
to tell me he was on his way to the POL point. I had a few
minutes' head start on him, so I told him that after I dropped
off the bag, I would meet him there.

The copilots were sitting in the aircraft. The crew chiefs
were refueling, and the gunners were checking the aircraft
over for hits. Grant and I walked away from the noise to try to
figure out how in the hell we were going to make this son of a
bitch work.

Darkness in the Orient does not come slowly. One minute
it's light, and the next it's dark. As we headed out to the AO, it
was already blacker than the inside of a whore's heart. W.T.
was giving me a long head start. A ladder extraction takes a
lot of time. At least we were back in our element. There was
nobody better at that kind of work than the two aircraft commanders who were in the process of doing what they got paid
to do. As Joe Friday of *Dragnet* might have said, "No brag,
ma'am. Just fact." Besides, we were the only two UH-1 aircraft with ladders in the division. Sometimes I doubted my
own wisdom.

We figured that we still had forty-eight people on the
ground. It was going to take us four trips apiece to get them
all out. The Cav troops, who had refused to leave the LZ,
would be the first ones extracted.

Eklund was keeping a steady supply of gunships on station
to give us covering fire. It was amazing. Earlier we couldn't
get any help at all, and now everybody and his damn dog was
there to assist. Even Dragon Six had been used sometime
during the day, but he hadn't been willing to risk his ass by
trying to take over the operation again.

Looking toward the Ruong Ruong as we left Camp Eagle
behind, I could barely make out the silhouettes of the moun-

tains. Damn, I hated night extractions! At least during the day, when someone was shooting at you, you couldn't see the muzzle flashes and the tracers as well. At night it looked like the Fourth of July. With W.T. and myself making four trips each into the PZ, there was going to be one hell of a celebration.

The gunships were still making runs, so it wasn't difficult to find the general area where we were to pick up the troops. At about two miles out I got on the radio. "Linwood Two-one, this is Kingsman Two-five. Give me a strobe."

There was a long pause before Tercero came back. "Two-five, Two-one. Negative strobe."

"Okay, Two-three. How about a flare?"

"Negative flares."

"Two-three, what in the hell do you have to mark the PZ with?"

"I've got a Zippo."

"A what?"

Then it dawned on me that in their haste to get on the aircraft, the LRPs forming the reaction force had taken nothing with them but their weapons and ammunition. So at approximately 1930 hours, on November 20, 1968, the M1-A1 Zippo Landing Zone Marking Device came into being.

From a distance of about two miles it was amazing how well the flame of that lighter showed up. The only problem was that if you held a lighter for very long, it got hotter than hell. Luckily, there were several other people on the ground who also had lighters.

The extraction went off like clockwork. Although we could see lights moving along the ridges heading for the ambush site, the Cobras and the F-4s held the NVA away from the PZ. I had never seen the NVA use flashlights to move about at night. They were offering some very tempting targets, and the gunships were taking them up on the offer. If they wanted to give their lives for Uncle Ho, so be it.

After the last of the reaction force had been dropped off at the Acid Pad, we repositioned to the Castle. It was 2145 hours. We'd been up for seventeen hours, and flying for over twelve straight hours. As soon as we shut down at the Castle, I was notified that I was to return to the LRP company for a debriefing.

All I wanted to do was put the aircraft to bed and then find one for myself; my ass was dragging. I was so tired that I didn't even want a drink. I left Cline and the rest of the crew to take care of the aircraft. It seemed that lately they'd been getting all of the dirty work. Their day had been just as long as mine. Well, at least they would be asleep by the time I returned.

After dropping off my gear, I went by Operations to check in and borrow the Operations officer's jeep. Driving back to the LRP company, I kept wondering how the operation could have gotten so screwed up. Who had dropped the ball? Was there anyone to point a finger at? Someone had to be blamed for the tragedy. Had Grant and I really done all we could? Were we responsible for any part of the operation that had gone wrong?

The questions kept piling up, and there didn't seem to be any clear answers. The only thing I was sure of was that we had lost some people. As of that moment, out of the thirty-five people we put in, three were dead, one was injured, and fourteen were wounded. Of those fourteen, how many would survive? God, I was so tired that I couldn't even think.

Walking into the Operations building, I was shocked at the number of people there. The building was packed. It didn't take me long to realize that the two lowest-ranking officers there were Captain Eklund and myself. Everyone else was a major or above. Normally, there would have been one or two officers down from division to attend the debriefing.

I was pondering just how interesting this could be when Maj. Gen. Melvin Zais walked into the room. Now there was no doubt about it being interesting. The team must have stumbled onto something big; the division commander doesn't sit in on debriefings at 2230 hours just because he has nothing better to do.

Think, damn it, think, I told myself. What had they said in the premission briefing? Ambush small NVA units. What else? Colonel Mot, commander of the 5th Regiment; that had to be it. Had we gotten him? That had to be it. The bag of documents. What was in that bag? If we'd gotten him, would the price we had paid be worth it?

As soon as everyone settled down, the LRP company commander, Captain Eklund, began the debriefing. He was upset but did an outstanding job. He covered the mission as it had been planned and executed. After covering the insertion of the LRP reaction force and that of the Cav platoon, he described the extraction. When he finally concluded his portion, it was thrown open for questions.

No one from the initial team was at the briefing; they were at the 22d Surgical Hospital or at Graves Registration. Tony Tercero and Tim Coleman, from the reaction force, were present. They had gone in on my aircraft and were the first two to reach the survivors. Fortunately, Tony had gotten dressed before coming to the briefing. He had gone into the mountains with only his boxer shorts and a pair of shower shoes. Coleman had been slightly wounded, but refused to remain at the hospital.

Tony described what he'd found when he reached the top of the hill. The devastation had been unbelievable. There were dead NVA all around the perimeter and down the hill toward the LZ. The artillery, gunships, and air strikes had shredded the jungle. The dense tropical forest now looked like the aftermath of a hurricane.

Coleman said that about halfway up the hill, a dead NVA officer was lying on his side. The man had a long diagonal scar on the right side of his face. A pearl-handled automatic pistol was still in his holster. He remembered that very well because he'd wanted to stop and get the pistol but there had been no time. The description of the dead NVA officer fit Colonel Mot. Tim had not been at the briefing prior to the team's going in so he would have had no knowledge of what or who they were looking for. It could not be confirmed, but there seemed a very good chance that Colonel Mot was no longer with us.

The bag of documents, which I'd brought out, indicated

that the people hit in the initial ambush were part of the 5th NVA Regimental Headquarters Company, which was being accompanied by the XO of the regiment. Papers in the bag confirmed that he was killed in the ambush.

General Zais asked if we knew what had caused the casualties suffered by the team. That question had been on our minds all day. It had been one hell of an explosion. A B-40 rocket or even ten B-40 rockets wouldn't have caused the collateral damage that had been done. The 2.75-inch rockets used by the Cobras were not large enough to cause the amount of devastation on the hill. With the Cobras working in the area at the time, the artillery had been cut off, so that left them out. The F-4s were not on station at the time of the explosion. No one knew what had happened.

I'd been one of the last to arrive for the debriefing, and as such, I was standing in the rear of the tent. It was a good thing that I was standing. If I'd been sitting, I would probably have fallen asleep.

I looked around, and the only people I could see in the tent who'd been involved in the air during the action were Captain Eklund and myself. Or so I thought. Before we had a chance to answer the general's question, a man sitting in the front of the tent stood up and started talking. He was wearing a major's gold oak leaves and Army aviator wings on his uniform. I'd never seen him before. As he began to speak, I knew exactly who he was. It was the commander of the ARA company, the same asshole Eklund had run out of the area earlier that day. As soon as he began, he started blaming the Cobras for firing rockets into the LRPs' position. The more he talked, the more irrational he became. In a short time he was like a small child throwing a temper tantrum. I couldn't believe that the general and his staff were letting this fool ramble on.

It had been a long and sad day, and I'd had as much of this son of a bitch as I could take. I started to move toward the front of the tent. I didn't know what I was going to do. More than likely, if I'd reached him, I would have knocked him on his ass, but I didn't get the chance.

Two other people were moving ahead of me. One was easy

to see. He was dressed in tiger-stripe fatigues and had white bandages on both hands running almost up to his elbows. It was Sp4. Billy B. Walkabout. The other one was S.Sgt. Bruce "Doc" Proctor, the company senior medic. Doc had gone to the hospital as soon as the extraction of the wounded had taken place. Walkabout had refused to stay in the hospital. I didn't know how long they'd been in the tent or how much of the debriefing they'd heard.

Doc walked up to the major and, without a word, dropped several pieces of metal fragments on the wooden table in front of him. There was not a sound in the tent other than the pieces of metal hitting the wood. Lying on the table were several pieces of rusty metal and a three-quarter-inch bolt. The major stood there looking at the fragments with his mouth open.

Doc said in a very quiet voice, "Major, you evidently don't know what the hell you're talking about. These were just taken out of Frank Souza's chest. The last time I checked, we didn't use this kind of shrapnel in our 2.75-inch rockets. So why don't you just sit down and shut the fuck up?"

The major couldn't speak. He just stood there with his mouth opening and closing like a fish out of water. He was having a very bad day. First, a captain had run his ass out of the AO, and now there was a twenty-one-year-old staff sergeant telling him the truth about himself right there in front of God and everybody. Some days it just doesn't pay to get out of bed.

Still, no one said anything. The major looked around as if trying to find someone to help him. The dumb-ass had dug his own grave, and there was not a soul in the tent who wanted to join him in it. He grabbed his hat off the table and quietly walked out of the tent. Boy, would I have loved to see his next OER (officer efficiency report).

Walkabout confirmed most of what had been covered in the debriefing: from the insertion the day before, the medevac of John Sours, the initial ambush, Venable being shot and extracted by McGuire rig, and waiting for the reaction force that did not come. He said that after about three hours, they started receiving heavy sniper fire and repeated probes. They remained at the ambush site far too long. The NVA knew exactly where they were. Contreros had called in artillery in an attempt to keep the pressure off the team. It worked for a little while, then the NVA started coming at them in force.

Walkabout also said there were more targets than he'd ever seen before. The NVA troops were beaten back time and time again. There were bodies all over the hillside. Contreros called for everybody to move up to the top of the hill. As they stood and started to move, the explosion occurred. Everyone had been hit. Billy said he didn't remember anything about the explosion, other than being slammed to the ground. He also described the conditions on the hilltop, and the ensuing fight until the reaction force arrived.

Doc Proctor gave an update on the casualties:

Sp4. Arthur J. Heringhausen Jr.—Killed in Action.

Sgt. Michael Dean Reiff—Killed in Action.

Sp4. Terry W. Clifton—Killed in Action.

S.Sgt. Albert D. Contreros Jr. was not expected to live. He had a dime-size hole behind his right ear, but the exit wound in the top of his head was much larger.

Sgt. Frank Souza was not expected to live. He'd been hit in the head, neck, and chest, and had lost his right lung. The exit wound was massive.

Sgt. Jim Venable was hit in the chest, neck, and arm.

Sp4. Steve Czepurny was hit in both feet.

Sp4. Riley Cox suffered massive shrapnel wounds that had dumped his intestines in his lap and severely shattered his right forearm. He had also been hit numerous times by small-arms fire.

Sp4. Jim Bacon had been severely wounded in his right leg just above the right knee.

Sp4. John Sours had suffered two broken ankles.

Sp4. Gary Linderer had multiple shrapnel wounds in his right leg and had been shot in the left thigh.

Sp4. Billy B. Walkabout had multiple shrapnel perforations of both hands. He had refused to stay in the hospital.

The six members of the reaction force who had been hit received painful but not life-threatening wounds.

Based on the information from Walkabout, and the type of wounds received by the LRPs who had been on the hill, it was determined that the explosive device that wiped out the team had to have been a large Chicom claymore mine of some type. The amount of damage caused by the explosion indicated that it had likely been a forty-pounder. Most likely the mine had been command-detonated, because most of the team members were moving to the top of the hill to tighten up the perimeter seconds before the explosion occurred.

All of the data, information, and speculation had been gone over with a fine-tooth comb. There were still a lot of unanswered questions. But all those that we could answer had been answered.

We knew what had transpired. We knew what our casualties were. We would never know the price the NVA had paid, but from what I'd seen, there were hundreds of NVA dead on the hill around the perimeter. There was no way to estimate the number of dead and wounded on the outlying hills and the ridge lines blasted by the Cobras and F-4s. The NVA wanted to dance, and they definitely paid the fiddler.

Everyone was leaving. I remained where I was in the rear of the building. I wanted to talk with Walkabout and Proctor about the people in the hospital. Needless to say, Ken Eklund was also waiting to talk to them.

When all of the people not assigned to the company had departed, I moved to the front of the tent where the company members were gathered. It was a very solemn group of people. We went over everything that had already been covered. It was almost like we were trying to make all of the events of the day go away. It didn't work.

As I walked to the door I saw someone standing off to one side. Oh, shit! It was General Zais. I thought, If he's still waiting, he must really be pissed. Nobody talked to a general officer as I'd done that day and got away with it. Well, they could shoot me, but they couldn't eat me. *That* was against the law. I stopped in front of the general, since there was no place I could run and hide, and said, "Good evening, sir."

General Zais looked at me and said, "Captain, I think we had a discussion on the radio this afternoon."

I replied, "No, sir, General. I did not have time for you this afternoon. I have the time now."

Shaking his head, he responded, "Captain, if you ever let anybody do to you what I tried to do today, I'll personally run your ass out of the Army. All I had to do was listen, and I would have gotten all of the information I needed."

I just stood there looking at him. For one of the few times in my life, I was speechless.

The general continued, "You look tired. I'll have you and the other air crew taken off duty for the next two days. You men have earned a rest."

"General, please don't do that. We still have a team in, and we're responsible for them."

Now the surprised look was on his face. "Okay, Captain," he replied. "Stay on until the team you have in comes out. Then you and Mr. Grant are taking some time off. I cannot afford to lose you two."

"General, I'm glad you understand. Thank you."

"No, Captain. Thank you." He turned and walked out of Operations.

I had read many books about war, some which went back to the times of Helen of Troy and the Trojan horse. I'd read about all the great leaders, about all the great men whose soldiers would follow them anywhere. But that was history, something that had happened in the distant past. That night I had met and talked to a man *I* would follow though the gates of hell.

Driving back to the company area, I was thinking that tomorrow was another day. Then I looked at my watch and saw that "tomorrow" was already here. A day had passed that I would never forget for the rest of my life, no matter how long or short that life might be.

Chapter
Twenty

There was no good reason to go to bed. In two and half hours we'd be back in the saddle again. Sitting in the mess tent by myself, I tried to figure out how I could block out the events of the past twenty-four hours. There was no solution; they would not go away. The events of the mission were so damn vivid. We had gotten away with so much, for so long, that I think we all knew that a catastrophe was just a matter of time. There was nothing that I or anybody else could have done about what happened. We would simply have to continue doing our jobs the best we knew how.

After the fourth cup of coffee I figured I still had time to shit, shower, shave, and get ready for the rest of the day. There was not any doubt that I needed to get cleaned up and put on a clean uniform. I smelled like a goat in rut.

We arrived back at the Acid Pad a little after 0600 hours. The atmosphere was about as I expected. No one really had anything to say. With eighteen casualties the previous day and a twelve-man heavy team and a six-man radio relay team still out there, there weren't very many people around the LRP company area. The air crews from the mission the day before wanted to know what the debriefing covered. I told them they would have to wait for Captain Eklund to brief them. I did not want to talk about it.

After breakfast we went to Operations and met with Eklund. He went over the debriefing with W.T. and the rest of the crew. He was still very upset, but somehow his West Point training allowed him to put most of his emotions on the back burner. He was very professional and to the point.

At the conclusion of the debriefing he asked me if I'd fly him to the hospital. We still had a team in, and he wanted an aircraft available in case they got into contact while he was there. Of course I agreed to take him; I would have gone to the hospital even if Eklund hadn't wanted to go. Grant asked if he could accompany us.

We left W.T.'s copilot and crew with his aircraft. They would have it cranked and ready to leave if it became necessary to go back to the Ruong Ruong. Looking at the sky, I hoped it would not happen that day. The weather had turned to garbage overnight. Off to the west, toward the mountains, the clouds were right down on the ground.

We parked the aircraft well off the helipad, making sure we wouldn't interfere with aircraft carrying wounded. It was the first time I'd been to the hospital. It was impressive; everything was so clean. We were used to living in the dirt and I was almost afraid to walk into the ward. I was sure someone would run me out so I wouldn't track in dirt. Eklund was leading the way. Hell, he looked worse than I did. I let Grant follow him. If they did not throw those two out, I was pretty sure I could get in.

I was walking fifteen to twenty feet behind them as we entered the ward. Beds lined both sides of the room, and all of them were occupied. I'd covered about a fourth of the ward when I heard someone in a very loud voice say, "Meacham, you dumb son of a bitch." That caught me by surprise. Stopping, I looked at my name tag. There was no mistaking it, that was my name. I looked at my collar and saw that I was still a captain in the United States Army. As far as I knew, no one there outranked me. So who in the hell was there who would talk to me like that?

The voice called again, "Hey, asshole, over here." Looking to my right, I saw the familiar face of one of the blackest men I'd ever known. The white bandage covering him from the

waist to the middle of his chest accented the color of his skin.
I hadn't seen the guy in four years.

Gerry Garrison and I had served together in Germany as
privates and Sp4s. and become close friends. When I'd arrived in Europe, Gerry was already assigned to the unit. For
some reason, we seemed to hit it off right from the start. He
took it upon himself to show me the ropes and we were
friends over the next three years. After Gerry rotated back to
the States, we lost contact. Now here he was, a sergeant, lying
in a hospital bed, wrapped in bandages, and grinning at me.

"Gerry, what in the hell happened to you?"

"Got shot by my own people." Gerry'd had a patrol working out of FSB Bastogne. When they were coming back to the
fire base a little after dark, someone on the bunker line heard
them and fired an M-79 round. He'd caught a piece of shrapnel in the side.

We talked for a while. Damn, it was good to see him. It
would have been better under different circumstances, but at
least he'd recover. I asked Gerry if there was anything I could
do for him or bring him. He said he could use some cigarettes
and I told him I'd bring him some when I came back to see
him. I never got back to the hospital, which has bothered me
to this day.

Eklund and W.T. were at the far end of the ward. As I got
closer I was surprised to see a man who was supposed to be
dying sitting up in his bed. Frank Souza was looking pretty
damn good when I walked up to him. He was getting his bandages changed. His only concern was how the other members
of his team were, and who, or what, had been the cause of the
team getting its shit blown away. After we told him what we
thought happened, he seemed to relax. "I knew the Cobras
didn't shoot us up," he said.

Jim Venable was in the same room, two beds down. I
hadn't expected to see him alive. He asked the same question,
although, since he'd been hit in the throat, he had a lot of
trouble talking.

I was feeling pretty damn good until I looked across to the
other side of the ward and saw a figure that looked like a

mummy. I could see his eyes. It was Riley Cox, the kid who'd been shot all to pieces. He was wrapped from head to toe. His right arm was in a cast, and he had tubes coming out of his chest and stomach.

I didn't know how many times he'd been hit, but it was just short of a miracle that he was still alive. I guess he'd lived up to his nickname—the Bulldozer, Dozer for short. The Dozer took a lot of killing.

True to form, he asked the same question as the other team members: How were his buddies? It was amazing, or maybe it was not so amazing, that all of them were more worried about their friends than about themselves.

There were also a couple of guys there from the reaction force who had been lightly wounded at the LZ. I talked to them for a short time. They said they'd be going back to their unit in a few days.

We stopped and talked to the chief surgeon on the way out. He told us that S. Sgt. Al Contreros had been flown to the hospital ship USS *Repose*, about fifteen miles off the coast from Da Nang. He died shortly after arriving on board.

Hopefully, God had made the right decision. I didn't think Al would have wanted to go home as a vegetable. He would have wanted to die as a soldier, and not be a burden to his loved ones. That's what I would have wanted under those circumstances.

Back at the LRP company area all I wanted to do was get some sleep. Using the skid as a headrest, I lay down by the aircraft and was asleep before my eyelids closed. My burnout point had been reached. I slept the deepest sleep I'd ever experienced. The LRPs told me later that on two separate occasions they'd tried to wake me. Finally, Eklund told them just to leave me alone and let me sleep it off. The way it sounded, he could have been talking about someone on a three-day drunk. Eventually, the noise of helicopters flying over caused me to open my eyes. Two Cobras were on short final to the Cav ramp. I had no idea how long I'd been out. I didn't even remember falling asleep.

Looking around, I could see I wasn't the only one who'd

sacked out. Grant and his crew, and my own crew, were all still asleep. I saw Eklund walking down the hill from the Operations tent toward the helipad. He must have seen me moving around. He wasn't carrying his weapon or map case, so I knew we wouldn't be going anywhere. I sat and waited.

Eklund came over, sat down on the ground, and looked at me. His first comment was typical. "Bill, you look like shit. How do you feel?"

"I'll live. How long have I been out?"

"About five hours. Feel like doing some flying?"

I looked toward the mountains. The weather was still bad. Clouds were covering the mountaintops, but there were some holes in them over Camp Eagle and farther to the east. I had a good idea where he wanted to go, but asked anyway. Ken pointed to the southwest, toward where Burnell's team was located.

Eklund filled me in on what had been going on while we were at the hospital and then while I'd been asleep. Burnell had been on the move since first light. He had married up with an infantry company that had established a defensive position on a small mountaintop.

Ken wanted to try to get at least six of the twelve-man team out of the field. With the loss of the eighteen men who'd been killed or wounded, there had to be a major reorganization of the teams within the company. In addition, quite a few of the old-timers were due to rotate back to the States.

I told him we'd go up and see how thick the clouds were. If we could see the mountaintop, we would try to get in and extract his people. But I didn't think we'd have very much luck.

We departed the Acid Pad around 1630 hours and headed east. There was a large hole in the clouds right over the airfield at Phu Bai. I contacted Ground-Control Approach and they vectored us up through the hole until we were VFR on top. It was good to know the GCA was operational; if that hole closed up, we'd need the GCA to get us back on the ground.

After breaking out on top of the clouds at three thousand feet, we turned and headed southwest. I knew that the highest mountain was approximately 2,500 feet. There were no mountaintops in sight, only a solid layer of clouds under us. We knew how to get in the general area, using airspeed, time, and heading. That would put us somewhere within the ballpark of where the team was located. The main problem was that their mountaintop was at only 2,200 feet. Eight hundred feet of it was solid overcast. No way in hell to get in there.

I talked to Burnie on the FM radio. Although we were above the clouds, he could hear us. I finally had to tell him that I couldn't get in. He asked me if I had any information on what had happened to Contreros and his team. Burnie and Contreros were as close as two men could get without being brothers. I didn't have the heart to tell him that Al was dead, so I lied. Then I gave the controls to Jim and I cried. Al had been my friend also.

I called Eklund, informed him of the weather conditions, and told him we'd have to try again the next day. At that point he released us. So all we had to do was find a way to get back on the ground. The clouds had moved in, and the holes over Phu Bai were no longer there. Hello, GCA. It was another time when our instrument training came into play. We broke out of the clouds at a thousand feet, terminated the approach with the GCA controller, and proceeded to the Castle.

W.T. was waiting when we landed. He helped us postflight the aircraft, and then we all headed for the club. We hadn't had a chance to sit back and relax for four days.

As tired as we were, Grant and I both knew we wouldn't be able to last, so we decided to get drunk as fast as possible and go to bed. It didn't take us nearly as long as we thought. It was a very short night.

The next morning both air crews were back at the Acid Pad by 0700 hours. It was getting to be almost like a regular job. I was tempted just to move my gear over there; it would have saved a hell of a lot of time.

Over breakfast Eklund informed Walkabout, Grant, and myself that we were to report to the division headquarters at 1000 hours for an awards ceremony.

I thought W.T. was going to have a fit. He hadn't shaved for two days and he needed a haircut. His uniform was in the same shape as mine, well-worn and dirty. Getting a haircut was out of the question. As far as the uniforms went, to hell with it. What you see is what you get.

W.T. headed toward the latrine to see if he could find soap and a towel. He returned after about twenty minutes, freshly shaven but bleeding from several small cuts on his face. I looked at him and asked, "What did you use to shave with, a broken beer bottle?"

He got that shit-eating grin on his face and replied, "Nope. I used my K-Bar."

About a dozen people were present to receive awards. The last three in line were Walkabout, Grant, and myself. Everyone was dressed in starched fatigues and spit-shined boots. Then there were the three of us.

General Zais presented the various awards to the people as he worked his way down the line. When he came to Walkabout, he pinned a Silver Star on his shirt and said, "Son, that was a very selfless and courageous act you performed on that mountain the other day. Soldiers like you have made, and still keep, the good reputation that this division has always had. This Silver Star is only a small token of our recognition of your bravery." After Billy saluted him, the general reached out to shake his hand. He realized then that both of Billy's hands were wrapped in bandages. He put his hand on Walkabout's shoulder and said, "Thank you. Thank you very much."

General Zais stopped in front of me and pinned the Distinguished Flying Cross on the left shirt pocket of my uniform. He returned my salute, and moved on to W. T. Grant, whom he presented with a DFC. After W.T. returned the salute, the general looked at us and said, "I want to thank you two gentlemen for getting those men off that mountain. You kept a bad situation from becoming a total disaster."

I could feel the tears welling up in my eyes. There was no doubt in my mind that the man meant every word that he said. He cared. He really cared.

Chapter
Twenty-one

In the afternoon, after the awards ceremony, we were back in the AO trying to extract Burnie's team. No luck. The clouds were still sitting on top of the mountain.

Eklund was concerned. The infantry company had been in place for three days and they wanted to get moving. Once they and the team moved off the mountaintop and headed down into the valley, it would be almost impossible to pick them up. We knew we'd hurt the NVA badly a couple of days before, but it wouldn't take them long to try to get even.

The next morning, November 23, we were back in the air. After flying around the area for close to two hours, we headed back to Camp Eagle for fuel.

I'd been talking to Burnie on the FM radio most of the morning. He was not in good shape. By now he'd heard about Contreros. I was relieved I wasn't the one who had to break the news to him. When I later got up the courage to tell him I was sorry, his only comment was, "They'll find out."

Not knowing what he meant, I asked, "Find out what?"

"Payback's a bitch."

I would have hated to be in the next NVA unit he happened across.

There was no use going back out that morning, so we waited by the Operations tent until midafternoon. The cloud cover over Camp Eagle and the area to the west seemed to be breaking up. I told Eklund we'd give it one more try. If that didn't work, there'd be nothing more we could do that day.

The base of the clouds was at fifteen hundred feet, and the tops were between 2,500 and 2,600 feet, with a few small holes in them. The trick was to find a way to reach the mountaintop where our people were located.

We flew back and forth over the area for almost an hour. Then there it was. Through the chin bubble I could see the top of the mountain about four hundred feet below. I could see people standing around on the bald mountaintop. If they were the good guys, it was the right place. If they weren't, well, things would get exciting in a hurry.

As soon as we set up our approach and entered the sucker hole, it lived up to its name and just disappeared. We were somewhere in the middle of that damn cloud. Everything was gray. You couldn't tell if you were moving forward, up or down, backward or sideways. It was a totally helpless and un-nerving feeling.

I needed some kind of reference point. Trying to hold the aircraft steady, I keyed the radio and told the RTO on the ground to pop a flare. In only a few seconds there was a bright glow coming from below. It seemed to cover an area of about three hundred meters in every direction. I let the aircraft descend toward the center of the glow.

As we continued slowly down, the glow seemed to get smaller. Then it disappeared completely. I called for another flare. The glow came back, only this time it was much smaller. We continued down. The second flare burned out and was replaced by a third. As the glow of the third flare died out, it took me a moment to realize that I was looking at the three burned-out canisters. I was on the ground. That had to be the softest landing I'd ever made. Or would ever make in the future. I had never felt the aircraft touch down.

There was nothing to see out the window. It was like being in a gray void or a world of gray dampness. It was eerie, as if time were standing still. I reached up and turned on the aircraft position lights so the people on the ground could see where we were. The last thing that I needed was for someone to walk into the tail rotor.

Burnell materialized next to my door. I hadn't seen him approach. He asked if I thought we'd be able to make it out, or if we would have to wait until the weather cleared. I told him I was leaving and if he wanted to go with me he'd better get his people on board. I had no doubt that the NVA had heard us come in. I was not about to shut the aircraft down and spend the night on that mountaintop.

It didn't take them long to load onto the aircraft. Burnell, Lieutenant Williams, Larry Chambers, John Burford, Kenn Miller, and Don Harris were sitting in the rear of the aircraft. None of them looked happy to be making this trip. I think they would have preferred to wait for the next ride. The only problem was that mine was the last bus for the rest of the day. No way was I going to spend the night on that goddamn mountaintop. I was going home. The people on board the aircraft had absolutely no say-so in the matter. As far as I was concerned, they were just passengers.

I'd been put in a situation in May, and then again in September, where I was forced to fly in the clouds. However, this mission was the first time I'd had to make an actual ITO (instrument takeoff).

It was something we'd practiced in flight school. But on the mountain, if I fucked up, I wouldn't get a pink slip and a chance to go back and try it again. On that mountain, if I did fuck up, I'd get a body bag. It was a time when I had to have blind faith in three things: my training, my instruments, and my ability. If any one of those was lacking, I might as well kiss my ass good-bye.

But all things considered, I was in pretty good shape: the weather was cool, we'd burned off half our fuel, and the team members had eaten most of their rations and consumed most of their water, so the load was fairly light.

Making an ITO required bringing the aircraft off the ground smoothly and establishing a positive rate of climb. That would be indicated on the vertical speed indicator (VSI). The artificial horizon was used to keep the aircraft level. Once the rate of climb was established, the nose of the aircraft was lowered slightly to gain forward airspeed. The ideal situation was eighty knots of forward airspeed and five-hundred-feet-per-minute rate of climb.

Taking a deep breath, I began pulling in power. There

was no need to look outside; nothing to see but the dark gray interior of the clouds. All my attention was focused on the instruments.

The three burned-out flares disappeared from beneath the chin bubble as the aircraft lifted off the ground. There was no sensation of movement. The only indication that we were flying came from the instruments inside the aircraft.

The VSI showed a rate of climb of two hundred feet per minute. I held that power setting and let the aircraft rise for about fifteen seconds, to ensure that we were well clear of the ground before letting the aircraft move into forward flight.

After cross-checking the VSI with the altimeter—it showed that we were in fact climbing—I eased the nose over slightly and applied a little more power. The airspeed indicator showed that we were starting to move forward at about twenty knots and the airspeed was increasing. I could feel the air starting to move past the open window of the aircraft. With the increase in power, the rate of climb began to increase also.

Knowing that the cloud tops were only four hundred to five hundred feet above us, I just held that power setting and let the aircraft climb. I was not in that big a hurry.

One of the things the instrument instructors in flight school had tried to beat into our heads was never to try to rush the aircraft. We were not to make any sudden or abrupt moves with the controls, just hold the aircraft steady and let it do all of the work. Damn, right then I was really glad that I'd stayed awake in those classes.

Everything seemed to be working as advertised. We were climbing at a rate of four hundred feet per minute and sixty knots forward airspeed. The grayness began getting lighter as we got closer to the tops of the clouds.

There was no talking or movement in the aircraft. I was sure everyone was wondering if I knew what the hell I was doing. Well, they were not the only ones. But it worked; it took only a little more than four minutes from the time we lifted off the mountaintop until we broke out on top of the clouds.

It was beautiful! The sun was a brilliant orange ball setting in the west. The sky was turning from a dark blue to a light violet. The aircraft was skimming the tops of the clouds. It was like running across a pure white cotton blanket that extended as far as the eye could see. The thought crossed my mind: I've died and gone to Heaven. Nothing on earth could be this beautiful.

Reality came back with a vengeance. I looked back into the rear of the aircraft. Burnell was staring into the clouds. I could only imagine what was going on in his head. The hate was clear in his eyes. I had never seen anyone so intense. Burnie and I had been friends before the mission began. I hoped we still were; I would hate to have the man as an enemy.

Lieutenant Williams, the junior RTO, was visibly upset. He'd been on several missions before, but nothing had affected him so strongly. He was sitting in the back of the aircraft with tears running down his face. Although it was not his team, they were his people, his friends.

Larry Chambers's grip on his M-60 machine gun was so hard that his knuckles were white. Larry was the company joker, but there were no jokes on his mind that flight. He was another one in a killing mood. He was crying. I didn't know if they were tears of sadness or tears of rage. Regardless, someone was going to pay. The four other team members were staring out into space.

It had been three days since Contreros and his team were chopped up. But that flight was the first time that Burnie or his team members had had a chance to show any emotions at all.

Shortly after we broke out of the clouds, I gave the controls to Ed Ragan and told him to take us home. Operations had replaced Jim Cline as my copilot. I guess they figured I'd worn him out. I had flown with Ed before, and knew that he was as solid and steady as they came. He reminded me a lot of Grant when he'd first joined the unit. Ed had watched, listened, and kept his mouth shut. He'd learned fast. The questions he asked were all mission-related. There was no bullshit. That was something I had no trouble living with.

After Ed took the controls, I sat back, lit a cigarette, then handed the pack to the people in the rear of the aircraft. The pack disappeared. I was lucky to get my lighter back. The tension was starting to subside.

As the aircraft skimmed the cloud tops, I wondered if we were making the same type of ripples as skipping a flat stone across a still pond, which I'd done as a kid. I closed my eyes and wished that I were a kid again.

It was the first time in eight months that I brought a team out of the field and no one was on the Acid Pad to meet them. Not a soul was in sight. I could feel the sadness and despair in the company. The six guys in the back of the aircraft made no move to leave as we shut the aircraft down. They just sat there as if there was no place to go.

After the blades were tied down, Burnie started walking up the hill, followed by the five other team members. His shoulders were bent and he looked like an old man. I couldn't help but think, He's a professional. He'll heal and come back stronger than ever.

As they reached the Operations tent, Captain Eklund came out to meet them. Eklund and Burnell stood talking. Burnie's head was bowed. After a few minutes Eklund put his arm around Burnie's shoulders and they disappeared into the tent.

I had no business in the Operations tent. I'd heard it all before; I headed to the Ranger Lounge for what I thought was a well-deserved drink. There was only one person there, the bartender. I ordered two shots of Jim Beam. He cracked the seal on a new bottle and poured two very large shots into one glass. I paid him, finished the drink in one swallow, and left.

It was like a ghost town. There was no one in the area. I started walking. I had no idea where I was going, but just felt the need to walk. Eventually I ended up at Contreros's hootch. I'd been there before, in better times, drinking, partying, and just raising hell. It was different now. The people who'd lived in the tent were no longer there. All were either dead or wounded. I stood there, trying to convince myself to leave, but couldn't. I had to go in and say good-bye.

It was dark in the hootch, like entering a shrine. The only

light was at the far end. Two people were going through the footlockers, sorting out the personal effects of the people who used to live in the tent. Personal things would be sent home to the families of the dead soldiers. Jim Schwartz and John Meszaros had either been given the job or had taken it upon themselves to do a job nobody else wanted to do.

They didn't see me enter, nor did they hear me leave. I went quietly back to the Ranger Lounge. As I entered, the bartender looked up. I walked behind the bar and picked up the bottle of Jim Beam that he'd opened earlier. I also picked up three glasses. I told him, "I need this for Contreros's hootch. What do I owe you?" He turned his back on me and went over to the tape deck he'd been listening to when I came in.

When I returned to the hootch, the tent was still dark. At the far end the two men were still doing a job that I would have tried to leave for someone else. This time I made sure they heard me enter. I walked the length of the room, set the bottle and three glasses on a footlocker. I knew I couldn't alleviate their pain, but maybe they would allow me to share in it.

Chapter
Twenty-two

On the morning of November 24, I was back at the Acid Pad. There would be no LRP missions for the next few weeks, of course. Captain Eklund and his remaining NCOs would have their hands full trying to rebuild the company with the replacements that would soon be arriving.

I knew I'd be involved in the training program. What we'd been doing for so many months, and had almost begun to take for granted, would have to be taught all over again. Rappelling, McGuire extractions, ladder insertions and extractions would have to be practiced until they became second nature. There would also be a lot of flying just to teach the new TLs and ATLs how to conduct a proper visual recon. They would have to learn how to select insertion and extraction points, possible ambush sites, and even their E&E routes from the air. Many other things covered in the training flights would be crucial to the team's survival.

Although we were leaving on a training mission, I was surprised that only one aircraft was assigned. Grant had been sent to support one of the line battalions. I guess Operations thought he needed to get away from the LRPs for a few days. I must admit that he, like myself, was getting close to burnout. I was getting so short that it didn't really matter; I was down to almost thirty days. W.T. still had nearly six months left. They must have figured I couldn't get into much trouble in the little time I had left if I was just doing training flights. As it turned out, it was an easy day. We did little actual flying; mainly just sitting around on standby.

After being released, I landed back at the Castle a little

after 1600 hours. I shut the aircraft down and headed for Operations to check on the next day's mission. When I walked into the tent, things got very quiet. Everyone stopped talking, looked at me, then looked away. What the hell was going on?

The Operations officer came over and asked me to step outside. I didn't like the way this was going. Once out of hearing from the rest, he said, "Bill, I've got a few things to cover with you, and I want you to hear me out before you come unglued. First, your orders are in. You're leaving Vietnam on the twenty-fourth of December. Second, Grant has been transferred. He's gone to the 3d Brigade at Camp Evans. There's nothing that you or he can do about it. The decision's final. And the last thing—just remember, don't kill the messenger—as of right now, you will not, under any circumstances, fly as the aircraft commander or copilot on any LRP missions. That is a direct order from the Old Man. He's going to let you continue with them for training purposes only, for as long as they want you. I guess it doesn't really matter that much. Next week the 2/17 Cav is going to be taking over most of the LRP mission support. Unless something comes up where the company *has* to use you, you are out of the combat flying business."

I think he was surprised when I turned and walked away without saying anything. My usual reaction, that is, blowing my stack, did not happen. But it seemed that my whole world was coming apart. I couldn't understand why it was happening. Or maybe I just didn't want to understand. In the last week everything seemed to have gone wrong, and now the one thing I lived for was being taken away from me. To my mind, I was the best there was at doing what I got paid for.

I left the Operations tent and headed for my hootch to drop off my flight gear, then walked to the Officers' Club. After I'd finished my third drink, I still couldn't, or wouldn't, make myself believe or accept what was happening to me.

I was sitting by myself, watching the door as people came in. It finally dawned on me that I didn't know any of them. Oh, I knew *who* they were—I'd flown with them too many times not to know their names—but I still didn't know them.

Without realizing what I was doing, I'd made it a point not to get to know them. All of the people that I had *known* were gone. This bunch was a group of total strangers.

I sat thinking of all the people who'd already departed, and those who'd been killed. I remembered the guys who taught me the tricks of the trade: Dick Washburn, John Dean, Jerry Seevers, Dave Greenlee . . . There were so many more.

I also thought of the pilots who'd been in the gun platoon before they were taken away from us in July. What a blow that had been! Those were people we'd come to know and trust. Literally, we'd put our lives in their hands. We would attempt anything as long as we knew we had the Lancer gunships covering us.

All of the battalion's gun platoons had been consolidated to form D Company of the 101st Aviation Battalion. God, we hated to lose those guys. There were many people who were also good friends: R. L. "Hootchmaid" Smith, Jim Post, Bill Turner, and Steve Martin.

As I continued to watch the door, they kept coming in. Young warriors, men who not long ago had been boys; boys who, if they lived long enough, would soon become men long before their time.

Had I been as good a teacher as the people who taught me? I hoped so. If one of those soldiers died because I hadn't done my job well enough, it would all have been in vain. How would I find out what happened to them after I went home? I knew I would wonder and worry about that for many years to come.

Only two other people had been in the company as long as I had: Capt. Ed Carpenter, who would be leaving the following week, and WO Jim Weaver. Jim would be going home a week after I left. Ed and Jim had been working in the aircraft maintenance section for some time, but they'd put in their time flying in the lift platoon before moving to other assignments.

Now that Grant was gone, there was nobody left I considered my equal. Sitting there, I realized I was lonesome. I'd never considered myself a loner, but that was what I'd become.

No one could teach me anything. I felt I knew it all; I was the best there was. I had set myself above all of the other pilots in the company. In doing so, I built a wall between myself and anyone who tried to get close to me.

Dave Poley entered the club, came over, and sat down at my table. Dave had flown Grant to Camp Evans. He and W.T. had been, and still were, very close. After a short time trying unsuccessfully to make friendly conversation, Dave gave up and left.

As he walked out the door I couldn't help thinking that I'd just finished talking to a dead man. Dave was one of the gutsiest pilots I knew, but there was a recklessness about him that I felt would someday be his downfall. He should have gone home in September, when he'd been scheduled to rotate; he extended. I understood his reasons for staying, but he should have gone. (On March 9, 1969, David Allen Poley was killed while on a resupply mission in support of the U.S. Marines in northern I Corps. He'd flown into an area covered with low-lying clouds and was not heard from again. The burned wreckage of his aircraft was found three days later. All five people on board were dead.)

The LRP training continued for the next week. The Cav was supplying the operational aircraft and crews for the LRP company. There was not much left for me to do. Eklund knew I was under orders and couldn't fly as an aircraft commander or copilot on any missions. But my orders said nothing about going along as a passenger to evaluate the pilots from the 2/17 Cav. Ken said he was concerned about my getting into trouble if I went along in the aircraft. I had to laugh as I told him, "Shit, Ken, I may bend the rules, but you know I don't break them. Besides, what are they going to do to me, send me to Vietnam or make me stop flying?"

The next morning I went along on a VR in the vicinity of Leech Island and the area just to the east. The Cav was flying in support of the LRPs. Ken and I were sitting in the back of the aircraft, looking for movement along any of the trails visible from the air. After searching for about an hour with no luck, we headed back toward Camp Eagle.

I was sitting on the left side of the aircraft watching the vegetation below when I caught a flash of black moving through the tall, brown elephant grass. The aircraft commander was flying from the left seat. He entered a hard left-hand turn to keep the target in sight.

The figure on the ground was trying to hide in the grass. As the aircraft continued making its descending turns, the figure began to move. I could see the black pajamas and the conical hat. The person could have easily been taken for a farmer or a woodcutter except for the AK-47 assault rifle he carried in his right hand. Great! We had a VC in the open. This would surely result in a kill.

Eklund and I were both hooked up to the intercom, so we could hear and talk to each other as well as to the aircraft crew. When we reached one thousand feet, I could see muzzle flashes as the VC began firing at us. The crew chief had his M-60 lined up on the bad guy and started to return fire. Ken was yelling over the intercom for us not to kill the VC. He wanted to try to take him prisoner. The damn VC must have heard him. As we reached two hundred feet, he dropped the weapon and put his hands up. He had nowhere else to go.

I still had my CAR-15 sighted on the VC, hoping that he would try to get away. The rotor wash from the landing helicopter blew off the man's conical hat. It was only then that I saw the long black hair. It was a woman, a goddamn woman.

I looked at Eklund and said, "This bitch is mine." Ken was screaming at me not to shoot. "Fuck it!" I told him. "She's mine." I guess I thought that by killing that one, it might help make up for the losses we had suffered on the twentieth.

Ken shouted at me, "Bill, if you kill her, I'll have you brought up on charges. I need that damn prisoner." With that, he was out of the aircraft and heading toward the VC. As soon as he hit the ground, I was right behind him. I was still hoping she would try to run. No such luck. Ken was the first to reach her. He knocked her to the ground and did a quick search while I recovered the AK-47. By the time I got back, Ken had her hands tied behind her back with his belt and had dragged her to the waiting helicopter. I got there just in time to help him pick her up and dump her into the aircraft.

I was so damn mad I couldn't see straight. I was as close to being in a rage as I'd ever been. I still wanted to kill the thing that was lying across from me. There was not one reason I could think of why she should still be alive while my friends were dead.

Eklund was watching me intently. He knew what I was thinking and what I would like to do. Suddenly I started to laugh. I laughed so hard that tears began running down my face. Ken must have thought I'd lost my mind. Knowing that I would like nothing better than to throw her out of the helicopter, he kept a tight grip on the VC's arm. When I continued to laugh, he finally asked, "What in the hell is wrong with you?"

It took a few minutes before I could reply. "Ken, when you finish with her, I want her."

Ken sat there shaking his head and said, "Bill, I can't let you kill her."

Still laughing aloud, I said, "Kill her! Hell, Ken, I don't want to kill her. Anyone with the kind of luck she has, I want to take to Las Vegas. I'd never have to work another day for the rest of my life."

Ken relaxed, but he must have thought I'd gone completely over the edge.

I had no idea who did the interrogation or what information the woman provided, but two days later we were told we'd be putting in a team. The team leader, Sgt. John Burford, was given four days to prepare for the mission. The other team members were Larry Chambers, John Looney, Larry Saenz, and John Meszaros. The area they were going into was called the "Game Preserve" because the hunting was always good there.

Meanwhile, I'd been working with the new pilots for three weeks. We'd flown practice insertions over and over, and I talked myself blue in the face trying to impress upon them the importance of the low-level approach. Get in and get out with the least amount of exposure time. For some reason, I didn't think they were listening.

The aircraft commander was a WO1 with about six months in country. He was a good pilot, but he seemed to have a problem taking instruction from what he thought was an old burned-out captain. I couldn't help thinking, How in the hell does he think I've lived long enough to become burned out?

With four days to go before the insertion, we trained and talked about the coming mission. It still seemed to me that the guy was listening but not hearing. His attitude seemed to be, "Okay, asshole, say anything you want to. I'm still going to fly the mission the way I see fit."

What could I say? After all, he was the aircraft commander. Well, I'd done all that I could. If he didn't want to listen, I couldn't force him. Besides, I wasn't going to be on the aircraft. I would be in the Operations tent listening to the insertion on the radio. Or so I thought.

But Eklund called me off to one side and asked me if I would be willing to go along as the belly man on the insertion. I said, "Ken, you've got to be out of your goddamn mind. I don't ride in the back of anybody's helicopter. What the hell are you trying to do, get me killed?"

He just looked at me and smiled. He knew that I wouldn't, or couldn't, turn down an opportunity to get right in the middle of whatever was going down. I had the feeling I'd just let myself be suckered into a situation that I thought I would never become involved in: I was going to be sitting in the back of a helicopter as a goddamn passenger, with absolutely no control or say as to what was going on.

To say that I was apprehensive about the mission was a gross understatement. I was amazed that I'd let myself be talked into agreeing to something so foolish. I got paid to fly the damn things, not ride around in the back and let somebody shoot at me.

Ken was concerned because he was still not comfortable with the Cav pilots taking over the mission. We had some long discussions regarding the situation, and I agreed with him. Oh, well. What was it they always said? Duty calls. Bull-shit. Anyway, flying the mission as belly man would be a hell of a lot better than sitting in the Operations tent and won-dering what was going on.

We boarded the aircraft at first light for what was supposed to be a quick mission. We were inserting a short team (five men) for a three-day patrol. Strictly reconnaissance. Avoid contact if at all possible. Knowing those guys as well as I did, I knew that was a joke.

The Game Preserve was not the place they sent a team for a walk in the sun; it was the best hunting grounds in our area of operation. When a team went in there, we knew it would bag some game.

It was an absolutely beautiful morning. The sun was just coming up over the ocean, turning the gray dawn a light shade of pink. There were no clouds in the sky, and just a light breeze out of the west. It was so peaceful. The war seemed far away until I looked into the five painted faces that were going out to find it.

I'd been in the back of the helicopter on training missions before, but that day was the first time I'd ever gone on a combat mission when I wasn't on the controls. And I still didn't feel good about the attitude of the guys sitting in the front seats. Maybe I was worrying about nothing. I would just have to wait and see.

The aircraft call sign was Assault One-three. We lifted off the Acid Pad for the fifteen-minute flight to the LZ, on a ridge at about the two-thousand-foot level. The ridge line ran north to south. We would make our approach from the east at eigh-teen hundred feet. That would put us a little below the LZ with the sun at our back. All we'd have to do was pop up over the crest, drop into the LZ, and within five seconds be on our way down the other side of the ridge. Unless the NVA hap-pened to have a man sitting in that clearing, they would never know we'd been there. Damn, wouldn't it be nice if they were all that easy? I knelt behind the pilot's seat watching the in-strument panel. I guess some habits just won't die. Any pilot I ever knew watched the flight instruments whenever he was in an aircraft and could see them.

The main problem with being in the rear of the aircraft was that the visibility through the windshield was very limited. However, the instruments never lie. They showed that we were heading south and climbing. Where in the hell were we going?

After about ten minutes we started a 180-degree turn back to the north. We leveled off at five thousand feet, and I could hear Eklund on the radio asking the aircraft commander the same thing I'd been wondering. "What in the hell are you doing?"

The pilot's reply was, "We are starting our approach now."

At that point I felt the aircraft start to descend. I couldn't believe it. This silly son of a bitch was setting up for a text-book approach: follow the ridge line, five-hundred-foot-a-minute descent, eighty knots forward airspeed. It was just like they taught it at Fort Rucker. However, we were not at Fort Rucker.

At the rate we were going, it would take six minutes to reach the LZ. Everybody and his goddamn dog would know we were coming. The guy flying would definitely get a pass-ing grade at Fort Rucker, but if he kept that shit up in Viet-nam, the only thing he would get would be a posthumous Purple Heart. Unfortunately, the same would be true for me and the other eight SOBs (souls on board) riding with him. Thank you, but no thank you.

Eklund asked why the approach was not going as briefed. He was already over the LZ and in a position to vector the in-sertion aircraft into the LZ. Our aircraft commander said that he thought this approach looked better to him and as the air-craft commander, he would make the decision on how to fly the mission.

That was exactly what I'd been afraid of. That shit just wasn't gonna work. With that much aircraft exposure time, the team would be compromised before they even got on the ground. I told the pilot over the intercom that I didn't think his approach was a very good idea, and that we should break off the approach and make the insertion as planned. His reply to me was the same as he'd told Eklund. The only thing I could think of was to get Ken to abort the mission.

"Linwood Six, this is Kingsman Two-five on Fox Mike."

"Two-five, this is Six. Go ahead."

"Six, abort the mission."

"Roger. Break. Assault One-three, this is Linwood Six. Abort your approach and return to base."

"Linwood Six, this is Assault One-three. We are continuing with the approach."

"One-three, Six. Abort the goddamn mission now."

The pilot did not bother to reply. He just kept flying toward the trees. We were about fifteen hundred feet above the ridge line and still descending at five hundred feet a minute. If ever a person was asking to be killed, that clown was. If he wanted to die, that was fine, but let him do it by himself. I didn't believe anyone on board wanted to join him. I knew damn well that I didn't.

I told him again to abort, and he told me to shut up. He said I was not part of the air crew and had nothing to say about the conduct of the mission. The copilot was looking at me and grinning. The grin faded as I drew my pistol and placed the muzzle in the middle of the pilot's neck just below the back of his helmet. I said very quietly, "Break off the approach right now or I'll blow your fucking head off."

The copilot was still watching as I pulled the hammer back. He must have sensed I wasn't kidding. I heard him key the intercom and say, "Joe, I think you had better do as he says. This silly son of a bitch is crazy. He'll do it."

The aircraft went into a right-hand turn, and we headed back toward Camp Eagle. Nothing was said on the flight back. Neither Sergeant Burford nor the rest of his team had heard anything over the radio or the intercom. I didn't know what, if anything, Eklund had told them on the company radio.

I was worried about what was going to happen once we got on the ground. I was sure there would be some sort of confrontation and probably a formal inquiry. I knew if the tables had been turned, I wouldn't have stood for it. Once again, it was wait and see.

As the aircraft touched down at the Acid Pad, I got off and walked about a hundred feet away. I waited there while the pilots shut the helicopter down. The LRP team had also departed the aircraft and moved off to one side. They stood there waiting and watching me. I had no idea what was going through their minds or how much they knew about what was going to happen. But one thing I knew for certain: I'd had enough of the asshole's bullshit for one day.

It had taken close to six minutes to shut the aircraft down. In that time, Eklund's C&C aircraft had also landed. He'd gotten out and was headed to where I stood waiting. Before he could reach me, the pilot and copilot from the aircraft I'd been a passenger on started walking toward me. Boy, were they pissed. When they got within about fifteen feet of me, I raised my CAR-15 and pointed it at the pilot's head. The two men stopped in midstride. Clearly they had not expected that. As my thumb slid the selector switch from the safety position to the full-automatic position, I said, "Do you have a problem?"

Before either one of them could reply, Eklund stepped between us. Ken looked at me and said, "Go up to the Operations tent and wait for me." I could tell he was in no mood for an argument.

As I turned to walk up the hill, I noticed that the team members had spread out. Although their weapons were not pointed at anyone, they could have been brought to bear in a heartbeat. It was a good feeling, knowing I didn't have to worry about watching my back.

I'd been at Operations for about ten minutes when I heard the helicopter crank and depart. Ken walked in a few minutes later and wanted to know what in the hell had happened while we were in the air. I told him that I'd threatened to shoot the dumb bastard to get him to break off the approach. Ken thought about it for a short time, then asked, "Would you really have shot him?"

I just looked at him. The question was so damn ridiculous it didn't even deserve an answer. I picked up my gear and started out of the tent. "I'm going to get something to eat. Are you coming?"

Later that morning, Ken sent word for me to come to Operations. He'd gone to the squadron headquarters of the 2/17 Cav and informed them that the air crew we'd flown with that morning was not suited for the work we were doing. Ken requested, and received, another aircraft and crew to proceed with the insertion at first light the next day. If he'd gone into detail with the headquarters aviation officer as to what transpired, he didn't say anything to me.

Early that afternoon the replacement aircraft and crew arrived at the Acid Pad. These people were not part of the division. They were, as we had been until July, under operational control (Op Con) to the 2d of the 17th Cav. They were from Delta Troop 1/1. The parent unit was the 1st Squadron, 1st Cavalry. Two of the warrant officers, John Eiss and Steve Michaus, had taken their orientation rides with me when they arrived in late July. We'd trained with those guys over the last three weeks, so they knew what to expect. Ken briefed the crew and told them I would be going along as the belly man. We conducted the VR with Sergeant Burford and me on board, then returned to the LRP company area.

The insertion the next day would go the same as the one that had been planned for this morning. We talked about how the approach would be made, and went over the map until everything seemed to be covered. Nothing was said about the incident earlier in the day. Maybe they didn't know anything about it, or maybe they just figured it was best to leave well enough alone. Man, what a shitty day it had been! I was getting too old for that kind of crap. And besides, I was too damned short.

The next morning everything went off like clockwork. Those guys really had their shit together. It made me feel good knowing that the team on the ground had a good crew working with them. It would be interesting to see how they handled a hot extraction, but if the way they worked that morning was any indication, they'd be all right.

For the rest of that afternoon and all of the next day we

stayed in the Operations tent listening to the radio. As always, the waiting was the hardest part. The team kept reporting negative contact, no sightings or movement. If everything went according to plan, we would extract the team in the late afternoon the next day.

I stayed until after the team reported that it had moved into the NDP for the night, then told Ken I'd be back at 0600 hours if he still wanted me to fly along as belly man. But he said he was sending another man from his unit as belly man. However, he still wanted me to go along on the extraction. Maybe the aborted insertion a few days earlier was bothering him; he didn't say. Anyway, it just suited the hell out of me. I would be able to go for a helicopter ride and get to just sit back and enjoy the scenery. What a hell of a deal!

I was sitting in the mess tent with the air crew the next morning when Ken came in. Everything was still on schedule. Burford had called in a negative sitrep at first light. He and Chambers were going to leave the rest of the team in the NDP while they conducted a short recon. Burford couldn't believe that the NVA had moved completely out of the Game Preserve.

Around 0900 hours a call came in from Looney, the team's senior RTO, requesting gunships. His voice was so calm and well controlled that the radio operator in the Operations tent didn't think he was serious. We could receive the transmissions directly from the field, but we had to go through a radio relay site for them to get our response. Looney's next transmission was so out of the norm it was almost funny. You could tell he was yelling into the handset. "What do I have to do to get those gunships, start cussing? All right, we've got beaucoup gooks less than fifty meters from our position and nowhere to run. Now, get those goddamn gunships out here, and get them out here now, asshole." As soon as Looney finished talking, I was out the door and heading for the aircraft. The pilot had gone when the first call came in. The blades were turning as I ran down the hill. The aircraft was lifting off the ground as I dove headfirst into the cargo compartment.

The aircraft commander was not about to sit on the ground waiting for me. Good man.

Departing the Acid Pad, we passed by the parking area for the 2/17th Cav. Two Cobra gunships were lifting off. Boy, was I ever glad to see them. I had no doubt we'd need them.

The flight into the Game Preserve didn't take long, but it did give me time to wonder what I was doing in the back of the damn helicopter. I should have been sitting back in my company area having a drink, or flying some milk run to Da Nang. But I didn't have enough sense to do that. With less than two weeks left in country, I had to be flying into a hot extraction in the back of someone else's aircraft. I was beginning to think that, maybe, I was going crazy.

The pilot was talking to the team on the ground. They'd popped a yellow smoke grenade and had the gunships working to the south of the smoke. A clearing about seventy-five meters to the north was going to serve as the extraction point.

As we set up our approach, I saw five men in tiger-stripe uniforms moving along the ridge line. I also saw several people in light brown uniforms moving along behind the LRPs. The NVA had gotten on the south side of the smoke, outside the area the gunships were working. Those people, if they were allowed to follow the team to the LZ, could turn out to be a real pain in the ass.

I told the pilot to contact the guns and let them know about the NVA. As the aircraft touched the ground, I yelled to the pilot, "Don't go away!" and jumped out the door. I hit the ground running.

A small path or trail ran along the top of the ridge. I followed it. At the time, I didn't think about booby traps or anything else. My main concern was marrying up with the team. I was not too concerned about their not knowing that I was one of the good guys. I was wearing a light gray flight jacket, no helmet, and I still had on my chicken plate, which was in a light-color canvas protective cover. I knew damn well that I didn't look like an NVA soldier.

I almost ran into the point man before I saw him. He was like a walking bush. He grinned at me, then kept moving toward the sound of the helicopter. Burford and Chambers were bringing up the rear.

Honest John, the guy who never got surprised or rattled, looked at me as if he thought I'd lost my mind. He asked, "Wild Bill, what in the fuck are you doing here?"

Without taking my eyes off the trail, I told him, "You've got company."

It could not have been five seconds later that three NVA soldiers came into view moving up the trail. Burford, Chambers, and I all fired at the same time. The three people in the light brown uniforms went down. At that range, we couldn't miss. I don't know who hit who, and it didn't really matter.

I continued firing until my magazine was empty, then I just stood there in somewhat of a daze. Finally, I put another magazine in my weapon and waited. As Burford popped another yellow smoke, I felt someone pulling on my arm; Chambers was tugging me up the trail toward the waiting aircraft. I couldn't take my eyes off the spot where the three NVA soldiers had gone down. I was fascinated. As the yellow smoke engulfed the trail, I fired one more magazine into the area where we'd seen the NVA. Then Chambers started pushing and yelling for me to get the hell out of there.

As I turned toward the aircraft, I looked up. That was when I understood why he was in such a hurry to get out of the area: one of the Cobras was just starting its gun run. They were going to fire on the smoke. At that point I didn't need any more urging. I took off at a dead run. I could hear the rockets impacting behind us as Larry shoved me into the cargo compartment of the helicopter.

The ground fell away as the aircraft lifted off. The sound of the rockets exploding, and the ripping sounds of the miniguns, soon faded in the distance, replaced by the thumping of the rotor blades.

I sat back trying to catch my breath, totally exhausted. I lit a cigarette, closed my eyes, and tried to relax. I thought, Damn, it's good to be alive.

The people we'd killed that day never entered my mind;

they were the enemy, and once you left them behind, they simply ceased to exist.

The flight back took only fifteen minutes. I didn't take part in the jubilation in the aircraft. Those guys were just letting off steam. The pressure of three days in the field, and then the firefight at the end, had to have been overwhelming for them. How could they keep going back time after time? I wondered. It was beyond me. The only thing I knew for sure was that I'd just been involved in my last LRP mission.

I sat through the debriefing, still wondering how they did it.

Burford and Chambers said that when they left their NDP that last morning to do a little area recon, they'd moved only about 150 meters when Chambers spotted a man sitting in the fog eating his breakfast. As he stood watching, Chambers saw another NVA, and then another. He said they looked like ghosts. The longer he watched, the more men he saw, as his eyes adjusted to the misty shadows. He realized that if they saw him, he was dead. There was no way he'd be able to take on that many enemy soldiers and come out alive. He carefully backed out of the NVA bivouac area and rejoined Burford, who had also spotted some of the NVA.

On their way back to where they'd left the other three team members at the NDP, Burford and Chambers had to cross an open area; thick bamboo on both sides prohibited movement to either side of the clearing. There was only one way, and that was straight across. They knew they couldn't help but leave a trail through the tall, damp grass. They also knew it would be only a matter of time before the NVA moved out and discovered where they had been observed.

They got through the clearing without being seen, and informed the other team members about what they'd just observed. Chambers moved back down to the edge of the clearing to see if anyone had picked up their trail.

Five minutes later a man stepped out of the tree line and discovered the trail left by the two LRPs. He studied the ground for a short time before disappearing back into the trees. Two minutes later a group of eight NVA soldiers, led by an officer, came out of the trees. They were less than fifty meters down the hill. At that moment Looney called for the gunships.

Burford sent three of the team members up the hill toward the pickup point while he and Chambers remained back to give covering fire. Once the three men started up the hill, the two remaining LRPs opened fire on the NVA. They could see little puffs of dust erupt as their bullets hit a number of the enemy soldiers. Some fell but the rest disappeared into the grass. They didn't know how many they hit, and decided not to stick around to find out.

Return fire soon erupted from the tree line. Burford estimated there were at least thirty weapons firing. At that point the gunships arrived on station and went to work, about the same time Chambers heard the sound of the UH-1 coming in. Burford then tossed out the yellow smoke and headed up the trail toward the landing helicopter.

I thought the debriefing was over until someone, possibly Chambers, made mention of some dumb-assed helicopter pilot doing a very bad impersonation of John Wayne leading a frontal charge of one coming to the rescue. That brought a laugh from everyone. Although they saw the humor in my actions, I think the men of the LRP company were pleased to know that the Kingsmen still tried to live up to their motto, "Deeds, not words!" even though we were no longer flying in support of them.

Chapter
Twenty-three

As far as I was concerned, it was over. I was through. No more LRP or FOB missions. No more sniffer missions, flying low-level over the mountainous jungle. If the company assigned me to fly combat assault missions, I would have no choice but to go. But I'd looked for trouble for the last time. I was tired and getting too complacent, as well as a little careless. That day had been a good example. I really had no business leaving the aircraft. That was not my job. I could see that if I kept doing things like that, sooner or later—probably sooner—I would get myself or someone else killed.

Eklund and I were sitting in the mess tent discussing my decision. Ken agreed with me, especially after the stunt I'd pulled that morning. Everything turned out all right, but I'd been completely out of my element. Ken offered to call my company and request that I remain with his unit for another week. That would prevent them from screwing around with me. It would also bring me to within five days of going home.

Although it would have been nice to remain with the LRP company for the next week, I knew it would be impossible. The first time they had a mission or a team in contact, I would be like an old fire horse that has to run to the smell of the smoke. Besides, if the company needed me to fly missions, I wanted to be there. It would not be right for someone else to have to do my job.

Over the next seven days I flew three missions. The first one was a combat assault that lasted all day. We were moving ARVNs around. As far as anyone knew, we did not receive any fire. I also flew two administrative missions to Da Nang.

At the end of the last flight, I was directed to turn in my flight gear. I had five days left in country. During that time, I would have to administratively clear both the company and battalion and turn in the rest of my gear.

After that I would have to catch a hop to Saigon, complete a little more paperwork, then get manifested on a flight back to the States. The final step would be boarding that good old civilian plane. Boy, was I looking forward to that.

There was not very much to do around the company during the day because everyone was out flying. After I'd finished turning in my gear and clearing post, I just sat in my hootch and drank. I made it a point to stay away from the LRP company. They did not need me anymore. They had new air crews and quite a few replacements for the soldiers they'd lost. Most of the old guys were gone. My being around would probably do more harm than good.

With nothing for me to do but drink, the days took a long time coming to an end. By the time the club opened in the evening, I would already be more than a little drunk, but I showed up anyway, just to finish the job.

Jim Weaver was going home a week or so after me. He was working in the aircraft maintenance section. Jim was not flying many missions anymore. He'd done so for nearly eight months, but the past few months he mostly did maintenance test flights.

After finishing his work for the day, he'd join me in my hootch or at the club. Weaver and I had been doing that from the time we joined the company. We'd gone through many bottles of rum in that period. It seemed that most, if not all, of our friends were gone. It was not the same anymore. It was no fun anymore. We were simply trying to forget everything by drowning our memories in alcohol.

When I checked with Operations, they told me I was scheduled out on a C-130 leaving Hue/Phu Bai at 0500 the next morning. They would have a jeep at the Operations tent at 0330 to take me to the airfield. It was only about a thirty-minute ride from Camp Eagle to Hue/Phu Bai airport.

Leaving Operations, I thought, Bullshit! There's no way in

hell I'm going to ride in a damn jeep at that time of the morning. Charlie still owns the night. And at 0330 hours it's sure as shit still night. I'll find my own way there.

As I walked back to my hootch, a helicopter was just landing. Now, a helicopter landing in our company area was nothing unusual, but that one had 3d Brigade markings on its tail boom. Before the pilot stepped out, I knew it was none other than William T. Grant. The son of a bitch had to be a mind reader.

W.T. was on his way to Da Nang on a bullshit ash-and-trash mission. He told me that as he got close to Camp Eagle, he'd gotten homesick. Besides, he knew I was getting ready to leave, and he didn't want me to get away without saying good-bye.

As soon as the aircraft was tied down, I took Grant and his crew up to my hootch. I handed each of them a cold beer, took one for myself, and sat down. I explained my situation to Grant, and asked if he might be able to find a way to stick around and take me to the airfield in the morning.

He sat there looking at the floor a minute, shaking his head. The copilot, a first lieutenant, started to say something. W.T. looked at him and said, "Lieutenant, don't say anything. This is part of your educational process. Just sit back, listen, and learn."

W.T. went on to explain that he had to get to Da Nang today, pick up some people, fly them around for a while, drop them off, then return to Camp Evans that night. The aircraft was already scheduled for a 0900 hours mission the next day.

Grant thought about it for a few minutes, looked at me, and said, "Okay. How do we do it?"

"Shit, W.T., it's easy. You go and do what you have to do in Da Nang. Then, on your way back, you'll develop a maintenance problem. You know the maintenance people here, so you stop and let them have a look at it."

Grant still was not too sure about this. "Then what happens?"

"Look, W.T., Jerry Staazt is still Maintenance officer. He owes me more money from playing poker than he'll ever be able to pay. I'll have him call your unit and tell them he's grounded your aircraft and will have it flyable late tonight."

"Do you think he'll do it?"

I couldn't help laughing. "Yeah, he'll do it. He'll even make the entries in your logbook, and make you look like some kind of a hero for wanting to get back to your unit for the 0900 mission."

Grant's crew chief was sitting there grinning. "Captain, I know a few of the guys in the Kingsmen. They wouldn't trade units for anything. Do you guys do this shit all the time?"

I had to think about that a moment. I looked at Grant to see if he wanted to try to explain how the unit worked and why it was such a goddamn great unit. He shook his head and just pointed at me.

I took a deep breath and said, "Mission accomplishment is the name of the game. We do whatever it takes. I've been with this unit for a year. In that time, I can think of only once when we didn't accomplish what we set out to do. On that day we had a maintenance aircraft following us on a combat assault when we were putting in at Fire Support Base Vehgel. They went one ridge line too far to the west. That day we lost our entire maintenance crew. Nine people were killed. We didn't have a recovery aircraft when we needed it. That's the only time that I can think of. Yes, we do this shit all of the time if it's the only way to accomplish the mission."

We sat there for a few minutes. Nobody seemed to have anything else to say. It was almost uncomfortable. Then the crew chief looked at W.T. and said, "You know, Mr. Grant, I have been feeling some weird vibrations in the rear of the aircraft. If they continue, I think maybe we'd better find someplace to stop and have them checked out."

W.T. and his crew stayed for another hour, then headed for Da Nang. He figured he wouldn't be back until around 2000 hours. I stood watching as Grant's Huey disappeared to the south, then I returned to my hootch. It had been nice having W.T. and his crew visit. I hadn't realized how much I'd missed his company. He hadn't been gone very long, only thirty days, but it seemed a hell of a lot longer.

Jim and I were sitting in the hootch doing our normal thing, having a drink, when the Operations officer walked in. He looked a little the worse for wear, so I told him to sit down and mixed him a very strong rum and Coke. He just sat there quietly, sipping his drink. I knew something was really bothering him, but had no idea what it could be. I finally broke the ice. "Okay, Tom, what's going on?"

He seemed unable to look at me. Finally, he swallowed and said, "Bill, I know you've been taken off flight status and you're leaving in the morning, but I need you and Jim to fly tonight."

I looked at Jim and we both started laughing. Then I replied, "For chrissake, is that all? Why in the hell didn't you just say so?"

Tom went on to explain that the mission that night was a maximum effort. Everything flyable would be in the air. The battalion would be inserting an entire infantry battalion in an attempt to bottle up a large group of NVA moving out of the mountains. The company had flyable aircraft, but was short air crews.

The insertion would start at 2000 hours. My job would be to put the Pathfinders on the ground in three separate landing zones thirty minutes before the combat assault. The Pathfinders were to set up the LZs for the lift ships. After I'd inserted the Pathfinders, I was to rejoin the company for the battalion lift. Once the combat assault was over, I would pick up the Pathfinders, drop them off, and return to the Castle. It sounded pretty good to me. Piece of cake.

Jim and I departed Camp Eagle at 1900 hours to pick up the Pathfinders and insert them. Then we returned to join the company. Up to that point, everything had gone as planned.

Once the battalion began its part of the operation, everything began to fall apart. First of all, no one was put into the right LZ. I believe the only place where we got lucky was when the NVA changed their plans and decided not to move that night. What a goddamn mess.

After all of the troops were put in, I picked up the Pathfinders and returned them to their company area. Grant met me when we landed. His first comment was, "Meacham, you stupid son of a bitch. What in the hell are you trying to do, get your dumb ass killed?" It went downhill from there.

I already had my bag packed. I didn't have much. In fact, it was a lot less than I had when I arrived in country. So with nothing to do, W.T. and I took a bottle of rum and sat on top of the bunker. We talked about everything under the moon.

Finally, it was time to go. At that time of the morning there was nobody from the company to see us off or for me to say good-bye to. We met W.T.'s crew at the aircraft and started to load on board. I'd just thrown my bag into the back and was climbing in when Grant pulled me back and pointed to the left front seat (the aircraft commander's seat). My last ride in a helicopter in Vietnam would not be as a passenger. It would be only a ten-minute flight, but one I would never forget.

After we'd cleared the company area, I turned the radio to the guard channel and used it for the first time when I was "not" in trouble. I don't know what made me want to use the radio. Possibly, just because it was so quiet. I keyed the transmit switch and made my last radio transmission: "Good morning, Vietnam. Be advised. Kingsman Two-five. Destination: Termination. Rotation. No holes. No ventilation. No alterations. I'm going home, y'all. Merry Christmas."

ALPHA   MIKE   FOXTROT

Epilogue

> God and the soldier we like adore,
> In time of trouble not before,
> When troubles ended and all things righted,
> God is forgotten and the soldier is slighted.

> —FRANCIS QUARLES
> 1592–1644

Some things never change. Unlike most of the soldiers with whom I served, I remained in the United States Army. The others came home, took off their funny green suits, threw them in the closet, and tried to begin their lives all over again. They had a very long, hard job ahead of them. Many are still trying.

After returning from Vietnam, I was assigned to Fort Gordon, Georgia, as a company commander for a student company. I lasted for six months in that position before requesting to be sent back to Southeast Asia. It seemed to me that was where I could do the most good. The request was granted, and in March 1970 I was back in Vietnam flying helicopters.

The Vietnam conflict officially ended in 1975. For many of us it has never ended, nor will it ever end; the nightmares will still come when least expected. The ghost of a friend will reach out and put his hand on your shoulder, just to let you know that the bond has not been broken and he is still with you. Then there are the sounds and smells that one cannot make go away. The sound of battle, the screams of the wounded and the dying. The smell of cordite and the sickening smell of death.

However, out of all of the bad, there is the good. The brotherhood that we formed with the men with whom we served. That brotherhood, where one man is willing to lay down his life for another, is something few men can share. I am extremely proud to have been accepted into this band of brothers.

There will be one last radio transmission:

"This is Kingsman Two-five. God love you all. Out."

Glossary

AA antiaircraft

AC aircraft commander, pilot

Acid Pad flat, hard-surfaced area designed to accommodate helicopter landings and takeoffs

AFVN Armed Forces radio and TV network in Vietnam

air burst an explosive device, such as a grenade, a bomb, an artillery round, or a mine, rigged to detonate above the ground to inflict maximum damage by expanding the range of shrapnel

air strike surface attack by fixed-wing fighter-bomber aircraft

AK-47 Communist-made 7.62 caliber automatic assault rifle. It was the primary individual weapon used by the NVA/VC forces.

AO area of operation; a defined geographical area where military operations are conducted for a specified period of time

ao dai traditional Vietnamese female dress, split up the side and worn over pants

ARA Aerial Rocket Artillery; military description of Huey gunship

Arc Light B-52 bombing mission

artillery fan area within range of supporting artillery

ARVN Army of the Republic of Vietnam

ATL Assistant team leader

BDA Bomb Damage Assessment. Special operations missions for the purpose of verifying results of an aerial bombing attack

beaucoup derived from French word for "very many"

berm high, earthen levee surrounding most large, permanent U.S. military installations as part of perimeter defense system

black box sensor devices planted along trails, roads, rivers, and at intersections and junctions to detect body heat, perspiration, or sound given off by passing enemy troops

blasting cap detonator inserted into claymore mines, grenades, satchel charges, and other explosive devices, which imitates the actual detonation

blood trail spoor sign left by passage or removal of enemy wounded and dead

blue line designation on maps of streams, rivers, and other natural waterways

body bag rubberized canvas or plastic bags used to remove dead U.S. casualties from the field to Graves Registration locations

boonies informal term for unsecured area outside U.S. military control

bush informal term for the jungle, also called boonies, boondocks, Indian country, or the field

butter bar second lieutenant

CA Combat Assault

CAR-15 commando version of M-16 assault rifle

C-3 or C-4 plastic explosives

C's or C-rats canned, individual rations

C&C Command and Control

CG Commanding General

CIB Combat Infantryman Badge

CID Criminal Investigation Division

CO Commanding Officer

CS riot control agent

cammies camouflaged jungle fatigues—blouses, pants, hats, or berets

canister round M-79 round containing numerous double-0 buckshot

Cav short for Cavalry

chieu hoi enemy soldier who has rallied to the South Vietnamese government

cherry new, inexperienced soldier recently arrived in a combat zone

Chicom designation for Chinese Communist or an item of Chinese Communist manufacture or origin

chopper informal term for any helicopter

chopper pad designated landing or takeoff platform for one or more helicopters

Chuck informal term describing the enemy; also Charles, Mister Charles, Victor Charles, VC

clacker informal term describing the electric firing device for claymore mine or a phoo gas barrel

claymore mine command-detonated, antipersonnel mine designed to saturate an area six to eight feet above the ground and over an area of sixty degrees across its front, with 750 steel ball bearings

cockadau Vietnamese slang meaning "kill"

cold term describing an area of operation or a landing zone devoid of any enemy sign or activity

commo communications

commo check radio operator's request to verify reception of his transmission

compromise enemy discovery of the presence of forces in its vicinity, thereby resulting in the termination of the mission and extraction of the team

concertina   coiled barbed wire strung for perimeter defense

contact   firing on or being fired on by the enemy

contour flying   low-level, high-speed, flight-adjusting altitude only for terrain features

conex   large steel container used to transport and store U.S. military supplies and equipment

daisy chain   more than one claymore mine wired together with det cord, to effect simultaneous detonation

DEROS   Date of Estimated Return from Overseas

det cord   detonator cord, demolition cord; timed-burn fuse used with plastique explosives or to daisy-chain claymore mines together

di di mau   Vietnamese phrase meaning "get out" or "go"

double canopy   primary jungle with a lower layer of undergrowth

dragging ass   slang term for physical exhaustion

deuce and a half   two-and-a-half-ton military transport truck

Dustoff   helicopter conducting a medical evacuation

early out   termination of military service prior to normal ETS

E&E   Escape and Evade

EM   Enlisted Man

ETS   Estimated Termination of Service

exfiltration   procedure of departing recon zone after completion of mission

extending   prolonging tour of combat duty beyond the normal DEROS

extraction   removal of troops from the field, usually by helicopter

F-4 or Fox-4   McDonnell-Douglas fighter-bomber that saw heavy use in Vietnam

FAC   Forward Air Controller

FNG   Fucking New Guy; slang term for inexperienced soldier newly arrived in a combat zone

FO   Forward Observer

FOB   Forward Observation Base

fast mover   U.S. fighter-bomber

fire base   forward artillery base, support base

firefly   helicopter mounting a searchlight and capable of dropping aerial flares

firefight   small-arms battle

fire mission   directed artillery barrage

foo gas or phoo gas   mixture of JP-4 aviation fuel and naphtha, which performs like napalm when detonated

frag   fragmentation grenade

free-fire zone   Area declared off limits to all personnel. Anyone encountered within its confines was assumed to be hostile and could be fired on without verification or authorization.

G-2 Division Intelligence section

G-3 Division Operations section

goofy grape slang for purple smoke

gook derogatory slang term for any Oriental person, especially VC or NVA; also, dink, slope, or zipperhead

go to cover move into heavy concealment

Graves Registration section of military service charged with reception, identification, and the disposition of U.S. military dead

grunt U.S. infantryman

gunship heavily armed helicopter used to support infantry troops or independently attack enemy units or positions

HE High Explosive

H&I Harassment and Interdiction, preplotted artillery fire designed to keep the enemy on edge and possibly catch him off balance

HQ Headquarters

heat tabs Heating tablets, small blue chemical disks that burn slowly and give off an intense, smokeless heat when ignited. Used for heating rations and boiling water.

heavy fire team three helicopter gunships

heavy team LRP team of ten or more personnel

helipad see "Acid Pad" or "chopper pad"

Ho Chi Minh Trail A vast network of roads and trails, running from southern North Vietnam, down through Laos, Cambodia, and South Vietnam and terminating just to the northwest of Saigon. It made up the transportation system that enabled the North Vietnamese Army to replace its losses of manpower, arms, and equipment.

hootch slang term for small civilian family or military shelter in Vietnam

hootchmaid slang term for Vietnamese women who maintained the living area for U.S. servicemen

horn term used to describe radio communications

hot term describing an area of operation or a landing zone where contact has been made with enemy troops

Huey UH-1 helicopter, primary helicopter troop transport in Vietnam

hump to walk on patrol, usually heavily laden and heavily armed; to perform a difficult task

I Corps northernmost military district in South Vietnam

II Corps central military district in South Vietnam

III Corps military district that includes Saigon, capital of South Vietnam

IV Corps southernmost military district in South Vietnam

IG Inspector General

in country American troops serving in Vietnam

Indian country anything outside the perimeter defenses

infiltrate procedure of entering a recon zone without detection by the enemy

insertion placement of combat or recon forces in the field, usually by helicopter

jungle penetrator metal cylinder with fold-out legs, attached by steel cable to a helicopter-mounted hoist, used to evacuate wounded soldiers from thick jungle terrain

K-Bar military knife used primarily by Marines, LRPs, and Rangers
KIA Killed in Action
kill zone target area of an ambush
killer team LRP team with primary mission of inflicting casualties upon the enemy through ambush or raid
Kit Carson Scout former VC/NVA soldier, repatriated to serve as a scout for U.S. combat forces
klick one thousand meters, a kilometer

LAW Light Antitank Weapon; single shot, disposable rocket launcher
LBE Load Bearing Equipment
LOH or LOACH Light Observation Helicopter (OH-6)
LP Listening Post
LRP Long Range Patrol
LRRP Long Range Reconnaissance Patrol; also a dehydrated ration used by special operations units
LZ Landing Zone
landline ground telephone communications between two points
lay dog going to cover after insertion to wait and listen for any sign of enemy movement or presence in the area
lifer a career soldier
Lima Charlie radio communications "loud and clear"
lock 'n' load to chamber a round in a weapon

M-16 lightweight automatic assault rifle used by U.S. forces in Vietnam; 5.56 caliber
M-60 medium 7.62 caliber belt-fed machine gun
M-79 single-shot, 40mm grenade launcher also called "blooper" or "thumper"
MACV Military Advisory Command, Vietnam
McGuire rig a nylon sling or seat attached to a 120-foot rope, used to extract special operations personnel from dense jungle under extreme conditions
MIA Missing in Action
mikes phonetic military designation for the letter M; usually means minutes or meters
MP Military Police
MPC Military Payment Certificate; funny money or script issued to U.S. military personnel in Vietnam

medevac   helicopter conducting a medical evacuation
monsoon   rainy season in Asia
Montagnard   see Yard

NCO   Noncommissioned Officer; ranks E-5 through E-9
NCOIC   Noncommissioned Officer in Charge
NDP   Night Defensive Position
Nam, or the Nam   short for Vietnam
nouc mam   rotten-smelling fish sauce used by the Vietnamese
number one   slang, means the very best
number ten   slang, means the very worst

OCS   Officer Candidate School
OP   Observation Post
one-oh-five   105mm howitzer
one-five-five   155mm artillery
one-seven-five   175mm artillery
op order   operations order, notice of an impending operation
overflight   Premission aerial scout of recon zone for the purpose of selecting primary and secondary landing zones and extraction points, determining route of march and locating possible trails and enemy supply
   depots, structures and emplacements; usually conducted by the team
   leader and his assistant team leader. The inserting helicopter crew flies the
   overflight.

PF   Popular Forces; South Vietnamese irregular forces
PLF   Parachute Landing Fall
POW   Prisoner of War
PRC-25 or Prick 25   portable radio used by American combat troops in
   the field
PSP   Perforated Steel Plating, used for airstrips, helicopter pads, bunker
   construction, and bridge matting
PT   Physical Training; Pilot Technique
PX   Post Exchange
PZ   Pickup Zone
peter pilot   copilot of a helicopter
piaster **or P**   Vietnamese currency
pig   affection slang nickname for the M-60 machine gun
pink team   airborne hunter-killer team consisting of one or more LOH
   scout helicopters, a Huey C&C helicopter, and two or more gunships
point   unit's advance man in line of march, or the scout in a combat patrol
Psy Ops   Psychological Operations unit
pull pitch   term used by helicopter pilots to take off
punji stakes   Sharpened bamboo stakes, hidden in grass, vegetation, in
   covered pits, or underwater, to penetrate the feet and lower legs of unwary
   troops. They were often dipped in feces to cause infection to the wound.

REMF   Rear Echelon Mother Fucker; derogatory slang term that combat troops called noncombat administrative and support troops

RPG   Communist-made rocket launcher, firing a B-40 rocket; used by both the VC and the NVA. It was effective against U.S. armor, fixed emplacements, helicopters, patrol boats, and infantry.

R&R   Rest and Recreation

RTO   Radio Telephone Operator

RZ   Recon or Reconnaissance Zone

radio relay team or X-ray team   communications unit, usually set up on a fire base, with the mission of relaying transmissions from the units in the field to their rear area command

rappel   controlled descent, by means of a rope, from a tall structure or a hovering helicopter

reaction force   military unit established to respond quickly to another unit's request for rescue or reinforcement

redlegs   informal name given to artillerymen

revetment   sandbagged or earthen blast wall erected to protect aircraft and helicopters from shrapnel and blasts caused by mortars, artillery, rockets, and satchel charges or demolitions

rock 'n' roll   slang term used to describe firing a weapon on full automatic

ruck or rucksack   infantryman's backpack

SAR   Search and Rescue

SFC   Sergeant First Class, E-7

SKS   Communist-made 7.62 caliber semiautomatic assault rifle used by the VC/NVA

SOG (MACV)   Studies and Observations Group; specialized in deep penetration patrols across the borders into South Vietnam's neighboring countries

SOI   Signal Operating Instruction; the booklet that contains the call signs and radio frequencies for units in Vietnam

SOP   Standard Operating Procedure

sapper   Specially trained enemy soldiers, with the mission to penetrate the perimeters of U.S. and Allied military installations by stealth and then cause as much damage as possible to aircraft, vehicles, supply depots, communication centers, command centers, and hard defense positions. They would utilize satchel charges, grenades, demolition charges, and RPGs to accomplish their mission; sapper attacks often preceded mass infantry assaults and took place under heavy shelling by their own mortar and rocket crews.

selector switch   a three-position device on the M-16 and CAR-15 enabling the operator to choose safe, semiautomatic, or automatic fire merely by thumbing it in ninety-degree increments

short or short-timer   term to describe a soldier whose time remaining in country is less than sixty days

single canopy   phrase used to describe low, dense jungle or forest growth, with no overhead cover from mature trees

sitrep   situation report; regular, scheduled communications check between a unit in the field and its rear command element, to inform it of their present status

Six   radio call sign for unit commander

slack   the second position in a line or march, or in a patrol formation; also means "go easy on"

slick   informal name for a Huey troop transport helicopter

smoke   informal name for a smoke grenade; they come in various colors, used to signal others, to mark positions, to determine wind direction, and to provide concealment

snake   informal name for Cobra gunship

snatch   to capture a prisoner

spider hole   one-man camouflaged enemy fighting position, often connected to other positions by means of a tunnel

spotter round   artillery or mortar shell producing a dense cloud of white smoke; used to mark targets or to assist units in establishing their correct location

Stars and Stripes   U.S. military newspaper

TDY   Temporary Duty

TL   Team Leader

TOC   Tactical Operations Center

tac air   fighter-bomber capability of the Air Force, Navy, and Marine aviation

toe popper   small, plastic, U.S.-made antipersonnel mine, designed to cripple rather than kill

tracer   ammunition containing a chemical composition to mark the flight of the projectile by a trail of smoke or fire

triple canopy   mature jungle or forest, with a third layer of ancient trees, often reaching heights of 200 feet or more

typhoon   Asian hurricane

VC or Viet Cong   slang names describing members of the People's Army of Vietnam; Victor Charles

WIA   Wounded in Action

WP, willie peter, willie pete, or willie papa   white phosphorus grenade, mortar round, or artillery rounds that explode into a spray of chemical fire, which ignites on contact with the air and can be extinguished only by removal of the source of oxygen

wait-a-minute vines   strong, barbed ground creepers that caught at the boots and clothing of American soldiers and retarded their forward movement

warning order   directive that gives final approval for an upcoming mission

white mice   derogatory slang term for the military police of the South Vietnamese government
World (the)   the States, USA, home

XO   Executive Officer
X-ray team   see "radio relay team"

Yard   short for "Montagnard," a French term for people who dwell in the
   highlands. In Vietnam the Montagnards belonged to a large number of
   ethnic minorities, most of whom had little love for the Vietnamese of the
   north or south.

WINGS OF THE EAGLE
A Kingsmen's Story

by W. T. Grant

As a member of the Kingsmen, the call sign for the 17th Assault Helicopter Company, helicopter pilot W. T. Grant regularly went into hot landing zones in Vietnam in 1968. He hovered in the lightly armed, thin-skinned Huey helicopter, braving enemy gunfire, until six men ran, hopped, or dragged themselves on board. First as peter pilot and then as full-fledged aircraft commander, Grant routinely flew McGuire rig extractions under enemy fire, inserts into combat zones exploding with mortar shells, and night operations in the enemy-infested A Shau Valley. This is his story of rescue in the steamy, bloody jungles of Vietnam.

THE PRICE OF EXIT
by Tom Marshall

For assault helicopter crews flying in and around the NVA-infested DMZ, the U.S. pullout from Vietnam in 1970–71 was a desperate time of selfless courage. Now former army warrant officer Tom Marshall of the Phoenix, C Company, 158th Aviation Battalion, 101st Airborne, captures the deadly mountain terrain, the long hours flown under enormous stress, the grim determination of hardened pilots combat-assaulting through walls of antiaircraft fire, the pickups amid exploding mortar shells and hails of AK fire, the nerve-racking string extractions of SOG teams from North Vietnam . . . and, through it all, the rising tension as helicopter pilots and crews are lost at an accelerating pace.

Available at bookstores everywhere.
Published by The Ballantine Publishing Group.

SEAWOLVES
First Choice

by Daniel E. Kelly

Created in 1967, the HAL-3 helicopter squadron—aka Seawolves—provided quick-reaction close air support to SEALs, PBR River Rats, and Special Forces advisers and their troops. During the five years of the unit's existence, the seven detachments of Seawolves amassed stunning statistics: 78,000 missions, 8,200 enemy kills, 8,700 sampans sunk, and 9,500 structures destroyed. These 200 men collected a total of 17,339 medals.

As a door gunner in the all-volunteer Seawolves, Daniel Kelly served with distinction until three bullets bought him a trip home. Here is his amazing story of the Seawolves—a harrowing tale of unsung heroism and undaunted courage in combat.

Available at bookstores everywhere.
Published by The Ballantine Publishing Group.

The bloody history of the 101st LRP/Rangers
by one of its own.

SIX SILENT MEN
Book One
by Reynel Martinez

In 1965, the 1st Brigade of the 101st Airborne Division
was detached from the division and assigned to Vietnam.
Reynel Martinez provides a personal account of the first
faltering steps of the brigade's provisional LRRP unit as
the men learn how to battle the VC and NVA while surviv-
ing the more pernicious orders of their own, occasionally
thoughtless, high-level commanders. SIX SILENT MEN:
Book One provides an often bloody but always honorable
chronicle of courage under fire.

The compelling chronicle continues in

SIX SILENT MEN
Book Two
By Kenn Miller

After working on their own in Vietnam for more than two
years, the 1st Brigade LRRPs were ordered to join forces
with the division once again in the summer of 1967. It was
a bitter pill to swallow for this formidable band of soldiers,
but swallow it they did as they went on to become one of
the most highly decorated companies in the history of the
101st.

Published by The Ballantine Publishing Group.
Available in your local bookstore.